Decision Making by the Modern Supreme Court

There are three general models of Supreme Court decision making: the legal model, the attitudinal model, and the strategic model. But each is somewhat incomplete. This book advances an integrated model of Supreme Court decision making that incorporates variables from each of the three models. In examining the modern Supreme Court, since *Brown v. Board of Education*, the book argues that decisions are a function of the sincere preferences of the justices, the nature of precedent, and the development of the particular issue, as well as separation of powers and the potential constraints posed by the president and Congress. To test this model, the authors examine all full signed civil liberties and economic decisions in the 1953–2000 period. *Decision Making by the Modern Supreme Court* argues and the results confirm that judicial decision making is more nuanced than the attitudinal or legal models have argued in the past.

Richard L. Pacelle, Jr., is Professor and Chair of the Department of Political Science at Georgia Southern University. His work is concerned with public law generally and the U.S. Supreme Court and separation of powers more specifically. He is the author of three previous books, *The Transformation of the Supreme Court's Agenda: From the New Deal to the Reagan Administration; The Supreme Court in American Politics: The Least Dangerous Branch of Government?* (winner of a 2002 *Choice* Outstanding Titles Award); and *Between Law and Politics: The Solicitor General and the Structuring of Race, Gender and Reproductive Rights Policy*, as well as a number of journal articles and chapters in edited volumes.

Brett W. Curry is Associate Professor of Political Science and Associate Director of the Justice Studies Program at Georgia Southern University. His areas of specialization include public law and separation of powers. His research has appeared in the *Journal of Politics, Law and Society Review, Politics and Policy, Presidential Studies Quarterly, American Politics Research*, and *Political Research Quarterly*.

Bryan W. Marshall is Associate Professor of Political Science at Miami University, Ohio. His areas of specialization include Congress, congressional-executive relations, separation of powers, and quantitative methods. Professor Marshall's book *Rules for War* (2005) looks at the effects of legislative rules on policy making. Professor Marshall also served as APSA's Steiger Congressional Fellow (2008–09), working for House Majority Whip, the Honorable Jim Clyburn.

Decision Making by the Modern Supreme Court

RICHARD L. PACELLE, JR.
Georgia Southern University

BRETT W. CURRY
Georgia Southern University

BRYAN W. MARSHALL
Miami University

CAMBRIDGE
UNIVERSITY PRESS

CAMBRIDGE UNIVERSITY PRESS
Cambridge, New York, Melbourne, Madrid, Cape Town,
Singapore, São Paulo, Delhi, Tokyo, Mexico City

Cambridge University Press
32 Avenue of the Americas, New York, NY 10013-2473, USA

www.cambridge.org
Information on this title: www.cambridge.org/9780521717717

First published 2011

Printed in the United States of America

A catalog record for this publication is available from the British Library.

Library of Congress Cataloging in Publication data
Pacelle, Richard L., 1954–
Decision making by the modern Supreme Court / Richard L. Pacelle, Jr., Brett W. Curry,
Bryan W. Marshall.
    p. cm.
Includes bibliographical references and index.
ISBN 978-0-521-88897-4 (hardback) – ISBN 978-0-521-71771-7 (paperback)
1. United States. Supreme Court – Decision making.   2. Judicial process – United States.
3. Political questions and judicial power – United States.   I. Curry, Brett W., 1978–
II. Marshall, Bryan W.   III. Title.
KF8748.P234   2011
347.73′26–dc22   2011015697

ISBN 978-0-521-88897-4 Hardback
ISBN 978-0-521-71771-7 Paperback

To Wayne – RLP
To Trent and Fiona – BWC
To Candace, Autumn, Evan, and Dylan – BWM

Contents

Acknowledgments

We owe a huge debt of gratitude to a number of people who helped with the gestation of this project. The University of Missouri–St. Louis provided a grant to help launch this project. We appreciate the faith and continued support of our editor at Cambridge, Eric Crahn. Ken Karpinski took over the production of the manuscript and we did not miss a beat. We also want to thank Laura Tendler who showed us how little we know about grammar. The reviewers suggested a series of important revisions and improvements. We did our best to incorporate all their suggestions. We know the manuscript is better for their assistance.

Over the years, we have presented many versions of the study at various conferences and profited from the comments of numerous colleagues. At the risk of forgetting one or two of them, we wish to thank Chris Zorn, Wendy Martinek, Chris Bonneau, Paul Wahlbeck, Ryan Owens, Chad King, and Kevin McGuire. A number of other colleagues, like Brandon Bartels, Kirk Randazzo, Christine Ludowise, Patrick Wohlfarth, and Banks Miller helped us with data, methods, and/or really smart suggestions. Mike MacKuen and Jim Stimson were gracious enough to share data with us. Sara Benesh provided us with some of her past research and it filled a critical gap in our work. The final result is better for their assistance. We wish we could blame them for some of the problems, but alas they are not responsible.

We all owe a great deal to the help of Larry Baum, who provided guidance long before this project was launched and patiently read multiple versions of chapters and papers. Any merit has his fingerprints, but he is blameless for any problems.

We had the help of former graduate students such as Marc Hendershot and Maureen Gilbride at UMSL and Jason Lawrence at Georgia Southern.

We want to thank, Heather Howard, the administrative assistant of the Department of Political Science at Georgia Southern, for all of her help. A number of our colleagues were also helpful in reading our work, providing support, or just knowing when to stay out of our way. Special thanks to Steve Engel, Dave Robertson, Mike MacKuen, Will Hazelton, Pat Haney, Christopher Kelly, Trent Davis, and Michele Hoyman.

Bryan wants to acknowledge all the help and support provided by his advisor, David Rohde. Bryan thanks his beautiful wife, Candace; his wonderful sons, Evan and Dylan; and his ever-so-talented daughter, Autumn – she reminds him every day how important and rewarding it is to be a dad. Bryan also thanks his mother and father who have made everything possible.

Brett would like to thank everyone who has contributed to his interest in law and courts over the years. In particular, the guidance provided by members of the Department of Political Science at Ohio State has proven invaluable, as have subsequent collaborations with Banks Miller, Nancy Scherer, Rich Pacelle, and Bryan Marshall. Larry Baum's mentorship and direction deserve particular mention. Brett is deeply indebted to him, as are many others. Friendships with many additional people, including Trent Davis, Bill Luce, Shawn Logan, and Kelly Thomas, have also helped make this book possible. Finally, Brett is extremely grateful for the love and support of his incredible family – particularly his parents, Bill and Judy, and his grandmother Bernice. He dedicates this book to another very special family.

Rich is pleased that he was smart enough to choose two great co-authors. He hopes that now that the book is finished the three of them can go back to being friends. Or at least speak to each other again. He is grateful for all those professors and mentors who went out of their way for him. Richard Curry (no relation to Brett as far as we know), Howard Reiter, Kent Newmyer, Fred Kort, George Cole, and Elliot Slotnick all played important roles in his development, as did the professors at Rutgers School of Law who systematically disabused him of the notion he wanted to be a lawyer. If not for each of them, someone else would be writing this book with Brett and Bryan.

As with Brett, Rich owes his most important intellectual debt to Larry Baum. Like Brett, Rich feels that deciding to go to Ohio State and study with Larry was one of his best decisions. Larry is a seminal figure in the public law area. He is also a brilliant teacher. As good a researcher and teacher as he is, he is an even better person.

Rich also wishes to thank his parents, Dick and Pat (like the Nixons, but only in name thankfully), and his sisters, Kim and Wendy. He owes the greatest debts to his wonderful wife Fenton. Like LeBron, Oprah, Cher, and Madonna, one name says it all. In addition to the support that spouses and families provide, the fact that she was an award-winning librarian was put to good use. Fenton was kind enough to index the book. We all appreciate her support, the lunches at the conferences, and her constantly positive attitude. I also appreciate the support of my boys, Russell and Craig. Occasionally, I corner them and tell them all about the Supreme Court. They are polite enough to listen for a few minutes before excusing themselves.

Rich dedicates his share of this book to a real American hero, his brother Wayne: My mother made a great choice when she picked him as her favorite child. Wayne and I were born in the two years when Willie Mays was MVP of the National League (look it up if you want to know how old we are). My father repeatedly said that he would kill Mays if he ever had another great season. When he was just 5 or 6, I was my brother's hero. Now he is mine. I made the wiser, more informed choice.

Wayne got a five-figure advance for his recent book. I told him my advance for this book was also five figures. What I may have neglected to tell him was that two of those figures were behind a decimal place. Wayne's book predictably became an Oprah's Book Club Choice. I sent her a copy of the manuscript for this book, hoping for a similar designation. I have not heard back from her yet.

The Supreme Court

The Nation's Balance Wheel

On the steps of the courthouse, she typically sits. Inside the courtroom, she usually stands. Regardless, she has a sword at her side, ready if necessary. She holds the scales of justice, and most often she is blindfolded. The Greeks called her Themes, the goddess of order and law. The Romans had a name that more closely reflects our language: Justicia. She is the symbol of the legal system in the United States. She represents the notion that justice is blind and should be meted out objectively, without regard to the identity of the supplicants. Whether known as Themes, Justicia, or Lady Justice, she is a normative icon.

If she has a modern embodiment in the American legal system, it is the nominee for a seat on the United States Supreme Court. Note that we did not say the justices of the Supreme Court; we said the nominees – most of them, anyway. When there is a vacancy on the Court, the stakes are high. Of course, if Justice truly were blind and prospective justices truly nonpartisan, it would not matter whom the president selected to ascend to the high bench as long as he or she were eminently qualified. And to the untrained eye, this is what appears to be the case, as the carnival that is the nomination process moves into the national limelight. When the nominee sits before the gatekeeper, the Senate Judiciary Committee, the chosen one appears to be the paragon of judicial temperament and objectivity. Sitting there with his or her metaphorical sword sheathed so as not to offend the exclusive elected club that holds the membership key to the more exclusive unelected club, the nominee promises to view every case on its merits. These individuals swear that they come with no agenda or preconceived ideas about the issues that will be on the docket should they become the newest justices. It is a well-orchestrated charade during which the nominee attempts to say nothing that will turn public opinion against the candidacy (Pacelle 2002).

The issue of who is nominated and who is confirmed is important because the Supreme Court is a significant policy maker. Its decisions choose between the two parties, allocating some value in that particular case. But, more importantly, the decision of the Court becomes the law of the land, a precedent that is to guide the lower courts in similar cases. Because the Court has only nine members, every change in its composition is potentially significant (Krehbiel 2007). Presidents understand that their most enduring legacy may be the justices they get on the Supreme Court. Senators understand that a new member can tip the balance, and they guard their constitutional prerogative of "advice and consent" (Abraham 2008; Epstein and Segal 2005).

There are essentially two debates about the nomination process and its results, one normative and the other empirical. The normative debate focuses on how justices should act. They should be objective, follow precedent, and practice judicial restraint. Indeed, the naïve legal model states that justices will "find" the law and that there is a determinative answer to every legal question in statutes, constitutional provisions, or extant precedents (Cross and Nelson 2001). A classic quote by Justice Owen Roberts sums up the view that the justices find the law, rather than make policy: "It is sometimes said that the court assumes a power to overrule or control the action of the people's representatives. This is a misconception.... When an act of Congress is appropriately challenged in the courts as not conforming to the constitutional mandate the judicial branch of the Government has only one duty – to lay the article of the Constitution which is invoked beside the statute which is challenged and to decide whether the latter squares with the former" (*United States v. Butler* 297 US at 62 [1936]).

The other debate – the empirical side – focuses on how justices actually decide cases. Students of judicial decision making often argue that justices come to the Court with ideological predispositions and then typically follow their sincere preferences when making decisions (Segal and Spaeth 1993, 2002). This naïve political model sees justices as unconstrained political actors furthering their deeply held policy goals through the cases that sit on their docket (Cross and Nelson 2001). Although he served at the same time as Justice Roberts, Chief Justice Charles Evans Hughes articulated a very divergent notion of the Court's authority and the importance of judicial preferences when he said: "We live under a Constitution, but the Constitution is what judges say it is" (Wolfe 1997, 30).

The fact that these different perspectives are labeled as "naïve" models of decision making suggests that they are straw arguments. We might ask, then, how far do these naïve views stray from reality? And how far does the normative view depart from the empirical reality? This brings us to the subject of this book. Regardless of what we think about how justices should operate, what factors actually explain decision making by the Supreme Court? We can pose the question of whether the Court is the keeper of the covenant or a bevy of Platonic guardians. Does the Court merely "maintain the constitutional shield," or does it "create a new living law"? We hate to give away the ending, but as we have hinted, it does both. Sometimes it is the guardian of the Constitution, and sometimes it is a council of elders hurling policy statements like so many lightning bolts from its marble palace in Washington, D.C.

This book examines institutional judicial decision making at the Supreme Court level. Our goal is to develop a theoretical accounting and empirical assessment of the primary factors explaining the collective decisions of the Court. In studies of judicial decision making, there has been a disconnect between individual and institutional levels of analysis. Perhaps we can see this disconnect most clearly when we consider the supposed independence of the Court and the justices. Lifetime tenure and the nomination process insulate individual justices and permit them to pursue their sincere policy preferences. Yet it is the institution that makes the decision, and it needs to attend to precedent, stabilize the law, and protect its legitimacy. The Court as an institution is hardly independent. The Court lacks the "sword and purse" and must rely on the other branches to fund or implement its directives. Thus, although the justices are free to vote according to their individual attitudes, the Court needs to pay attention to its limitations as an institution. Borrowing from individual decision-making literature and institutional-level models, we construct an integrative model of Supreme Court decision making.

Our integrative model unites key components of the contemporary decision-making models of the Court (i.e., attitudinal, legal, and strategic models). In particular, our contribution highlights the importance of the context of the Court's decision (constitutional vs. statutory) and the importance or salience of various issues to the Court. In general, one can think of issue area and decision context as conditions that create both opportunities and constraints with respect to the Court's power to affect policy and the interpretation of law. In broad brushstrokes, the integrated model explains how these conditions differentially affect the impact of legal, attitudinal, and strategic factors on the Court's decision

Other approaches

making. The analysis illustrates that issue area – the salience of certain issues over others to the Court – and the decision context (constitutional vs. statutory) do matter a great deal in understanding the effects of attitudinal, legal, and strategic factors. The impact of judicial preferences does vary across constitutional and statutory decision contexts. Moreover, the effects of legal factors like precedent and issue evolution are not constant but vary in important ways depending on the salience or centrality of the issues to the Court and its institutional power. We also find evidence that the Court behaves strategically in a larger separation-of-powers system. The evidence suggests that the Court anticipates the political constraints (and opportunities) imposed by the president and majorities in Congress. Indeed, the impact of strategic factors on Court decisions is not constant but varies across issues and the constitutional or statutory decision context.

On the following pages, we take the reader on a brief sojourn to examine how the Supreme Court became so powerful and how it walks the fine line between interpreting the law and the Constitution on the one hand and making public policy on the other. Then we discuss how key factors offer opportunities and constraints on the Court's exercise of its institutional power. In effect, these represent important factors from the contemporary judicial decision-making models that are discussed in greater detail in Chapter 2.

BECOMING THE "SUPREME" COURT

The Supreme Court's status as a major policy maker should not really surprise anyone, except maybe the nominees we discussed at the beginning of this chapter. If the public did not know that the Court was a major actor in the policy-making process, the decision in the *Bush v. Gore* (2000) case probably removed any lingering doubt. In truth, most schoolchildren and even some political science majors can name major decisions like *Roe v. Wade* (1973) and *Brown v. Board of Education* (1954). Even occasional viewers of police dramas have heard of the *Miranda* rights and likely can recite them verbatim. Baseball fans might know *Flood v. Kuhn* (1972), which dramatically altered the power structure of the sport (Goldman 2008). All represented major pronouncements from the Supreme Court.

That the Court has evolved in that way or would come to have such a luxurious home would come as a surprise to Alexander Hamilton and John Jay, to say nothing of James Madison. By the time he was elected president, Madison knew that the Court was a legitimate source of power, but prior to being the defendant in *Marbury v. Madison* (1803), he might not have guessed it. In "Federalist 78," Hamilton referred to the judiciary as "the least dangerous branch of government." Jay, the third and often forgotten co-author of the *Federalist Papers*, was able to see the weaknesses of the institution up close when George Washington nominated him to be the first chief justice of the United States. The Court adjourned after just nine days during its first term because it had nothing to do. That was a week longer than the second term in 1790. No cases were decided by the Court in 1791 or 1792. Nominees refused the honor of joining the Court, and those who were tricked into serving soon fled to run for governor or return to the state legislature. Jay left, claiming the Court lacked the "energy, weight, and dignity" to influence national affairs (Pacelle 2002, 82). As a symbolic reflection of this impotence, the Court was reduced to holding its official meetings and oral arguments in an anteroom in the congressional building.

This would change with the ascension of John Marshall. Marshall, like William Marbury (of *Marbury v. Madison* fame), was one of the famous midnight appointments made as the Federalists were going into exile. With his decision in *Marbury*, Marshall claimed an impressive power for the fledgling Court: judicial review. In a series of other decisions that included such landmarks as *Martin v. Hunter's Lessee* (1816), *McCulloch v. Maryland* (1819), *Gibbons v. Ogden* (1824), and *Barron v. Baltimore* (1833), the Marshall Court redefined federalism and animated national power. If there was any doubt about the power of the Supreme Court, it was soon dispelled. It is a testimony to Marshall that the largest statue in the new building that he for all intents and purposes made necessary is of the chief justice himself. He did more than any president of his time (he served much longer) to structure the evolution of American government and influence public policy.

The authority of the Court has waxed and waned over the years. The Court marched in lockstep with the ruling majority at times (Powe 2009). Yet there were periods when the Court was at odds with the elected branches (Casper 1976; Dahl 1957). Occasionally, there were self-inflicted wounds when the Court exercised authority that maneuvered the institution into difficult straits. The modern Supreme Court is a far cry from the "least dangerous branch." In fact, it would be closer to reality to regard it as an imperial judiciary rather than an ineffective or powerless one.

Thus, we start with the premise that the Court is an important policy maker. Given that, we want to understand how the Court arrives at the decisions that become the law of the land. The process is fairly well known, so we concentrate on which factors influence the Court and under what conditions. With an eye on the existing literature, we examine the decision making of the "modern" Supreme Court as a function of a number of factors. We start with the premise that the law matters. We are very cognizant of the fact that who is on the Court matters. We also hypothesize that the system of checks and balances just might mean that Congress and the president exert some influence as well.

What events and associated dates have transformed the modern United States Supreme Court? The list would be quite lengthy. For the sake of brevity, let's choose three: 1925, 1937–38, and 1954. In 1925, Congress, which has control over the Court's appellate jurisdiction, passed the so-called Judges Bill, which fundamentally redefined the Supreme Court's role by repealing much of the Court's mandatory jurisdiction and creating the discretionary writ of *certiorari* (Pacelle 1991; Perry 1991). This would help the Court increasingly become a constitutional tribunal. It would also help usher in long periods of judicial activism (Keck 2004; Powe 2000).

In 1937, the Court that had emasculated the New Deal was openly threatened by President Franklin D. Roosevelt in his thinly veiled "Court reorganization plan" (better known as the "Court-packing plan"). Eventually, the Court capitulated and began upholding the building blocks of the New Deal (Baker 1967). In the wake of this retreat and a series of subsequent retirements, Roosevelt was able to accomplish his goal of building a new majority without altering the size of the institution.[1] With no changes in membership, the Court reversed its own precedents.

Having played and apparently lost a game of constitutional brinksmanship, the Court seemed relegated to return to Hamilton's promise as "the least dangerous branch of government." Instead, it began the protracted process of rebuilding its institutional legitimacy and redefining its role. In an otherwise forgettable case involving filled milk products (*United States v. Carolene Products* [1938]), Justice Harlan Fiske Stone penned his famous "Footnote Four," arguing that the Court should show deference to the elected branches in matters involving economic policy. However, he continued, in matters involving the rights of insular minorities, the Court needed to be vigilant and protect civil rights and liberties. Stone was, in effect, advocating a double standard for the Court. Civil

---

[1] McKenna (2002) argues that Roosevelt's selection of Hugo Black was designed to bring the Court into disrepute and to undercut its institutional authority.

rights and civil liberties would be held in a "preferred position" by the post–New Deal Court (Mason 1956; Pacelle 1991).

The imperative of Footnote Four would have a number of significant effects on the Supreme Court. First, it would elevate civil rights and individual liberties to the center of the Court's agenda. To do that, the Court would have to de-emphasize economic issues (Benson 1970; Pacelle 1991). A second and related effect was the expedition of the process by which the Supreme Court became a constitutional court. The Court would extricate itself from the economic issues that were largely statutory in favor of individual liberties and civil rights cases, which would necessitate interpretation of the Bill of Rights and the Fourteenth Amendment. Finally, because of the preferred position doctrine, the Court would be proactive in monitoring legislative activity that might restrict individual liberties – the essence of judicial activism (Pacelle 2002).

The year 1954 was, of course, best known for the landmark *Brown v. Board of Education* decision. With that decision, the Court validated the promise of Footnote Four in many ways. The Court's decision was unanimous, a symbolic gesture of unity to demonstrate resolve to the public and the elected branches (Schwartz 1983). The substance of the decision was widely applauded, but the decision was controversial because the Court did not confine it to the four corners of the Constitution. Nor did the Court abide by the prevailing precedent.

Within five years of the *Brown* decision, in another civil rights case, *Cooper v. Aaron* (1958), the Court asserted that it was the ultimate arbiter of constitutional questions (Powe 2000). To protect the civil rights of African Americans, particularly in the South, the Court revisited the process of selective incorporation of the Bill of Rights (Cortner 1981; Walker 1990). The primacy of civil rights and individual liberties cases would force the hand of the other branches of government as well (but see Rosenberg [2008]). Congress eventually would pass an omnibus civil rights act. The president would enforce integration, and the solicitor general (SG) would consistently support civil rights initiatives for thirty years (Pacelle 2003).

These events, which contributed to the transformation of the Supreme Court as an institution, are noteworthy for a number of reasons. Most notably for our purposes, two of the three events were launched externally. The creation of the writ of *certiorari* and the changes in the Court's jurisdiction were part of the constitutional power given to Congress. The "Court-packing plan" came from the president's constitutional authority to choose the justices of the Supreme Court. These events are a reminder

that the Court operates in a system that both imposes significant constraints and provides wide-ranging opportunities. The *Brown* decision
was internally generated by the Court, although one could argue that the
Court was responding in part to the deafening silence of the other two
branches. Certainly, the *Brown* decision was not met by any subsequent
silence. There were questions as to whether the president would enforce
the decision. There were numerous attempts by members of Congress to
undermine the decision or give aid and comfort to those who would seek
to resist it (Canon and Johnson 1999; Powe 2000).

Yet 1954 is the beginning, not the end, of our analysis. The modern
Court has not been a stagnant institution. This brief sojourn through the
history of the Supreme Court is meant to highlight a few things: First,
the Court may have started out as a weak afterthought of the Framers,
but today it plays a significant role in policy making. Second, the most
effective way to change constitutional interpretation is to change the
composition of the Court. Third, there are periods that saw significant
changes in the composition of the Court, but they did not reveal wholesale
changes in precedent or in the law. Thus, the Court appears to be aware of
the limitations on its power and cognizant of its duty to stabilize the law.
We seek to construct a model that will reconcile these disparate ideas.

This book is not a history of the Supreme Court. There are many
fine volumes that cover that. This study seeks to examine systematically
the factors that influence judicial decision making under a variety of
circumstances. We examine the modern Supreme Court, the one that was
birthed with *Brown v. Board of Education*. It is the Court that delivered
on the promise of Footnote Four, became a major campaign issue, had
significant swings in ideological composition, and changed doctrine and
the political theories underlying constitutional interpretation. It is a Court
that has dealt with a modern, powerful president (Skowronek 1997) and
a Congress whose power has fluctuated (Dodd 1986). This provides an
ideal context for our analysis, which sets out to assess how the Court
exercises its powers differentially across issue areas and depending on
whether the cases require constitutional or statutory interpretation.

By any definition, the Supreme Court contributes to the construction of
public policy in the United States. In some areas of the law, the Court plays
a more interstitial role, filling in the gaps. Since Footnote Four, the Court
has taken a less central role in economic policy. In other areas, the Court
is more of the primary branch of government, assuming a leadership role.
When the Court announced the preferred position doctrine, it established
itself as the foremost institution in constructing individual liberties and
civil rights policy. On constitutional issues, in a pair of decisions that

virtually bookend the years of this study,[2] the Court announced that it has the last word on the Constitution. How does the Court interact with the other branches of government when it is involved in the process of constructing doctrine? When, if ever, does precedent play a role in the Court's decisions? How important is the ideological composition of the Court? Is the Supreme Court a court of laws or a super legislature? Does it make a difference if we look at constitutional decisions versus statutory ones? Are the factors that govern economic decisions different from those that govern civil rights and individual liberties? We consider these and other questions in this study. In particular, we examine the impact of a variety of factors on the decisions of the modern Supreme Court (1954–2000).

THE CONTEXT FOR SUPREME COURT DECISION MAKING

In Chapter 2, we will discuss the three models of decision making that dominate the literature. By way of a little preview and, more importantly, to establish a context for our research, we introduce them here. The three traditional models of decision making are the legal model, the attitudinal model, and the strategic model. The legal model holds to the primacy of legitimate factors like precedent and close adherence to neutral principles of decision making. The legal model is premised on the idea that the law matters and the Court strives for consistency and legitimacy in its decisions. By contrast, the attitudinal model argues that the justices are free to act on their own sincere policy preferences. Justices are not constrained by precedent or overly concerned about the other branches; rather, they seek to issue policy directives that are consistent with their collective preferences. The strategic model (and we speak generically of a strategic model, though there are many) places the Court in the context of separation of powers and checks and balances. Such models argue that the Court needs to act in a responsible manner and occasionally trim its policy preferences to avoid any retaliation from the other branches of government.

We find merit in each of these individual models. But none of them alone, in our opinion, is sufficient to provide a nuanced view of Supreme Court decision making. Our study is different and, we hope, important on a number of levels. First, on the epistemological level, the models reflect the history of political science and the different approaches that have

---

[2] The Court made this position explicit in *Cooper v. Aaron* (1958) (Powe 2000, 160) and reiterated it in *City of Boerne v. Flores* (1997).

dominated the discipline (Murphy and Tanenhaus 1972). Second, we examine decision making from the institutional rather than the individual perspective. Third, this study focuses on both governmental institutions and Supreme Court decision making. Fourth, this is an integrative model of decision making that combines the legal, attitudinal, and strategic models of judicial behavior. Finally, the study has theoretical significance for democratic theory, separation of powers scholarship, the appropriate role for and the legitimacy of the Supreme Court, and the protection of individual rights and liberties (Clayton and Gillman 1999; Franklin and Kosaki 1989; Gillman and Clayton 1999; Pacelle 2002; Silverstein 2009; Smith 1985; Sunstein 1993).

Each of the models of decision making is predicated on notions of how the Supreme Court works and the environment in which it operates. Before we investigate the three models in detail and develop our own integrated model in the next chapters, we briefly sketch out in this next section the key legal and strategic considerations that make up the Court's environment. In essence, these features provide both opportunities and constraints that powerfully shape the Court's incentives in making decisions.

Next.

OPPORTUNITIES AND CONSTRAINTS: THE SUPREME COURT'S ENVIRONMENT

Despite lifetime tenure, the marble palace, and the general goodwill the public feels toward the institution, the United States Supreme Court does not exist in a vacuum. The Court can be constrained by existing precedent, case facts, the evolution of the particular issue, Congress, and the president. Yet it is important to note that these factors can also serve as opportunities for the Court. When precedents are favorable, issues have developed in a particular manner, and Congress and/or the president is ideologically aligned with the current majority, the Court can more easily pursue its policy designs. We need to establish the context for the Court to help us build a model of institutional decision making. We consider the roles of precedent, issue evolution, the president, and Congress in influencing the Supreme Court.

Precedent

How important is precedent? There are typically two views of precedent. The first, sometimes referred to as the weak view, holds that precedent carries little or no weight in constitutional law. It is just one of a number of factors that justices consider in making a decision. The strong view sees precedent as determinative of decisions. Although this has some normative appeal, it has very little empirical support (Gerhardt 2008, 3–5). Judges, at least at the lower court levels, seem to treat precedent seriously (e.g., Benesh and Reddick 2002; Hettinger, Lindquist, and Martinek 2006; Songer and Haire 1992). For example, Hansford and Spriggs (2006, 122) find that "the Supreme Court's treatment of its precedents matters because it has a real effect on how the lower courts then use that precedent." If this is so, then it is likely that Supreme Court justices view precedent as important in constraining lower court judges and maybe their successors (Gerhardt 2008). This is often referred to as vertical *stare decisis*, and it is hard to imagine the system functioning without it.

Most litigants also treat precedent seriously (Knight and Epstein 1996). As repeat players, they press for advantages in the system. They play the odds, seeking to establish favorable rules and precedents (Galanter 1974), and they may have to maneuver around adverse precedents. Consider the National Association for the Advancement of Colored People (NAACP) as it began to mount its litigation campaign to build toward equality. The Legal Defense Fund (LDF), the litigation arm of the NAACP, had to deal with an adverse precedent that was deeply rooted in Southern law. *Plessy v. Ferguson* (1896) virtually mandated the separation of the races. It required separate but equal facilities. Everyone knew that institutions in the South followed the former but ignored the latter. The LDF tried to find a wedge to advance equal protection of the law despite that adverse precedent.

The carefully crafted strategy of the LDF began with attempts to get individual African American graduate and law students into segregated universities. In their briefs and arguments, LDF attorneys never asked the Court to overrule *Plessy*. Rather, they told the justices they respected the viability of the precedent and asked the Court to distinguish the particular case from the general principle (Wasby 1995). This turned out to be a successful strategy. The LDF opened a door of opportunity, and eventually the Court pushed that door wide open in *Brown v. Board of Education*. *Brown* would turn out to be what some have called a "super-precedent" that had lasting power and swept across a variety of domains (Landes and Posner 1976).

In *Brown*, the Court rid itself, at least in the realm of education, of the albatross that was *Plessy*. This illustrates that precedent can be an enormous opportunity as well as the constraint it was prior to *Brown*.

When the Court announces a new precedent, it typically commits to it in the short term. A new precedent may signal a shift in priorities to other institutional actors. A new precedent will prompt repeat players to bring the next round of litigation in hopes of expanding the nascent precedent or, for opponents, containing the damage. It may also have spillover effects, as it did in *Brown*, leading to advances and new precedents in related areas of law (Pacelle 1991, 2009).

Legal precedent plays an undeniably critical role in structuring the behavior of actors before the Supreme Court. The Court's opinions rely heavily on precedent (Phelps and Gates 1991); litigants and *amici curiae* structure legal arguments around existing case law (Epstein and Knight 1997, 1999); and lower courts are expected to make decisions that fall within the boundaries of controlling cases (Songer, Segal, and Cameron 1994). More generally, precedent provides the American legal system with continuity and stability. Without precedent as an anchor, *stare decisis* would be a fiction, law would be unpredictable, and lawyers, lower court judges, and ordinary citizens would be incapable of navigating the terrain developed by new and different legal problems. Rather, each case would require *de novo* consideration, and the judicial system would be incapable of functioning efficiently under that additional pressure (Collins 2008; Hansford and Spriggs 2006; Landes and Posner 1976).

At the same time, the extent of precedent's importance remains hotly debated. Although litigants and lower court judges appear to pay attention to precedent, justices on the Supreme Court do not necessarily feel bound by it. Some refer to this as horizontal *stare decisis*. According to the most traditional analysts, precedent is sacrosanct. These scholars acknowledge the historical reality that the Court has overturned several notable precedents including *Plessy*, *Adkins v. Children's Hospital* (1923, overturned in 1937), and *Bowers v. Hardwick* (1986, overturned in 2003), yet they point to the fact that, in the aggregate, the Court nevertheless overturns very few precedents (Ball 1978). When the Court does overturn precedent, it discusses its reasons for doing so. Perhaps intervening cases have so weakened the precedent that it has been all but overruled *sub silencio*, or circumstances have shown it to be unworkable or badly reasoned (see *United States v. Gaudin* 1995; *Agostini v. Felton* 1997). In any case, by going out of its way to explain such reversals, the Court highlights their rarity.

Other analysts maintain that precedent is instrumental – that it is but a normative concept designed to obscure the primacy of sincere policy preferences. These scholars argue that, rather than finding controlling precedents and using those cases to reach dispassionate decisions, justices vote in a manner consistent with their policy preferences and then find precedents that lend support to that conclusion (Segal and Spaeth 2002). In other words, justices (or perhaps their clerks) scour the *U.S. Reports* for precedents that coincide with their policy attitudes.

Scholars in this tradition base their views on several propositions. They argue that precedents appear on both sides of virtually every appellate court controversy. As such, they contend that arguments about the impact of precedent on judicial decisions are nonfalsifiable or untestable (Segal and Spaeth 2002, 47). Justices may rely on precedent as the primary explanation for Court decisions, but skeptics note that justices rarely invoke precedents that might weaken their argument or of which they disapprove (Segal, Spaeth, and Benesh 2005, 30). Of course, if justices are confronted with adverse precedent, they may opt to overturn it. But even if a precedent is not overturned, the Supreme Court may "distinguish" a given case and, thus, limit the precedent's application (Baum 2010, 120). When the Burger Court authorized a "good faith exception" to the exclusionary rule in *United States v. Leon* (1984), it did not reverse the core precedents. Rather, it distinguished the facts of *Leon* and held that those facts created a particular exception to the exclusionary rule's general requirements (Pacelle 2004).

But as soon as the Court establishes a new precedent, as it did in *Brown*, it has the additional goal of protecting that precedent's long-term viability from attack by future Court majorities. By protecting and expanding the new precedent's scope and weaving it deeply into the fabric of additional precedents, the Court can make it increasingly difficult for future justices who may wish to abandon the existing standard to do so. Soon-to-be justice Samuel Alito (2006) made this point during his confirmation hearings, noting, "When a precedent is reaffirmed, each time it's reaffirmed that is a factor that should be taken into account in making the judgment about *stare decisis*. And when a precedent is reaffirmed on the ground that *stare decisis* precludes or counsels against reexamination of the merits of the precedent, then I agree that that is a precedent on precedent."

There is a missing piece to the puzzle. If the proponents of the attitudinal model are correct, then the justices are trying to pursue their sincere preferences. How do they do that? If justices are primarily interested in reading their sincere policy preferences into the law, this occurs through precedent and legal interpretation. Thus, justices have to respect their colleagues' precedents if they expect their brethren to respect theirs.

Thus, Gerhardt (2008, 79–86) argues that there is a "golden rule" of precedent.

Despite its importance, few would argue that precedent is always determinative of decisions. Collins (2008, 82–86) advocates a legal persuasion model. In this view, there is not a single correct answer to a case. Rather, the legal persuasion model is based on the expectation that "justices will find some arguments more persuasive than others and make good faith efforts to endorse those positions, regardless of whether the outcomes are at odds with their ideological preferences" (Collins 2008, 86). It is likely that *stare decisis* provides a sort of "gravitational effect" on justices (Aldisert 1990; Segal, Spaeth, and Benesh 2005, 29). Indeed, in his testimony before the Senate Judiciary Committee, Alito (2006) "[did not] want to leave the impression that *stare decisis* is an inexorable command because the Supreme Court has said that it is not." The Supreme Court's interpretations of precedent cannot be completely decoupled from judicial policy preferences (Hansford and Spriggs 2006, 56), but precedent may constrain judicial choices by limiting the universe of legally defensible alternatives (Hansford and Spriggs 2006, 74; van Hees and Steunenberg 2000).

Issue Evolution

In discussing precedent, we argue that law matters. Similarly, in discussing cases, we emphasize that facts matter. More difficult cases make it harder for the Court to reach a liberal economic or a pro–civil rights or pro–civil liberties decision (Segal 1984, 1986). The Court has established a long line of precedents that give protection to citizens from warrantless searches of their homes. The same level of protection does not hold for automobiles. The latter is a more difficult issue for the Court to decide. It is important when understanding the potential impact of precedent and the other branches in influencing Court decisions to control for the facts of the case.[3] In some cases, the violation of one's rights or liberties is so severe that even the least sympathetic justice would have to side with the claimant. There are some occasions when the government has followed the procedures scrupulously, and the substance of its actions is beyond reproach. In these cases, even the most civil liberties–oriented justice

---

[3] Dimensional analysis is typically used to demonstrate the impact of values and attitudes. Analysts use a Guttman scale that starts with the assumption that items are arranged in an order so that an individual who agrees with a particular item also agrees with items of easier or lower rank order.

would have to concede the state's action met constitutional muster. Of course, these clear cases seldom reach the Supreme Court. Lower courts settle most of them, leaving the cases that raise the more difficult questions and require the refined balancing acts for the Supreme Court.

The construction of judicial doctrine and Supreme Court policy has been compared to piecing together a giant mosaic. Public policy is normally associated with landmark Court decisions, like *Roe v. Wade, Mapp v. Ohio*, or *Brown*, or seminal legislation, like the Civil Rights Act (CRA) or the Patriot Act, disregarding the processes that made such important pronouncements possible and the work necessary to flesh out the questions left in the wake of the landmarks (but see Baumgartner and Jones [1993] and Kingdon [1995]). Supreme Court decisions and congressional legislation, no matter how significant, raise more questions than they answer. Landmark decisions like *Brown, Roe*, and *Mapp* were far from the last word in their respective areas of law. In fact, each preceded an explosion of litigation and Court attention in the areas of school desegregation, reproductive rights, and search and seizure, respectively (Pacelle 1991). Thus, it is useful to view judicial doctrine and policy as evolving through a series of decisions and a number of stages (Pacelle 2009).

The notion of policy evolution is implicit in many studies of the president (Light 1982; Skowronek 1997), Congress (Kingdon 1995; Sinclair 1989), and the bureaucracy (Ripley and Franklin 1982, 1990; Wood and Waterman 1993, 1994). Studies of the outputs of the elected branches (M. Smith 1993; Walker 1977) show how policy is built in stages. Analyses of specific areas of law (Cortner 1981; Graber 1991; Haiman 1981; Hoff 1991; Kritzer and Richards 2003, 2005; McCloskey 1960; Richards and Kritzer 2002; Wahlbeck 1997) demonstrate how current decisions are layered on existing precedents to flesh out the Court's policy.

The judicial behavior literature, most notably analyses of decision making by justices (Schubert 1965, 1974; Segal and Spaeth 2002) and analyses of the facts of cases (Ignagni 1993, 1994; Kort 1957; Segal 1984, 1986), lends credence to the processes by which issues evolve and become more complex over time (Baum 1988, 1992). These studies implicitly or explicitly demonstrate that differing fact or case situations have a significant impact on the decisions of individual justices and the Court as a whole (George and Epstein 1992).

Traditionally, a case law focus overemphasizes the importance of landmark decisions. Policy and policy change are not individual events or a single landmark decision, but rather a series of decisions. Landmark decisions interrupt the previous stationary pattern and initiate a new pattern of development. Thus, policy is better defined as the sum total of legislative or judicial initiatives in a given area. To be sure, seminal decisions alter the dynamics of policy making, affect the authoritative allocation of values, and expand, narrow, or in some cases overturn previous policy. They are not, however, the last word in that substantive area of law (Baird 2004; Pacelle 1991). The changes in doctrine are visible and serve as the beginning or the acceleration of the dynamic that underlies the development of that issue (Kahn 1994; Kritzer and Richards 2003, 2005).

Studies of the Supreme Court typically offer generalizations that appear to govern every circumstance. In practice, the behavior of justices and litigants varies as a function of different conditions or situations (Baird 2004; Epstein and Kobylka 1992; Kobylka 1987; Pacelle 2003; Richards and Kritzer 2002). This framework considers the evolution of policy in the Supreme Court by examining the expected behavior of justices and repeat player litigants in different contextual settings. This perspective maintains that the Court's decisions are a function of the individual preferences of the justices as well as the institutional norms and rules that affect the Court's work (Pacelle 2009).

The notion of policy evolution makes a great deal of sense. Supreme Court policy is doctrine woven from a number of decisions over time. Litigants have the incentive to bring cases to further their litigation goals. Justices have the desire to see their constitutional visions put into the law. But they have an institutional obligation to build doctrine in a coherent fashion. The Court's decisions settle individual disputes. But its doctrine develops policy, creates precedents, and guides lower courts and litigants. The opinions help actors overcome uncertainty in their decision-making processes (Hansford and Spriggs 2006, 3).

The creation and development of doctrine demands multiple rounds of litigation and may be interrupted or influenced by the actions of the other branches of government. The individual cases that reach the Court are not decided in isolation. Rather, doctrine is built over a period of time. A given policy is born of related issues and subsequently spawns other issues. As a result, decisions in one area can often have ripple effects on other areas (Pacelle 1991, 2009).

Justices and litigants have a strong incentive to see their policy designs reflected in the interpretation of the Constitution. They seek the opportunities to create favorable decisions. At the same time, they face a variety of constraints. Policy evolves in predictable ways and follows basic patterns of development. At the initial stage, policy is unstable. Justices and litigants search for a niche for the new issue. Often it comes from a related area of law. The Court needs to stabilize doctrine to guide the lower courts and let citizens know the extent of their rights. Ultimately, the Court lays down the fundamental principle that guides the future development of doctrine. As soon as the central standard has been established, the Court applies it as the cases get more difficult. The issue may get attached to other issues, reintroducing instability to the emerging doctrine and inconsistency in decision making (Pacelle 2009).

The Supreme Court and the President

It had been a couple of years since the unanimous Supreme Court hurled its lightning bolt from its marble palace. In the area of public education, the Court held, separate but equal had no place. It was a mighty symbolic blow for equal protection. However, though the Court had taken the moral high ground, there was no guarantee that its decision would be faithfully implemented. Indeed, when attempts were made to desegregate the public schools in Little Rock, Arkansas, the white political establishment resisted. The Court had made a major pronouncement that was being openly flaunted. Would the president come to the aid of the Court and put executive power and the bully pulpit behind the desegregation efforts?

Dwight Eisenhower was leery of the potential impact of the pending *Brown* case. When the Supreme Court invited the U.S. government to provide its views in an *amicus curiae* brief, Eisenhower wanted to decline the invitation. Attorney General Herbert Brownell told him that was not possible (Pacelle 2003). On the eve of the oral arguments for the case, Eisenhower invited Chief Justice Earl Warren to the White House, ostensibly for dinner. Warren was seated between the president and former SG John Davis. It just so happened that Davis was arguing the case on behalf of the school districts against desegregation. They implored Warren to resist the impulse to desegregate the schools (Newton 2006; White 1982). Eisenhower was not too happy when the Court announced that in the realm of education, separate but equal was inherently unequal and unconstitutional. There was a question of whether Eisenhower would fulfill the part of his oath that required him to faithfully execute the laws of the United States (Nichols 2007).

In the political game that is checks and balances, the president has a number of resources that can be brought to bear to try and influence the Court. Eisenhower apparently failed at two. First, he could not rein in the solicitor general. Second, the president can also stamp his imprint on the Court through the appointment of justices. If Eisenhower's goal was to keep the status quo in race relations, Earl Warren turned out to be a very bad choice. Because the Court lacks the sword and the purse, it is dependent on Congress and the president to see its directives are carried out. Thus, Eisenhower had another chance to undermine *Brown* by dragging his feet or even using active noncompliance. Reluctantly, Eisenhower sent federal troops to ensure that the decision be implemented.

Dahl (1957) noted that the Supreme Court cannot long hold out against majority sentiment to the contrary (but see Casper 1976). According to Dahl, the president's responsibility for making nominations to the Court is the most important factor contributing to this reality. In addition, presidential appointments to the Court often give chief executives an invisible hand over the development of legal and public policy long after their terms have ended (Krehbiel 2007). Consider Franklin Roosevelt's role in shaping the trajectory of American constitutional law in the past century. When the Roosevelt presidency began, the Court was populated by Republican appointees who had an affinity for *laissez faire* economic policies and showed little interest in addressing matters of civil liberties or rights (Cushman 1998; Leuchtenburg 1995). By the close of his twelve years in the White House, Roosevelt had appointed all but one member of the U.S. Supreme Court. Those appointments changed the face of the Court's jurisprudence for decades to come by validating a more expansive view of federal governmental power (Benson 1970). Ultimately, and arguably of greater consequence, Roosevelt appointees Hugo Black and William Douglas remained central to the Court's treatment of civil rights and civil liberties issues into the 1970s (Ball 2000; Pacelle 1991). Indeed, many of the precedents they helped to establish remain viable today. Thus, a president's powerful imprint may remain influential on the Court not just through appointees who outlive his tenure, but also through legal precedents that are established because of those appointments.

Not all presidents have the opportunity to shape the Court to this extent, but a president may need to make only one or two judicial appointments to change the ideological balance of the Court and impact its decisional trends (Krehbiel 2007; Silverstein 1994). Regardless, presidents do not always get what they want when their nominees take their seats on the bench. History is replete with examples of presidents who expressed disappointment with their judicial selections. Eisenhower, for example, pointedly referred to two of his Court nominations (Warren and William Brennan) as mistakes, going so far as to call his 1953 nomination of

Earl Warren "the biggest damn-fool mistake I ever made." Eisenhower's predecessor, Harry Truman, was even blunter in assessing the performance of his second nominee to the Court, Justice Tom C. Clark: "He hasn't made one right decision that I can think of.... It's just that he's such a dumb son of a bitch" (O'Brien 2005, 83). Still, the evidence suggests that justices tend to reflect the views of the presidents who select them (Epstein and Segal 2005, 121; Yates 2002). When justices do not reflect those views, it tends to be because they were chosen by presidents who had nonideological criteria such as religion or regional ties in mind.

Although presidential power over Supreme Court nominations represents an important aspect of the synergy between the executive and judicial branches, there are a number of other ways that presidents can interact with the Court. Because of the increased activism of the Supreme Court, the potential impact of its decisions is broad and sweeping. Those decisions, however, must be implemented, and the enforcement power is the province of the president and the executive branch. If the president does not like a decision, he may choose not to enforce it (Canon and Johnson 1999). Indeed, history books report that Andrew Jackson, upset by the *Worcester v. Georgia* decision, growled, "John Marshall has made his decision, now let him enforce it."[4] Presumably, then, the Court will consider the potential response of the president when it makes a decision.

In a related fashion, the president can help protect the Court's legitimacy through his behavior and his use of the bully pulpit. When Eisenhower sent troops, albeit reluctantly, to Little Rock, this lent strong symbolic support to the Court's race desegregation decisions. President John F. Kennedy sent a similar message in 1962 when he dispatched several thousand troops to enforce desegregation at the University of Mississippi (Baum 2010, 210). As the nation's chief executive, presidents also have the capacity to oversee implementation of Supreme Court decisions by executive branch agencies and departments. For example, the Court's decision in *Frontiero v. Richardson* (1973) required the U.S. Air Force to implement a policy it had originally opposed; ultimately, presidential oversight ensured the Air Force's compliance with that decision (Carp, Stidham, and Manning 2004, 375).

The president also has a check through the Justice Department and the executive branch's representative in the Supreme Court, the SG. The

---

[4] Clearly the president did not comply with the Court's decision, but his oft-repeated remarks may be apocryphal.

SG brings cases on behalf of the U.S. government, and because he or she is a presidential appointee who answers to the attorney general, there is the potential for executive influence. The increased activism of the Court and the rise of the institutional presidency have magnified the potential influence of the Office of the Solicitor General (OSG) (Pacelle 2003; Ubertaccio 2005). The president may try to use the SG to pursue his agenda through the Court. Because of the volume of litigation the government is involved with, the SG plays a major role in helping the Court control its docket. In particular, analysts argue that the SG can use *amicus* briefs to advance the president's agenda before the Court (Bailey, Kamoie, and Maltzman 2005; Pacelle 2003; Segal 1990; Wohlfarth 2009; Yates 2002).[5] In recognition of the Office's influence before the Court, the SG is routinely referred to as the Court's "tenth justice."

The president speaks with one voice. This provides him with important opportunities to use the bully pulpit (Kernell 2006). It can also introduce some meaningful constraints. We tend to heap too much praise on our presidents when things are going well and hold them accountable for things that may be beyond their control. The nation's lawgiver, Congress, also has resources that might influence the direction of Court decisions (Rosenberg 2008).

Congress and the Supreme Court

Like the president, Congress represents another important component in the Court's environment – a potentially powerful "principal" that the Court must consider in making its decisions. A discussion of Congress's powers and the role of politics can provide considerable insight into the Court's relationship with Congress. We use these as a backdrop to explore how and why Congress should matter to the Court's decision making.

The sequence in the Constitution establishing Congress as the first of three branches of government was much more than random happenstance. Congress is first for a reason (Mann and Ornstein 2006). The legislative branch would not only give voice to the great variety of policy tastes and intensities in the Republic, but it also would regulate its powers

---

[5] But Pacelle (2003) argues that there are multiple forms of *amici* and that only some can be used to advance the president's agenda. Indeed, in many areas of law, the position the SG adopts when filing *amicus* briefs does not reflect that of the president (Pacelle 2006).

from within as well as between the other institutions to better serve the public good. To achieve such ends, the Framers' design established a set of institutional dichotomies with respect to power and politics. Congress is the most powerful branch constitutionally, but it also is the most dependent on politics relative to the other branches. The constitutional powers of the presidency are far more ambiguous and seemingly less significant. However, the executive branch typically has the upper hand politically because presidents do not face the same collective action dilemmas in exercising their powers that Congress does. The framework relegated the Court to a lesser status, making it constitutionally weaker but more insulated from politics.

In no uncertain terms, the dichotomies encouraged by the Constitution placed Congress atop the institutional pecking order. For example, there is more than a little irony in what is widely recognized as the "Judicial Article" because it invokes congressional power over the courts no fewer than four times. To the extent that federal power was exercised during the first 150 years after the founding, it was usually exercised through Congress. In fact, Woodrow Wilson's extraordinary nineteenth-century text was a testament to *Congressional Government* (1885), which was just that – government by Congress. However, history has witnessed fairly astonishing swings in the institutional balance of power over time. On the heels of two world wars and a Great Depression, congressional government has given way to presidential government. Importantly, politics has played no small role in explaining the changing power relations between branches (Shepsle 2006).

Thus, the evolution of institutional power is importantly affected by both the constitutional framework and politics (Moe and Howell 1999). Despite its relatively dominant constitutional powers, the modern Congress seems clearly positioned on the losing end of a zero-sum struggle for power with the other branches. The president and the Court are much less likely to be deferential to the legislative branch compared to the days of Wilson's *Congressional Government*. In Scigliano's (1971) terms, the president and the Court have entered a "natural alliance" favoring coordinate construction on their own terms as opposed to those of Congress. Through their power over judicial appointment and implementation, presidents seem better equipped to shape the behavior of the Court as compared to Congress. Indeed, as Moe and Howell (1999, 869) argue, "Congress does not have a club over the Court's head. The president does."

Yet the fact that Congress does not hold a club over the Court clearly not mean that Congress has no power over the Court – the record is clear on that score. For Congress, it is a matter of *political will* or motivation to use its power. When the political incentives are aligned in its favor, Congress's constitutional powers may be even more intimidating than a club to beat the other institutions into submission. In those relatively rare instances when politics motivates Congress to act as a unified institution, its power may loom more like a loaded gun in the closet than a blunt club.

The relationship between Congress and the Court echoes the competing themes of agency independence and congressional control that are found in literature on the bureaucracy (e.g., Weingast and Moran 1983). For Congress, there usually exists a tension between politics and power. This tension reflects a significant collective action problem that often allows politics to trump an institutional willingness to exercise power. Both the executive and judicial branches have responded to Congress's collective weakness by enhancing their own institutional powers and discretion. Indeed, there is considerable theoretical and empirical work that suggests that the Court's decisions are driven by judicial preferences and free from congressional constraints (Segal and Spaeth 1993). In this view, the Court's independence in decision making results from Congress's lack of willingness due to collective transaction costs as well as its inability to overcome multiple veto points (Segal 1997). Despite this competing view, there remains ample reason to recognize the important role of the Congress.

The Court recognizes Congress's significant power and remains strategically wary of how a changing political environment could awaken the sleeping legislative giant. In this view, Congress presents the Court with a number of potential constraints. This is thought to be particularly true of statutory decisions, in which a simple congressional majority can reverse the Court's rulings. For example, William Eskridge (1991a, 1991b, 1994) argues that, in interpreting statutes, the Court does not necessarily pay attention to the intent of the Congress that passed the law in question, but to the sitting Congress. After all, he reasons, that current Congress is the one that could retaliate.[6]

---

[6] Congressional reversals of the Supreme Court's statutory decisions are unusual and require overwhelmingly high levels of interest and attention on the part of legislators (Note 1958, 337). The recent phenomenon of divided government has contributed to this difficulty as well, because even if Congress passes legislation overturning a statutory decision of the Court, opposite-party presidents may veto that retaliatory legislation (Fiorina 1996; Peterson 1990).

In contrast, because Congress can only reverse the Court's constitutional decisions by the extraordinarily difficult process of constitutional amendment, those decisions are thought to give the Court greater freedom to pursue its sincere policy preferences. Yet even in the realm of constitutional cases, there are reasons to doubt claims of unfettered judicial independence. For one, Congress need not challenge the Court's decisions head-on. As an example, Congress has been unable to muster sufficient support for a constitutional amendment overturning the *Roe v. Wade* decision. However, it did pass the Hyde Amendment to cut off federal funding for abortion. That action, validated by the Court in *Harris v. McRae* (1980), did not overturn *Roe*, but it severely limited the exercise of reproductive rights (Hoff 1991, 302–305). Thus, while the chances are remote that a constitutional decision will be overturned directly, Congress can engage in what Meernik and Ignagni (1997) call "coordinate construction" of the Constitution (Barnes 2004; Pickerill 2004). Members of Congress and interest groups offer their interpretation of the Constitution to rival that of the Court. Bartels (2001, 8) finds that Congress has tried to pass legislation to reverse constitutional decisions in almost a quarter of the instances. Of those attempts, about a third were successful. These are not insignificant numbers.

The Constitution gives Congress a number of other opportunities to influence the Supreme Court. The Senate's role in the confirmation process is the most visible of these tools. Beyond affecting the Court's composition, Congress has significant coercive "sticks" available to it, and some are more consequential than others. For example, Congress has the constitutional ability to impeach and remove Supreme Court justices, although only one justice has been impeached and no justice has ever been removed from office (Baum 2010, 63). The Constitution gives Congress the power to set the Supreme Court's size, and although Congress has been reluctant to flex that power, Roosevelt's Court-packing plan serves as a reminder of its potential importance.

The Constitution also prohibits Congress from diminishing the salaries of the justices during their tenure. The Framers believed that such a guarantee, along with the assurance of tenure during good behavior, was critical to maintaining the Court's independence (Federalist 79). However, Toma (1991) contends that Congress uses its "power of the purse" to communicate its general approval or disapproval of the Court's decisions and doctrinal trends. Although this budgetary power is by no means a decisive check, it is a reminder of one way in which Congress can retaliate against the Court (Schmidhauser and Berg 1972, 16). It also illustrates that, "as long as the Congress controls the purse strings, members of the Supreme Court will not be totally autonomous agents" (Toma 1991, 146).

In addition, Congress's jurisdictional control over the Supreme Court may represent an important check on judicial independence. Congress is empowered to pass legislation regulating the Court's appellate jurisdiction. Whereas there is debate about the scope of Congress's power to curb the Court's constitutional jurisdiction under the Constitution's "Exceptions Clause," its ability to alter its statutory jurisdiction is well established (Lovell 2003). Many of the successful attempts have been conceived in a neutral fashion to assist the Court in handling its growing caseload. But some attempts at jurisdictional alteration were motivated by the desire to strip the Court of jurisdiction to entertain certain classes of constitutional cases. Typically, these "Court-stripping" efforts have been motivated by opposition to a particular decision or series of decisions. Whether Congress can constitutionally strip the Court of jurisdiction over specific constitutional cases is uncertain, and it has not successfully done so since *Ex parte McCardle* (1869) (Fallon, Meltzer, and Shapiro 1996, 365–370). Yet that has not deterred Congress from trying. Many controversial issues reach the Supreme Court. The Court's decisions are bound to provoke a response and have led members of Congress to introduce legislation to limit or deny jurisdiction (Katzmann 1997). Indeed, since 2004, three such Court-stripping measures have passed the House of Representatives (Curry 2005).

These efforts generally have been unsuccessful, but they are nevertheless consequential. When powerful members of Congress lend their support to such jurisdictional measures, it creates a precedent for attacking the Court and, by extension, its legitimacy. Moreover, it poisons institutional relations between the branches. As Justice O'Connor (2005) observed shortly before her retirement, "In all the years of my life, I don't think I've ever seen relations as strained as they are now between the Judiciary and some members of Congress." She went on to note that " . . . there are efforts being made currently to limit federal court jurisdiction to decide certain issues on an issue-by-issue basis in areas that some members of Congress think that the federal courts should not be involved [with]. That's . . . worrisome." In effect, these attacks undermine respect for the judiciary as an institution. On a few occasions, the Court has retreated in subsequent cases, thus giving Congress a short-term victory (Murphy 1962). Nevertheless, the Court necessarily keeps a wary eye on congressional actions that could undermine its respect and legitimacy – the Court's most precious institutional resource.

CONCLUSION

The modern Supreme Court, which we have defined as post–*Brown v. Board of Education*, has become a very powerful institution. It has been at the center of issues like civil rights and individual liberties. It has been at the forefront of drawing the lines between national and subnational government and in balancing liberty with order. It is or should be an issue in every presidential election.

The ideological composition of the Supreme Court is widely considered the most important factor in its decision making. Although the statue of justice may be blindfolded and impartial, the justices of the Supreme Court are not. Presidents make their nominations on the basis of a number of different factors. If the ideological predilection of the nominee is not one of them, then the president is forfeiting an opportunity to shape the direction of American law (Rehnquist 2002).

Some theories of decision making, which we discuss more fully in Chapter 2, hold that the ideological views of the justices are the sole determinant of decision making. Indeed, studies show that justices are relatively consistent in their decision making across their careers (Rohde and Spaeth 1976; Segal and Spaeth 2002; but see Epstein, Hoekstra, Segal, and Spaeth 1998). But is there something about being a judge, something about taking the oath and donning the robe, that makes the decision making calculus a little more complicated? And if so, what are the factors that might lead a justice to migrate from his or her sincere preferences in making a decision on the merits of a given case? Justices might be influenced by the precedent that governs the particular area of law. Perhaps the facts of the case would induce the justices to move from their sincere preferences. It is possible that the justices might react to the president or to Congress and make a decision that would avoid antagonizing the other branches. For example, research shows that the SG, a presidential appointment, has a remarkable degree of success regardless of the composition of the Court (McGuire 1995; Pacelle 2003; Salokar 1992; Segal 1988).

The Supreme Court is a complex, often mysterious, quasireligious institution. It is fundamentally undemocratic in that its members are unelected and have life tenure. Its authority to interpret the law and the Constitution give it a measure of legitimacy. But the Court must guard that legitimacy. The fact that its decisions help shape public policy gives it an important measure of power. The Court's exercise of that power can enhance or diminish its legitimacy.

The lifetime tenure of the justices seems to insulate them and, in effect, free them to pursue their sincere policy preferences. Yet there is a potential collective action problem – if justices pursue their policy designs without regard to political consequences or institutional constraints, they run the risk of weakening the Court. A weakened Court reduces the ability of the justices to pursue their individual and collective goals. Justices as individuals are relatively consistent in their decision making, and their behavior can be defined as ideologically coherent. But are the collective decisions the mere sum of nine autonomous ideologies? We are skeptical. We think the trappings of the "law," the need to attend to precedent, the symbols attendant to the judiciary, and the structural constraints imposed by the Framers make a difference. Our task is to investigate this skepticism and see if it is warranted. The purpose of our integrative model is to provide insight into how these strategic, legal, and political conditions shape the Court's decisions.

Heuristic Models of Judicial Decision Making

You really should visit the Vatican. While you are there, be sure to pause for a few moments to marvel at Raphael's "School of Athens" in the *Stanza della Signatura*. According to James Beck (1993, 78), "[A]mong the handful of masterpieces of the period, the picture has few equals." In the center of this fresco, the greatest thinkers, philosophers, scientists, and mathematicians of antiquity flank Plato and Aristotle. Plato, who bears an uncanny (and intended) resemblance to Leonardo da Vinci, is pointing at the sky. His partner in conversation, Aristotle, has his palm down and is pointing toward earth. These gestures are designed to represent their different philosophical ideals. Plato seems to represent normative ideals, whereas Aristotle is grounded in the empirical world. We do not think they were discussing judicial decision making, but they could have been. The normative-empirical debate has raged throughout political science for decades and has helped to shape the way scholars have studied the Supreme Court.

If they had been discussing decision making on the modern Supreme Court, Plato would have been arguing that the Court uses precedents and grounds its decisions in the law. The Court follows legal interpretations and exercises restraint in its decision making. To the contrary, Aristotle would have responded, the Court is a collection of individuals who can follow their own political preferences and are not strictly bound by legal factors. They are unconstrained and free to pursue their conception of the good society. They are free to adopt the tenets that are normally associated with judicial activism.

The notions of activism and restraint are approaches to judicial decision making. In part, they speak in relative terms of the relationship of the Supreme Court with the other branches of government as well as with Courts that came before. A Court that is deferential to the elected branches and follows precedent exhibits judicial restraint. An activist Court is one that is willing to ignore its own precedents and substitute its judgment for that of the elected branches. Activism and restraint have become loaded words. They are normative in that restraint is expected to be the way courts act, whereas activism is supposed to violate the very spirit of the Constitution. At the same time, they have an empirical basis. Analysts agree that the Warren (Belknap 2005; Bickel 1962) and Rehnquist Courts (Keck 2004) were activist tribunals. For large portions of the post-*Brown* period, the Court exercised both activism and restraint, often at the same time. In fact, as we argue, the Court was particular in its activism, largely directing it to civil rights and civil liberties while adopting restraint in economic cases. Indeed, this was the central tenet of the "preferred position" doctrine enunciated in Footnote Four of the *Carolene Products* decision (Pacelle 1991).

The normative view of how the Court should act has viability because the general public largely accepts it as reality. The activity surrounding the nomination process does little to strip away the veneer. Proponents of the attitudinal model argue that their perspective better reflects reality. They have the empirical data to back their claims. But do they err too far in the other direction by arguing that the legal factors have no impact? We examine the three models of decision making and consider their strengths and weaknesses as a prelude to building an integrative model that we think better reflects reality by borrowing components from each of the existing models.

MODELS OF SUPREME COURT DECISION MAKING

The burgeoning judicial literature has provided significant insight into the complex conditions and factors affecting judicial behavior. From this rich body of work, three central explanations of decision making have developed. To sketch out these models, we begin with first principles – the assumptions they make about judicial motivations (Baum 1997; Hausegger and Baum 1999).

As we noted, there are three typical explanations for a judicial decision: the legal model, the attitudinal model, and strategic models, such as separation-of-powers models. Although notions of separation of powers and checks and balances play a role in all three, the attitudinal model is largely internal to the Court. The strategic model accepts the individual motivation to pursue sincere preferences, but it also posits that the Court is cognizant of external forces. The legal model holds that the Court is supposed to rely on its previous decisions, but it is also supposed to be deferential to the elected branches of government.

The Legal Model

Variants of the legal model suggest that the law is the dominant factor for the justices to consider in rendering decisions. The legal model is based on the normative idea that putting on the robes makes a Supreme Court justice different from other governmental officials, such as members of Congress. Because they are unelected and have lifetime tenure (the very attributes that proponents of the attitudinal model feel free justices to act on their sincere preferences), the justices should avoid "making the law." In a sense, these approaches ask the justices to "find" the law and suggest where they might do so (Pacelle 2002). Legal factors represent a variety of different approaches that ask the justices to consult the Constitution, statutes, and precedents. Because these approaches to decision making invoke the consultation of some "higher" authority, they are considered part of what is referred to as "interpretivism." Interpretivism, the preferred normative ideal, refers to staying within the four corners of the Constitution (or the statute). Judges should remain faithful to "the norms derived from the written Constitution" (Grey 1975, 703). The most dominant legal factors include the intent of the framers, the use of neutral principles, and precedent. In each of these instances, the justices are asked to move beyond their sincere policy preferences in making decisions.

The legal model is typically portrayed as a series of constraints on a justice's sincere preferences. But it can be a motivating factor for justices as well (Gillman 1993; McCann 1999). The so-called "legal realists"[1] refuted the idea that judges lack discretion in their decision making and argued that judges in effect "make" the law. Yet at the same time, the legal realists argued that although personal views were important, maybe even paramount, justices would take things like precedent into account (Murphy and Tanenhaus 1972). A radical strain of the legal realists felt that justices were completely unconstrained and could simply exercise

---

[1] The "legal realists," writing in the early twentieth century, were among the first to challenge the normative orthodoxy that justices followed a strict legal model and carefully weighed the laws and facts in each case before reaching a disinterested decision. The realists accepted the influence of a variety of factors on decision making.

their policy views (Clayton 1999). Using slightly different grounds, proponents of the attitudinal model argue that the legal model represents a normative view of how justices should act but is a far cry from how they actually make decisions.

Perhaps the best known of the legal approaches suggests that justices should consult the original intent of the framers of the Constitution or the intent of the legislators in passing a statute. Legislative and framers' intent asks the justices to construe the statutory or constitutional provisions according to the preferences of those who originally drafted and supported them (Spaeth 1995, 300). When the justices face a question that involves the Constitution, they need to try to understand what the framers meant by the provision in question. Because the Constitution is supposed to be the central charter of American government, the justices should consult it. The framers chose their language deliberately as a guide to future generations. Using original intent fosters stability in the law and grounds decisions in the Constitution rather than leaving them to the values of the justices (but see Scalia 1997).

Proponents of restraint feel bound to search for meaning within the four corners of the Constitution. Justices who subscribe to judicial restraint would search for the intent of the framers and adapt it pragmatically to the current context. Justices can infer powers and rights from the structures and relationships created by the Constitution (McKeever 1993, 30–31). Thus, in theory, using the intent of the framers ostensibly takes unfettered discretion out of the hands of the unelected justices. And if one believes that the framers of the Constitution were an eighteenth-century version of "the best and the brightest" (Roche 1964), the importance of paying respect to their ideas gains further credence. Proponents of following the text of the Constitution or a statute argue that the language of the provisions should be a constraint on interpretation. They maintain that principles can be gleaned directly from the text or from the precedents that have been established to build the doctrine related to those provisions (Schauer 1985).

Many theorists argue that there is a set of fundamental values and neutral principles that can be inferred from the overall spirit of the Constitution. For example, analysts often argue that justices, when faced with questions, should err on the side of promoting democratic values (Bickel 1962). Accordingly, protecting political speech and voting rights would be paramount objectives for the Court. Herbert Wechsler (1959) advocated the use of neutral principles to tether justices to some abiding standards, saying that the Court is "bound to function otherwise than as a naked power organ." Thus, neutral principles can help prevent the Court from being turned into a "third legislative chamber."

Justices who try to ground decisions on broader principles that go beyond their personal views might develop a viewpoint based on the general philosophical underpinnings of the Constitution rather than on explicit provisions of the document. Some justices treat the Constitution as a document of aspiration, containing moral principles to endure for ages (Goldstein 1995, 276). The Constitution is supposed to provide enduring principles, even if its provisions do not provide specific answers to particular cases. In addition, the decisions of the justices are thought to be more legitimate if they follow a principled process of decision making in discovering and enunciating the shared, enduring values of society (Bickel 1962, 58).

If the Court merely follows the sincere policy preferences of its members, in Robert Bork's (1971, 4–7) view it has taken "an institutionalized role as perpetrator of limited coups d'etat." Bork (1971) argues that if the Court lacks a reasoned theory derived from the Constitution, it violates Madisonian ideals. The value choices should flow from the framers of the Constitution, not from the current justices of the Court. Such principled decisions are necessary because the Court is unelected. Bork argues that principled decision making need not come from a legislative or elected body. To the question that some might raise to contest his argument, Bork (1971, 11) replies that yes, we are at the mercy of legislative majorities. The voters have the final say, able to throw the rascals out if they fail to do the electorate's bidding or stray too far from their mandates (but see Pacelle 2002, 64–65).

Finally, other than the Constitution or a statute, legal factors would include precedent. Under the doctrine of *stare decisis*, judges are to be governed by similar previous decisions. When a case comes to the Supreme Court, justices should seek relevant precedents and apply them to the situation at hand. Following precedent creates stability and introduces predictability into the law. According to Harlan Fiske Stone, "The rule of *stare decisis* embodies a wise policy because it is often more important that a rule of law be settled than that it be settled right" (Epstein and Walker 1998b, 27). Lower court judges will know what is expected of them, and citizens will know the extent of their rights if the law is consistent.

As we noted, the doctrine of *stare decisis* takes some discretion away from unelected justices and provides the necessary direction for lower court judges when they have to apply the principles to similar cases

(Hettinger, Lindquist, and Martinek 2006). Everyone in the legal system understands the importance of precedent. In arguing cases, lawyers raise the precedents most favorable to their side (Knight and Epstein 1996). In deciding cases, justices cite the precedents most relevant to their decisions. According to Sheldon Goldman, "The rule of precedent symbolizes that we are dealing with a court of law as distinguished from a legislative body" (Epstein and Walker 1998a, 21). Thus, precedent is an important anchor. Not only would *stare decisis* be used to connect similar cases, but precedents that resulted from legal reasoning, neutral principles, original intent, and plain language and were followed by the Court would also invest further legitimacy in those approaches and the decisions as well as in the Court itself.

Critiques of the Legal Model and Its Approaches. Although there are normative reasons to want justices to act in detached ways and avoid substituting their own policy preferences for those of elected officials, not everyone accepts the legal model and its components. There are vigorous debates in the academy regarding which of these approaches is the best, and there are philosophical and empirical arguments to consider in each instance. There are also debates about whether any of the objective approaches is even possible. It turns out that such disputes are not merely normative intellectual debates. In a speech at Georgetown Law School in 1986, Justice William Brennan charged that then-Attorney General Edwin Meese's call for a jurisprudence of original intention was "arrogance cloaked as humility."

The full-blown legal model that holds that positive law and precedent are determinative is a straw person that is quite easy to attack and refute. As Hansford and Spriggs (2006) and Gerhardt (2008) maintain that most student of the Court regard precedent and the legal model in stark black and white terms. Either the Court abides by the legal model and strictly applies existing precedent, or neither has any relevance. But our view is more nuanced and complex. We argue that precedent and legal factors play a role but are part of a broader calculus that the Court and individual justices must undertake.

Proponents of the attitudinal and strategic models marshal the appropriate data and arguments to demonstrate that justices do not abide by these legal factors. Typically, there are three major criticisms of the legal model. First, there is the argument that the legal model is a normative ideal rather than an empirical description. Segal, Spaeth, and Benesh (2005, 17) argue that this myth has been devised "to sustain and rationalize" the awesome exercise of power by today's judiciary. Second, and perhaps worse, some argue that justices shroud themselves in these acceptable canons of interpretation, while in reality using them as cloaks for their naked political preferences. To the extent that justices actively propagate this myth, it can have deleterious effects for the polity. Third, critics argue that the legal model cannot be empirically verified.

In addition to the general attacks on the legal model, there are specific criticisms directed toward particular legal approaches. One of the major critiques of original intent is the question of who is responsible for that intent (Segal and Spaeth 1993). Do James Madison's convention papers, authored years after the convention, constitute a reliable and widely shared (among the framers) notion of the discussions? Was there a consensus on what particular provisions meant? If we take *The Federalist Papers* as authority, we see that Madison and Hamilton wrote in different tones and soon joined different political parties. Also, it is important to remember that *The Federalist Papers* were written as propaganda tracts to build support for the nascent Constitution (Robertson 2005). The task is even more daunting when the goal is inferring the intent of legislation. Members of Congress insert whatever they want in committee hearings or the *Congressional Record* to create legislative history and intent. Additionally, presidents have taken to issuing signing statements to contribute their interpretation for courts and executive agencies to consider (Whittington 2007, 39).

There are also a few clear problems with the idea of adhering to a strict reading of the language of the Constitution or a statute. First, language is seldom unambiguous, and trying to think back a few centuries would be a difficult task even if the words were clear. Second, the text, particularly of the Constitution, does not often give bright-line answers to modern problems. Finally, if the language in question is found in the text and precedents, no one can be sure if the latter was created not directly from the text, but from the policy preferences of the justices who molded the doctrine. Sanford Levinson (1982) argues that texts may not create the interpretation, but rather the opposite may be true: The interpretation creates or, more precisely, "rewrites" the text. If the language is in legislation, the problems can be magnified. Given separation of powers and checks and balances, it is important to remember how a bill becomes law. Legislation must navigate its way through subcommittees and committees, the floor of the House and Senate, a conference committee, and then avoid a presidential veto. The language is bound to be vague and open-ended. Then it has to be interpreted by the administrative agency (or agencies) charged with implementing the law across a variety of different jurisdictions, and the members of the administrative agencies, like the justices, are not elected. Whose interpretation of the language is to be given preference?

There are also some problems with attributing too much to precedent. First, empirically, as George and Epstein (1992) note, if justices followed precedent, the law would never change. If *Barron v. Baltimore* were still the governing principle, no parts of the Bill of Rights would have been incorporated to the states. Second, there is a larger problem: The cases before the Supreme Court are seldom direct reflections of previous decisions. A case that is a carbon copy of a previous decision typically will not reach the Supreme Court, because a lower court will be able to resolve it. Therefore, the cases that do reach the justices are those that raise difficult questions that lie in the gray areas between existing precedents. This frees the justices to exercise their sincere preferences (Pacelle, Marshall, and Curry 2007).

The attempt to ground decision making in neutral principles, the intent of the framers, or *stare decisis* is designed to accomplish a number of things. First, it constrains decision making. This is important, in part, because the justices are unelected. Second, these approaches represent attempts to tie decisions to interpretivism and thus to the four corners of the statute or the Constitution. This would, of course, restrict the sincere policy preferences of the justices. Third, to the extent that justices can glean the meaning that the framers intended, it contributes to the legitimacy of democratically elected institutions and positions the judicial branch above the political fray. Finally, using enduring principles and precedent ensures continuity in the law.

The Attitudinal Model

As the strongest proponents of the attitudinal model, Segal and Spaeth (1993) argue that interpretivist factors are merely cloaks that justices pull over themselves to deflect criticism. They argue that original intent, precedent, and neutral principles are not the determinants of decisions but rather rationales to cover the exercise of naked policy preferences. Methodologically, they claim that these legal factors cannot be measured and, thus, cannot be evaluated in any systematic fashion. Rather, they argue, the justices on the Supreme Court have reached the pinnacle of their careers and have lifetime tenure. Therefore, they are free to pursue policy goals in making their decisions. Presidents choose justices who will reflect their views and carry them forward long after their terms in the White House have ended (Epstein and Segal 2005; Rehnquist 2002).

The dominant paradigm at the individual level is the attitudinal model. Beginning with some relatively rudimentary box scores of justices' decisions, Pritchett (1948) blazed a trail for the study of individual-level decision making. In many ways, the work on judicial decision making had a parallel in the voting literature. Students of voting behavior tried to understand why American voters cast their votes in certain ways. They examined voting from psychological and sociological perspectives to explain and predict behavior (Berelson, Lazarsfeld, and McPhee 1954; Campbell et al. 1960). In a similar fashion, analysts looked at the backgrounds of justices to see if the variation in their age, schooling, religion, region, socioeconomic status, race, or partisan affiliation would yield any leverage on understanding decision making (Tate 1981; Tate and Handberg 1991). Although Supreme Court justices tend to be a rather homogenous lot – white males with upper-class backgrounds from elite law schools – there were some factors that explained variation. The main independent variable that influenced decision making was party identification. Justices who had been Republicans in their partisan lives were more likely to decide cases in a conservative manner. There was one problem with that variable: It seemed too much like an attitude or a value. After all, people presumably affiliate with a party because of their ideological predilections.

In its purest form, the attitudinal model states that the justices are totally unencumbered in deciding cases. It has theoretical and practical primacy: Supreme Court appointments are considered among the most important actions of a president, providing an opportunity to move the median justice (Krehbiel 2007) and stamp his imprint on the Court for up to a generation (Abraham 2008). For proponents of the attitudinal model, the justices' long-held values and attitudes are the explanation for their decisions in individual cases (Rohde and Spaeth 1976; Segal and Spaeth 2002).

Attitudes are "a set of interrelated beliefs about at least one object and the situation in which it is encountered.... Values are a set of interrelated attitudes" (Rohde and Spaeth 1976, 76). According to Segal and Spaeth (1993, 216), there are two sets of attitudes that have to be considered: attitudes toward objects and attitudes toward situations. Attitude objects include the litigants who appear before the Court. Attitude situations rely heavily on the case facts. The justices' decisions occur at the intersection of the two. Of course, traditional legal model theorists could argue that one potential situation would be the need to attend to precedent, which might interrupt the use of policy preferences.

The attitudinal models were at the forefront of the behavioral revolution in political science. Behavioralism shifted the focus "from legalistic institutional description and normative prescription" to the empirical and a search for systematic patterns (Goldman and Sarat 1989, 383). From Fred Kort's (1957) use of discriminant analysis and Boolean algebra (Kort 1963) to Glendon Schubert's (1962, 1965, 1974) i-points and j-points to the dimensional analysis of Rohde and Spaeth (1976) to Segal and Spaeth's (2002) refined models, analysts have tried to explain decision making with the goal of predicting decisions. The case was the stimulus, and the attitudes of the justice yielded the response: the decision. Cases were arrayed from the easiest to the most difficult, according to some form of Guttman scaling. The idea was that if the justice would vote for a hard case, he (and they were all hes for the early studies) would support anything easier (Goldman and Jahnige 1985).

The empirical evidence suggests that individual justices are very consistent in their decision making. They have fixed preferences in a unidimensional issue space (Rohde and Spaeth 1976; Schubert 1965, 1974, but see Epstein et al. 1998). Justices show consistency in their decisions within different dimensions or certain issues. But some issues "scale" better than others. Civil rights and civil liberties issues tend to show a great deal of ideological constraint among individual justices. By contrast, in economic cases and issues, the progression is not as neat and the decisions are not as consistent (Ducat and Dudley 1987; Hagle and Spaeth 1992, 1993). In addition, there are greater numbers of unanimous economic decisions, which led to their exclusion from dimensional analyses (but see Brenner and Arrington 1987).

The attitudinal theory sees justices as single-minded political actors who are more interested in their policy goals than in legal goals. Their votes in the cases are "direct expressions of their preferences" (Baum 1997, 25). For proponents of the attitudinal model, the explanation is simple: A single variable explains individual-level decision making. Segal and Spaeth (1996a, 973) maintain that "because the Supreme Court sits atop the judicial hierarchy, and because in the types of cases that reach the Supreme Court legal factors such as text, intent, and precedent are typically ambiguous, justices are free to make decisions based on their personal policy preferences."

Critiques of the Attitudinal Model. There are a number of critiques of the attitudinal model. Some are directed at the general theory, others at the construction of the model or the interpretation of the empirical results. On the broadest level, there is the critique that the model is too simplistic and too exclusive of other possible contributing factors (Baum 1997). Critics claim that the attitudinal model fails to capture the milieu in which the justices operate (Gillman and Clayton 1999). Most analysts' perspectives rest on the belief that, although exogenous forces like attitudes play a role, other factors – both endogenous and exogenous – structure decisions as well. Legal precedent, case difficulty, concern for the other branches, and the maintenance of institutional legitimacy are additional factors that may influence Supreme Court decision making. Some argue that the attitudinal model is much better at prediction than explanation. Indeed, the attitudinal model devotes no real attention to how attitudes are constituted (Rosenberg 1994). Nor does it admit that institutional forces or the law might influence judicial attitudes. The model's reliance on individual votes obscures the importance of the Court's collective opinion as a definitive policy pronouncement, which is curious in that Segal and Spaeth make policy positions the critical focus of their theory (Hansford and Spriggs 2006; Maltzman, Spriggs, and Wahlbeck 2000).

Whether or not justices exit the Court with the same preferences they had when they entered remains an open question from the attitudinal perspective.[2] Some studies have shown that justices alter their decision patterns over time (Blasecki 1990; Epstein et al. 1998; Greenhouse 2005; Maveety 1996; Ulmer 1973, 1979). Some argue that even if attitudes are fixed over time, the consistency in judicial voting may not be strictly due to personal policy preferences. At a minimum, decisions could also be a composite function of other factors. Consistency could be a function of attempts to follow precedent. Rosenberg (1994) suggests that what the attitudinal model calls "'subjective preferences' may be nothing more than honest attempts to apply a consistent interpretive philosophy to the facts." Thus, it is unclear whether preferred judicial outcomes drive one's choice of interpretative philosophy or if it is the interpretative philosophy that yields the judicial outcomes. Critics argue that the attitudinal model can describe behavior but not the motivation or foundations of those actions (Smith 1994).

---

[2] It has been a central tenet of the attitudinal model that values and attitudes are enduring, which is why they are important in governing behavior. To the extent that they are malleable over time, attitudes become less central as determinants of decision making.

In their outright rejection of the impact of any legal factors, indeed going so far as to suggest that the justices are openly disingenuous for claiming to use them, Segal and Spaeth have been accused of overplaying their hand. Rogers Smith (1994, 9) hoists them on their own petard, claiming that judges might use their attitudes in more peripheral ways, as opposed to the claim that legal factors play not the slightest role: "[J]udges must use their values to give content to concepts they find in the law, even when their preferences might be against those concepts being there."

The attitudinal models also have tended to be rather static. Most such models view attitudes as fixed and unchanging. Moreover, if the attitudinal model were taken to its logical conclusion, an impassioned oral argument or a brilliantly structured brief would have no impact; *amicus* briefs from well-heeled repeat players would not sway many justices. Particularly strong precedents, clear language, or unusually unambiguous original intent would have no influence on decision making if the extreme attitudinal claims were correct. Some studies have looked at different issue areas and found that cases did not scale as well (Ducat and Dudley 1987; Dudley and Ducat 1986), meaning that the justices were not as consistent in their behavior. This suggests that some other factors might be present, at least in those areas of law.

There are also methodological challenges in measuring and testing the central claim of the attitudinal model. If attitudes constitute the main independent variable, how do we discover these attitudes? The early models used the votes of justices to infer the attitudes of the justices to explain votes.[3] Although the models had strong predictive validity, critics were quick to note that using votes to explain votes was tautological. The scales that were used excluded unanimous cases. This is problematic because in unanimous cases, ideological opposites would unite. If justices with divergent attitudes vote together, it may be the case that other factors are at work (but see Brenner and Arrington 1987). Second, the large number of split decisions is a more recent phenomenon. Thus, if the Court's decisions were dominated by unanimous decisions for more than a century, attitudinal models might simply be a recent construct (but see Segal, Spaeth, and Benesh 2005).

Most analysts concede the role that attitudes and values play in individual-level decision making. Still, it is likely that not all individual

---

[3] Segal and Cover (1989) ultimately developed an external measure of ideology (as a proxy for the attitudes) from newspaper editorials. This was updated (and backdated) by Segal, Epstein, Cameron, and Spaeth (1995), but Epstein and Mershon (1996) show that this measure is only related to civil rights and civil liberties decisions.

decisions are based on attitudes. If they were, we would not see many unanimous decisions. Furthermore, the Court's collective decisions seem to be more than the mere sum total of nine individual attitudes. In addition, as George and Epstein (1992) note, the extralegal or attitudinal model suggests an unaltered dynamic: Doctrinal change is expected to be constant and in the direction of ideological changes on the Court. The fact that the Court overturns very few precedents suggests that the attitudinal model may have limitations.

Even the father of the behavioral revolution in public law, C. Herman Pritchett, rejected the radical strain of legal realism that claimed that justices merely exercised their sincere political preferences, with no regard for legal factors. In Pritchett's view, justices only occasionally had the unfettered discretion to exercise their policy preferences. Pritchett argued that when there was legal or factual ambiguity or the constitutional or statutory provisions in question were vague, justices had the freedom to step away from the legal factors and exercise their preferences (Goldman and Sarat 1989, 383). Of course, proponents of the attitudinal model can claim without exaggeration that such ambiguities and vagueness occur quite often.

Strategic Models of Decision Making

Whereas the attitudinal model holds that justices vote in accordance with their sincere policy preferences, strategic models of Supreme Court decision making posit that the decisions of the Court and its justices are subject to a number of internal and external constraints. In other words, although justices are indeed policy oriented, strategic models of judicial behavior depict members of the Supreme Court as rational, sophisticated actors. These models draw on the rational choice paradigm and emphasize "the interdependence of judicial choice" (Segal, Spaeth, and Benesh 2005, 35).

This perspective has a number of important implications both for the behavior of individual justices and for the Court's institutional position within the separation-of-powers framework. At the individual level, the main unifying theme of these models is that "justices are strategic actors who realize that their ability to achieve their goals depends on a consideration of the preferences of others, of the choices they expect others to make, and of the institutional context in which they act" (Epstein and Knight 1998, xiii). Of greater relevance to our research, scholars have extended this assumption to the Court's aggregate behavior, noting that the Court may temper its collective sincere policy preferences if necessary and that it will act strategically to avoid external retaliation (Eskridge 1994; Spiller and Gely 1992). However, before outlining these potential external constraints on the Court's decision making, we briefly consider the role of strategic considerations in structuring interactions among the justices themselves.

Strategic Action Inside the Court. Beginning in earnest with the publication of Walter Murphy's *Elements of Judicial Strategy* (1964), scholars of judicial behavior have suggested a number of ways in which Supreme Court justices may engage in strategic intra-Court behavior (Epstein and Knight 1998; Hammond, Bonneau, and Sheehan 2005; Howard 1968; Maltzman, Spriggs, and Wahlbeck 2000). Justices are thought to be strategic when they "take into account the effects of their choices on collective results . . . in order to achieve the most desirable results in their own court and in government as a whole" (Baum 1997, 90). In sum, strategic models of decision making suggest that justices move from their sincere preferences in response to colleagues or that the Court migrates ideologically from its preferred policy position to preempt a potential adverse response from the elected branches.

Justices can bargain or act strategically at a number of junctures in the decision-making process. They may act tactically in granting or denying *certiorari* (Perry 1991). They can bargain or act strategically in their votes on the merits of the issue (Epstein and Knight 1998). Perhaps the most obvious and explicit bargaining occurs regarding the language in the opinions or the threat to write a separate opinion, whether a concurrence or dissent. The majority opinion is the most important pronouncement from the Court and sets precedent. Justices can defect from the majority over the tone or sweep of the opinion (Maltzman, Spriggs, and Wahlbeck 2000). They may threaten to write a separate opinion, which can confound lower courts. Rational choice models of all types often make the unrealistic assumption that every actor has full and complete knowledge of the behavior of the other actors. If there is one branch of government where this assumption can be approximated, it is the Court. Justices have relatively full information and a good sense of how their colleagues will vote.

One of the most discussed manifestations of strategic action within the Supreme Court concerns the issue of case selection. Specifically, research on judicial behavior has examined the relationship between justices' votes at the *cert* stage and their preferences on the merits. According to this reasoning, a justice who may wish to reverse a lower court decision nevertheless votes to deny *certiorari* because she realizes that her preferred case outcome is unlikely to prevail at the merits stage (Caldeira, Wright, and Zorn 1999; Krol and Brenner 1990; Perry 1991). Thus, although that justice's preferred policy position – overruling the lower court decision – did not obtain, her strategic action of defensively denying *cert* may have prevented an affirmance that would have taken on precedential value. Had that justice neglected strategic considerations altogether and acted solely according to her sincere policy preferences, that behavior would have made it harder to achieve her goals. Alternatively, a strategic justice may vote to hear a case – or pursue an "aggressive grant" of *certiorari* – when he thinks his preferred policy outcome will be reflected in the Court's ultimate decision on the merits (Boucher and Segal 1995; Caldeira, Wright, and Zorn 1999).

Studies show that justices may change their positions between the initial vote in conference and the final vote on the merits. According to a study by J. Woodford Howard (1968), this "fluidity" occurred in about 10 percent of the votes (on average, one vote in every case). Of course, this flies in the face of the attitudinal model, which argues that attitudes are immutable (but see Brenner 1980). Instead, some analysts argue that justices bargain, persuade others, and use their sanctions (votes and the threat to write a separate opinion) (Murphy 1964, 43–68). Danelski (1978) argues that the chief justice has the position to exercise task and/or social leadership. Some justices, by virtue of their personalities (e.g., Brennan) or their position on the Court (e.g., O'Connor), may be well suited to exercise influence. All of these factors may represent strategic activity on the individual level. Even if one generally accepts the attitudinal model, some level of inconsistency may occur because of the rise of new issues or cases that bring multiple issues and force justices to choose which one is dominant.

The development of the Court's opinions, from the initial assignment stage through the bargaining process that ultimately produces the Court's authoritative ruling, represents the other major avenue for strategic action among the justices. The leading treatment of such questions hypothesizes that "justices will try to secure opinions that are as close as possible to their policy positions by basing their decisions in part on the positions and actions of their colleagues" (Maltzman, Spriggs, and Wahlbeck 2000, 17). In assessing considerations regarding majority opinion assignment, the initial opinion draft, responses to that draft, and subsequent reactions to revisions, Maltzman, Spriggs, and Wahlbeck (2000) paint a portrait of justices who, constrained by various small-group dynamics, sometimes espouse policy positions that are not wholly consistent with their sincere preferences (but see Hammond, Bonneau, and Sheehan 2005).

Strategic Action and the Separation of Powers. Strategic accounts of judicial behavior also recognize that Supreme Court decision making cannot be fully explained without considering the separation-of-powers framework within which the Court is nested. Although the Court and its justices would like to make all decisions based on sincere policy values, strategic models of judicial behavior recognize that the Court as an institution does not have a completely free hand in policy making. If the Court's decisions are to be respected and enforced, it collectively must consider the position of the president who will be charged with implementing the decision and the Congress that can resist or even overturn a decision with which it disagrees (Eskridge 1994). In these strategic models (also known as separation-of-powers models), there is the expectation that the Court will temper its sincere policy preferences if necessary and act strategically to avoid retaliation from the other branches (Epstein and Knight 1998).

A number of studies that have examined the applicability of external constraints and strategic considerations to the Court's decision making have produced mixed results. Most scholars believe that strategic considerations are at their acme when the Court engages in statutory interpretation (Fisher and Devins 1992; Rogers 2001), because Congress can overturn such decisions by a simple majority. Thus, the Court is thought to adjust its preferred outcome in statutory cases to get closer to a point Congress and/or the president will find acceptable. Because supermajorities are required to enact amendments reversing the Court's constitutional decisions, those issues are generally thought to provide the Court with greater freedom to pursue its sincere preferences (but see Epstein, Knight, and Martin 2001; Martin 2006).

Not all analysts believe that strategic considerations are confined to statutory cases, however. Some have suggested that "the sharp distinction between constitutional and statutory cases is flawed" (Friedman and Harvey 2003, 127) and that, even if the congressional constraint is more imposing in statutory cases, strategic concerns need not be irrelevant in constitutional cases (Epstein and Knight 1998, 141). Others have noted that the Court may actually be likelier to proceed cautiously in constitutional cases (Epstein, Knight, and Martin 2001). Although the barriers to congressional action are more onerous in constitutional cases, successfully overriding such a decision would have much deeper and longer-lasting consequences for the Court's role in the construction of public policy – it would permanently remove the Court's ability to shape policy in that particular legal area (Martin 2006).

Setting aside this distinction between constitutional and statutory decisions for a moment, strategic perspectives on judicial behavior posit that "justices deviate from their personal preferences when those preferences are not shared by the members of the ruling regime" (Epstein, Knight, and Martin 2001, 610). Justices prefer to vote their sincere preferences, but strategic models argue that there are constraints on those preferences. If the elected branches find themselves sufficiently dissatisfied with a particular decision, they may respond by overriding it. The result of that override would produce a policy outcome diametrically at odds with the Court's preferences.

Even if such a decision is not overridden, the elected branches may still exercise other checks on the Court. Many of these avenues were described in Chapter 1, but we underscore several of them here. Congress might engage in "coordinate construction" of the Constitution, whereby members of Congress and interest groups offer interpretations of the Constitution to rival those of the Court (Barnes 2004; Meernik and Ignagni 1997; Pickerill 2004). The executive branch may refuse to enforce the decision or undertake that enforcement halfheartedly. Congress also has the ability to circumvent Court decisions without overturning them (Keynes with Miller 1989; Murphy 1962, 1964; Whittington 2007). Most notably, Congress can introduce blocking legislation to limit the impact of decisions it opposes.

On the contrary, had the Court taken these external preferences into account and tempered its statutory or constitutional decision accordingly, no such response would have occurred. Thus, strategic models of judicial behavior posit that, in terms of ultimate policy outcomes, the Court prefers to act rationally and secure "half a loaf" rather than exhibit unbending adherence to its sincere preferences and obtain "no loaf at all" (Epstein and Knight 1998).

At the same time, not every challenge to a Supreme Court decision is emblematic of conflict. Although Congress can overturn statutory decisions by a simple majority and has a variety of weapons at its disposal to limit the impact of constitutional rulings, Congress and the Court are part of a colloquy that permits them "to promise and deliver more constitutional justice" than either branch alone could provide (Sager 2004, 7). Similarly, congressional overrides of Court decisions and judicial contraction or expansion of legislative language are not necessarily adversarial processes (Murphy 1964; Pickerill 2004). Hausegger and Baum (1999) point out that the Supreme Court occasionally invites Congress to reverse its statutory decisions. Therefore, the Court and Congress are often partners in piecing together policy. Congress passes legislation, and the process of circumventing numerous committees, the floor of each chamber, and a presidential veto often means that legislation will be written in broad terms. Courts and executive agencies must interpret and animate those vague provisions. There can be honest disagreements and a desire to solve outstanding problems. Consequently, some of the strategic behavior of the Court may actually be done in the spirit of cooperation (Pickerill 2004).

Much of the strategic model's support has been theoretical or has come from close analyses of particular decisions (e.g., Cohen and Spitzer 1994; Eskridge 1991a; 1991b Eskridge and Frickey 1994; Gely and Spiller 1990.) In addition, because of the reasons discussed above, the bulk of empirical research that does exist focuses on statutory cases (Eskridge 1994; Hansford and Damore 2000; Hansford and Spriggs 2007; Spiller and Gely 1992; but see Epstein, Knight, and Martin 2001). Bergara, Richman, and Spiller (2003) provide evidence in support of strategic behavior and find that the Supreme Court and its justices are often constrained by congressional preferences in statutory cases. Eskridge (1991a, 1991b) found evidence of strategic Court behavior in civil rights cases brought on statutory grounds. Spiller and Gely (1992) found that the Court's decisions in labor relations cases were subject to congressional constraints. Spiller and Spitzer (1992) concluded that, in addition to impacting decisions substantively, the preferences of actors in the Court's political environment can even influence the legal rationale on which the Court bases its decision.

The strategic model we test focuses more narrowly on the Court's behavior in response to the other branches, whereas the broader separation-of-powers models tend to be characterized by formal predictions from equilibrium and have broader implications for the efficacy of policy change and policy making more generally. Our analysis limits the focus to the median justice, the medians of both congressional chambers, and the president as opposed to other possible pivots (e.g., supermajority pivots) and thus represents a more conservative test of the strategic model. In the standard treatment of the separation-of-powers model, the pivot point represents the ideological location of key member(s) whose support could change the policy status quo. When making a decision, the Court tries to anticipate how the pivotal players will react and thus tries to assess the likelihood that its decision could be overridden. The likelihood of the Court being overridden is typically a function of the spatial location of the Court's policy position relative to the set of feasible policies that Congress and the president would have no incentive to overturn – the Pareto set. Thus, the Court is relatively free to change policy within the Pareto set, but when decisions fall outside the Pareto set, the Court is likely to be overturned.

Criticisms of Strategic Accounts of Judicial Decision Making. Despite their theoretical plausibility, strategic models of judicial behavior have been criticized on a number of fronts. Most fundamentally, critics of these separation-of-powers models argue that, however intuitive the logic behind them may seem, they "bear only the most incidental relationship to reality (and even that statement arguably grossly overstates their connection)" (Segal, Spaeth, and Benesh 2005, 37). Such critiques rest on one or more of the following considerations: the difficulties inherent in forecasting the behavior of those on whose actions strategic calculations may depend, the uniqueness of the Supreme Court and its decision making, and disconnects between certain empirical findings and the theoretical claims of strategic models.

For strategic considerations to be effective, the Court and its justices must make reasonably accurate predictions about the behavior of others (Epstein and Knight 1998). As Baum (1997, 96–97) notes, this is no small task – particularly with respect to predicting responses from Congress and/or the president. As one of nine proverbial scorpions in a bottle, a justice may be well equipped to forecast the presumptive behavior of his fellow justices because of their close proximity and repeated interactions. Making accurate predictions about the responses of external actors is arguably much more challenging. Although members of the Court could rely on general ideological or partisan cues to approximate Congress's ideal policy point, they can hardly be expected to calibrate their predictions with the specificity of measures such as Poole and Rosenthal's DW-NOMINATE scores (see Chapter 3) or tailor their actions to the requirements of any number of spatial models. Elections only exacerbate these difficulties because they require justices to anticipate ideological changes and update their strategic calculations in light of them (Baum 1997, 97). Moreover, it is unlikely that ideology fully captures the Court's relationship with the other branches, particularly in all areas of law (Baum 1997, 121–122).

Assuming that members of the Court are able to determine the ideal policy points of these external actors, another difficulty remains. Even stipulating that a majority of Congress wishes to weaken or overturn a given Court decision, separation-of-powers models rarely consider the complexities attendant to enacting such legislation. In other words, strategic models treat congressional retaliation as a given as long as the Court's activity diverges sufficiently from legislative policy preferences. However, as Segal and Spaeth (2002, 106–107) point out, enacting such legislation is *not* costless. It takes time and energy to retaliate against a Court decision, and legislators may opt to channel those resources elsewhere even as they remain dissatisfied with a given decision. There are also a number of practical barriers to such responses. A good deal must "go right" in order to override a Court decision. If an override measure fails at just one stage – in committee, on the floor of the House, on the Senate floor, or through veto by the president – the status quo, set by the Court, remains. Given these barriers to retaliation, the Court may consider the possibility of retaliation a gamble it is willing to take.

The special nature of decision making on the Supreme Court also poses difficulties for the plausibility of strategic accounts of judicial behavior. Many of the rational choice propositions that underlie the strategic model were first applied to congressional behavior and later transplanted to the judicial context. But there are important differences in legislative and judicial behavior that may be consequential for the applicability of strategic models to judicial decision making. As but one example, justices, unlike members of Congress, typically are not confined to choosing between dichotomous outcomes. Therefore, "to the extent that judges vote strategically, departures from their preferred positions can be (and probably tend to be) more limited and less stark than in the legislature" (Baum 1997, 91).

Attitudinalists push this critique further and assert that the members of the Court, unconcerned with higher ambition and armed with the guarantees of lifetime tenure and stable salaries, simply do not have much incentive to behave strategically (Segal 1997). Even if justices recognize – as they must – that Congress will occasionally respond to its decisions, it is far from certain that such knowledge will impel the Court to behave strategically. Justices may acknowledge the potential for legislative reactions but view them as being too intermittent or too idiosyncratic to justify factoring them into their decision-making calculus (Baum 1997, 97, 120). Even if a decision is overridden, the Court does not always comply with that override, nor does an override necessarily cause lower courts to cease relying on the initial precedent (Hansford and Spriggs 2007).

A third objection to these strategic conceptualizations asserts that their theoretical claims have not been consistently evidenced in empirical examinations of judicial decision making. Segal's (1997) critique concludes that the decisions of individual justices are not constrained by the positions of Congress or the president with respect to statutory decisions, and a number of other scholarly treatments have also yielded mixed results (e.g., Hansford and Damore 2000). Although Sala and Spriggs (2004, 205) "maintain that there are strong theoretical reasons to expect that the justices act strategically in the context of the separation-of-powers game," they find no evidence for the separation-of-powers hypothesis in their assessment of statutory cases from 1946 to 1999. Critics further argue that much of the research that is supportive of strategic accounts of judicial behavior (Bergara, Richman, and Spiller 2003; Spiller and Gely 1992) has been limited to areas of statutory law and that the simplifying assumptions of such research may yield inaccurate conclusions about judicial deference to Congress (Segal and Spaeth 2002, 105–106; see Harvey and Friedman 2006).

Responses to Criticisms of Strategic Models. Empirical examinations of the strategic model have indeed produced mixed results, and such examinations have grown increasingly sophisticated in recent years. Certainly, more extensive research must be undertaken, and adherents to the strategic model believe that such research will ultimately validate their view of Supreme Court decision making. At this stage, most empirical assessments of separation-of-powers models have focused on the Court's role in statutory interpretation. However, the scope of that scholarship is widening as it begins to consider the role of strategic factors in structuring the Court's constitutional decisions as well (e.g., Epstein, Knight, and Martin 2001; Martin 2006). In combination with specific historical examples of strategic action on the Court vis-à-vis the other branches (e.g., Epstein and Walker 1995; Knight and Epstein 1996), extant research indicates that this separation-of-powers framework is a plausible explanation of decision making – at least under some circumstances.

Proponents of the strategic model offer a number of points in response to these criticisms. Most would acknowledge the difficulty of forecasting the behavior of other actors with strict precision but respond that there are several ways justices might glean the general state of external preferences. Briefs of the parties in a case and *amici curiae* are one such source. According to Epstein and Knight's (1998, 145) analysis of a sample of cases, more than three-quarters of briefs submitted to the Court in both constitutional and nonconstitutional cases contained some information about the preferences of other political actors (see also Epstein and Knight 1999). Members of Congress may file *amicus curiae* briefs before the Supreme Court as well, providing the Court with a direct indication of congressional preferences (Scourfield McLauchlan 2005; Spill Solberg, and Heberlig 2004). Oral arguments before the Court may also communicate information to the justices on the preferences of these external actors (Johnson 2004).

Finally, the solicitor general can transmit the views of the elected branches to the Court in a variety of ways. If the SG is arguing on behalf of legislation, the Office will have to vet and represent the position of Congress as well as the agency in question. And, of course, because the SG is answerable to the attorney general, it is likely that the president's views will be closely considered (Pacelle 2003). Drew Days (1994–95, 493), who served as Clinton's first SG, noted that though presidents typically do not micromanage the Office, "given the way that the decision-making process works, by the time a case has reached the point of possible appellate court or Supreme Court review, the policy concerns of the President have usually been fully presented to the Solicitor General by his appointees in the affected departments and agencies." If the Court's members desire information on the preferences of external actors, these avenues provide them with relatively convenient ways to obtain that information. Indeed, on occasion, the Court will issue a "call for the view of the solicitor general" (CVSG) asking the government for its position on a particular issue (Pacelle 2006).

The nature of Supreme Court decision making and a lack of consistency in empirical findings stemming from tests of the strategic model have led to questions about the model's viability. However, for its proponents, those arguments are overdrawn. Fundamentally, if one assumes that members of the Court are "single-minded seekers of legal policy," justices ought to rely on strategy to influence the ultimate state of that policy (Epstein, Knight, and Martin 2001, 591). Individual justices may be insulated from direct reprisal, but members of the Court realize that the collective decisions that emerge from the Marble Palace must be filtered through the other branches before being translated into public policy. Rather than reflecting the Court's independence from the elected branches, perhaps the low incidence of legislative overrides that many attitudinalists cite is itself evidence that the Court *does* anticipate reactions from the other branches and only occasionally rules in spite of them.[4]

Proponents of the strategic model have also taken issue with several empirical studies that purport to refute the model's viability. Segal's (1997) challenge to separation-of-powers models has been a particularly inviting target. These advocates of strategic considerations criticize Segal's study for undertaking an individual-level critique of what is, fundamentally, an institutional model. This brings us full circle to the dilemma that we identified at the outset: the disconnection between the individual or micro-level analysis of the justices and the institutional or macro-level perspective of the Court.

CONCLUSION

Where does this leave us? Was Plato correct about judicial decision making on the modern Supreme Court? Was Aristotle closer to reality, or could he just predict and not explain? In many ways, the battle of the competing models has been a battle of straw persons (Brisbin 1996). The attitudinal model and the legal model are exclusive explanations for judicial decision making. Each is dismissive of the influence of the other. The strategic models seem preferable if only because they recognize a more nuanced process of decision making that takes a variety of factors into account. However, it is hard to dismiss the charge that the justices might not be as sophisticated as some of the models posit.

We argue that each of the models has a great deal to contribute, but that each is lacking on its own. Individual or micro-level analysis has concentrated on the individual values and attitudes of the justices and the facts of the case. The macro-level analysis has concentrated on institutional factors and the impact of the environment. Individual justices cast votes, but there are institutional and environmental factors that may constrain them (Gibson 1991, 277). The policy preferences of the justices are clearly important and likely the most significant factor in decision making. But these are judges socialized into the norms of the legal community. When they don their robes, their behavior has to be affected in some way. Law matters and legal factors play some role in the decision

---

[4] Considerable debate exists regarding the frequency with which Congress overrides the Supreme Court's statutory decisions (e.g., Eskridge 1991b) and, to a lesser extent, challenges its constitutional ones (Meernik and Ignagni 1997).

calculus of the justices. The Court operates in an environment and faces a number of constraints that structure its institutional decisions.

We are interested in the interplay of the micro and macro levels. Our task is to borrow the best parts from each model and meld them into a single integrative model of decision making on the modern Supreme Court. We combine an analysis of micro-level variables like the attitudes of the justices and the facts of the case with macro-level concerns such as precedent and the policy positions of the other branches of government. Then we want to go a couple of steps further. The legal and attitudinal models implicitly (or explicitly) note that different issues can and do yield different patterns. For instance, in some areas, there are large numbers of unanimous decisions. In addition, some issues scale better than others. We seek to test that proposition by examining civil rights and civil liberties issues and economic cases separately. We argue that the Court will treat the issues that are more salient to it differently from the less salient cases.

Similarly, the strategic models explicitly account for differences between cases decided on statutory grounds and those that are constitutional in nature. There is the general notion that the Court is more likely to act strategically when facing statutory cases because of institutional constraints. By contrast, when deciding constitutional issues, the Court is thought to have a wider swath of discretion. We also test this proposition by differentiating between constitutional and statutory decisions. We hypothesize that the Court will act differently when it is more constrained. We then look at the interaction of these two dimensions to see how the Court reacts to salient cases with few constraints, salient cases with many constraints, less salient cases with few constraints, and less salient cases with significant constraints. We begin that task in Chapter 3 by laying out the general model and discussing how our variables are operationalized.

3

Building an Integrated Model of Decision Making

Each of the three models of decision making has something to contribute to the study of judicial behavior. We have made the argument that decision making on the modern Supreme Court (since *Brown v. Board of Education*) is more complex than either the attitudinal or the legal model standing alone and incorporates a wider range of factors than the strategic models. How, then, do we link the design of the framers, the practical realities of American politics, and these conceptual models of decision making? In this chapter, we build an integrative model that accounts for the major factors in the Court's environment. We discuss the variables that we see as critical to helping us understand decision making and present the measures we use to approximate those variables.

We analyze decision making within the context of neo-institutional research (March and Olsen 1984; Walker, Epstein, and Dixon 1988), which treats the Court as an actor whose behavior can be explained systematically. We begin with the premise that Gibson (1983, 9) advanced: Justices' decisions "are a function of what they prefer to do, tempered by what they think they ought to do, but constrained by what they perceive is feasible to do." In translating this premise to institutional decision making, we argue that judicial behavior is a function of substantive preferences and structural considerations. Substantive preferences are at the heart of the attitudinal model. Although they are arguably the most important factor, the institution is also constrained by structural considerations like the scope of judicial power and the need to both impose doctrinal stability and protect its legitimacy by seeing that its decisions are implemented and respected. The prevailing view in the literature has been that structural considerations are subordinate to substantive policy

	Salience of the Issue	
Grounds for Decision	More Salient	Less Salient
Constitutional	*Scenario 1* Dominance of Attitudinal Variables	*Scenario 4* Strategic to Avoid Institutional Response
Statutory	*Scenario 3* Strategic to Avoid Policy Response	*Scenario 2* Dominance of Legal Variables

FIGURE 3.1. *Expectations for Supreme Court Decision Making Under Different Conditions*

preferences. What the Court does, then, is the product of multiple forces that are intertwined and operate in complicated ways to shape decisions (Baum 1997, 2006).

With regard to Supreme Court decision making, there appear to be four possible scenarios, which are shown in Figure 3.1. If the attitudinal variable is as strong as its proponents maintain, we will expect no differences between the Court's treatment of statutory and constitutional cases (Segal 1997). In Scenario 1, the sincere preferences of the Court will dominate decision making. Therefore, extralegal factors will overwhelm the legal factors. Similarly, in Scenario 2, if proponents of the full-blown legal model are correct, the Court will face constraints that are associated with following precedent or "finding" the law. Thus, if these normative constraints are in force, the Court may not distinguish between statutory and constitutional cases. The Court will adhere to precedent regardless of the type of case. Legal factors will dominate and push extralegal factors to the periphery of the decision-making calculus. Those who subscribe to the full-blown strategic model might also argue that the Court is constrained regardless of the type of case.

It is, however, the in-between scenarios that are the most intriguing. The dominant one, Scenario 3, reflects the strategic model but also has elements of the legal and attitudinal models. This scenario maintains that the Court is largely free to act on its sincere preferences in constitutional decisions but must hew to a more circumspect position in statutory cases. Martin (2006) argues for a different perspective, namely, that the Court needs to be more cautious and guarded in its constitutional decisions because the costs of reversal in those cases would be so much more onerous for the institution. Thus, according to Scenario 4, the Court is more constrained in constitutional cases because it has more to lose if it is reversed. By building an integrative model of institutional decision making, we can test for the relative impact of attitudinal, legal, and strategic factors as well as determine which of the scenarios guides decision making in the post-*Brown* Supreme Court.

We consider three issues: whether attitudinal variables crowd out the effects of strategic and legal variables, whether there are differences in the weight accorded to each of these variables across constitutional and statutory cases, and whether different factors control when the Court examines civil liberties as opposed to economic cases.

THEORETICAL MODEL OF SUPREME COURT DECISION MAKING

Supreme Court decisions result from the interplay of a variety of legal and extralegal factors. We theorize that the Court's decisions are a function of the ideological predilections of the justices, tempered perhaps by the positions of the president and Congress and structured by the facts of the particular case on the plenary docket and the existing legal principles, precedents, and tests in the particular issue area. In Chapter 1, we discussed the practical realities of American government and separation of powers. We examined the weaknesses inherent in the Court and the potential checks that the other two branches can bring to bear to restrain or influence the judicial branch.

We also examined the normative and practical effects of precedent and the empirical impact of issue evolution. Justices would presumably be guided by the "golden rule" of precedent – respecting one another's opinions (Gerhardt 2008). Also, precedent makes the law predictable for litigants and those who have to implement the decisions. Repeat players who use the judiciary to advance their preferred policy position try to play the odds and seek favorable precedents that penetrate through the system (Galanter 1974).

We also discussed the evolution of issue areas over time. Cases in discrete issue areas tend to arise in a systematic fashion. They start with relatively easy facts and get progressively more difficult over time (Pacelle 2009). It is important to consider this in building a model that considers the various factors influencing decision making (Pacelle, Marshall, and Curry 2007). In each of the substantive chapters (beginning with Chapter 4), we examine the specifics of issue evolution and precedent in each of the four areas of law: constitutional civil rights and civil liberties, statutory individual liberties and civil rights, constitutional economic cases, and statutory economic cases. We expect that the relative impact of these factors will vary across the four different areas.

The impact of the president, Congress, and the Court will be consistent across each of the areas. Of course, the president, Congress, and the Court may care more about some issues (civil liberties) than others (economic). They may be more constrained in some issues (statutory) than others (constitutional), but the identity and ideological preferences of the institutional actors will be consistent.

RESEARCH DESIGN

As noted, we consider three research questions embedded in our four scenarios: 1) Do legal or attitudinal variables act exclusively to explain decision making; 2) are there differences in the weight accorded to each of these variables across constitutional and statutory cases; and 3) do different factors control when the Court examines civil liberties, seen as more salient to the justices, as opposed to economic cases? We use an integrative perspective to consider the range of factors to help us address these questions.

Our analysis examines a significant portion of the Court's plenary docket: constitutional and statutory economic and civil liberties and civil rights cases in the period from 1953 to 2000 as determined by the Supreme Court Data Base. We use the case as the unit of analysis.[1] The data base includes 4,494 cases, of which 1,512 are constitutional civil liberties and civil rights cases and 1,115 are statutory civil rights and individual liberties cases.[2] The total also includes 235 constitutional economic decisions and 1,632 economic statutory cases, the universe of orally argued full decisions for the 1953–2000 terms.[3]

The dependent variable throughout our study is the ideological direction of the Court's decision, coded 1 for liberal decisions and 0 for

---

[1] The Supreme Court Data Base uses the issue as the unit of analysis. We opt for the decision as the unit of analysis. We selected cases on the basis of the issue area. Among the Fifth Amendment cases that were identified through this filter were a number of eminent domain decisions. We preferred to view them as economic cases for purposes of the analysis.

[2] We have confined part of the analysis in this book to the federal nonconstitutional cases and excluded state civil rights and civil liberties cases. This leaves us with an N of 605 cases for that part of the analysis.

[3] Economic issues include state and federal taxation issues, eminent domain cases, federal and state regulation, contract clause, and a series of ordinary economic disputes.

conservative decisions. Because the dependent variable has only two values, all of our analyses utilize logistic regression (Long 1997). Across the time frame of the study, slightly more than 51 percent of the constitutional civil rights and civil liberties decisions were liberal. The distribution of the dependent variable for the nonconstitutional civil rights and individual liberties cases was slightly less liberal, with 47 percent of these being coded as pro–civil rights or pro–individual liberties decisions. Economic cases were characterized by more liberal decisions than the civil liberties and civil rights cases. The distribution of liberal decisions for both constitutional and statutory economic cases was nearly 60 percent for each group in the time period.

We model the Court's decisions as a function of its ideological composition, the evolution of the specific issue, existing precedent,[4] and the policy positions of the president and Congress. In this fashion, we incorporate variables from the attitudinal, legal, and strategic models. To assess the importance of judicial preferences and whether the Court responds strategically to the ideological position of the other branches in making decisions, we need measures for the policy positions of the Court, Congress, and the president. The measurement of preferences is critical for analyses that, like this one, seek to understand the effects of strategic behavior in the context of the separation of powers. Indeed, positive political theorists and empiricists of many stripes have long sought valid measures of sincere political preferences to assess a vast array of research questions. Our most difficult choice was between using the Common Space scores and the Bailey bridge measures.

For theoretical and analytical reasons, we utilize the NOMINATE Common Space measures created by Epstein and colleagues (2007). The Common Space measures are derived from a nonlinear transformation of the Martin-Quinn (2002) scores that are based on the Poole and Rosenthal (1997) DW-NOMINATE technique originally created to measure the ideological scores for Congress and the president.[5] The Poole and

---

[4] Distinguishing the effects of legal precedent from judicial preferences in explaining the Court's behavior is an important question for public law scholars (see Brenner and Spaeth 1995; Segal and Spaeth 1993). Congressional scholars face a problem in distinguishing the effects of political party from congressional preferences in explaining Congress' behavior. Krehbiel (1993) has challenged congressional scholars to demonstrate that party effects matter independent of the effects of preferences in explaining congressional behavior. We have tried to meet that same standard here by showing legal precedent matters independent of judicial preferences and under varying conditions.

[5] Given some of the issues raised by Bailey (2007), we examined multiple measures. The models, whether using the Segal-Cover (1989) scores (Segal, Epstein, Cameron, and

Rosenthal measure is based on the median member of the House and Senate, and the Common Space measure is based on the median justice. Therefore, the Common Space scores provide a common metric to allow comparisons of ideology across institutions.[6]

The Bailey scores are derived from information resulting from civil rights and civil liberties behaviors. In particular, Bailey's estimation procedure utilizes bridge information in the issue areas of crime, civil rights, free speech, religion, abortion, and privacy (Bailey and Maltzman forthcoming). An important part of our theoretical focus is how variation in issues may condition the extent that the Court's preferences or other institutional actor preferences influence the Court's decision making. Thus, our design seeks to assess a very wide range of possible issues, from civil rights and civil liberties to regulation and economic issues.[7]

Beyond our theoretical/design focus, we also have examined the data to determine if our findings are robust. For the general model, there are no substantive differences between the Common Space and Bailey measures. The comparative results are very similar, with only a few modest changes in civil rights and individual liberties cases, in which the pattern tends to strengthen the strategic model results. In economic cases, the results diverge a bit, likely a function of the fact that the Bailey measures do not incorporate information from non–civil rights and individual liberties issues.

By and large, the differences between the two measures are modest. Using the Bailey measure would allow us to push the strategic line of argument further and make bolder claims in some areas, but we prefer to err on the conservative side in line with where our theory has led us. Therefore, based on our theoretical focus and the relative robustness we

Spaeth 1995), Baum adjusted scores (1988; 1992), or Martin and Quinn (2002) for the ideology of the Court, yield comparable results. Similarly, we tried two measures of presidential liberalism – those of Segal, Timpone, and Howard (2000) and Erikson, MacKuen, and Stimson (2002) – with no significant changes in the coefficients. Thus, our results are robust.

[6] For ease of interpretation, we multiplied the Common Space and NOMINATE scores by − 1 to make them compatible with the other measures that run from − 1 (conservative) to 1 (liberal) for variables like precedent or 0 (conservative) or 1 (liberal) for the dependent variable.

[7] It is also true that there are potential disadvantages to using the NOMINATE Common Space measures. For instance, the Common Space scaling technique seemingly does not sufficiently resolve the problem of explaining votes with votes (Epstein et al. 2007; Maltzman and Shipan 2008). But given that our theoretical perspective focuses on how the Court and other institutional actors' preferences will have differential effects across issues, we think the trade-off remains in favor of using the Common Space measures.

found empirically across our theoretical conditions, we think the strongest case is for the use of the Common Space measures.

Although we argue that the attitudinal variable is not the sole determinant of decision making, we fully expect it to be the most important determinant. Furthermore, we believe it will be more consequential in constitutional than in nonconstitutional cases and in salient rather than less salient cases, controlling for the other variables. The variable for the president should be positively related to the Court's decisions and strongly significant, particularly in the more salient civil rights and individual liberties cases. We expect that variable to be statistically significant whether the cases are statutory or constitutional, given the close connection between the branches and the role of the SG (Pacelle 2003; Scigliano 1971). We expect the variable to have less impact in the less salient economic cases, whether they are constitutional or statutory.

To the extent that the strategic model is correct, changes in congressional ideology (as measured by the NOMINATE scores) should be positively related to the nonconstitutional decisions, controlling for the other variables. We also expect the variables for Congress to be statistically significant in the economic cases because they are more salient to Congress than to the Court. In particular, economic issues will be salient to the relevant committees in Congress that serve as agents for the institution (Maltzman 1997). Many of the studies of congressional decision making demonstrate floor deference to committee decisions (Clausen 1973; Kingdon 1989). For the constitutional decisions, changes in congressional ideology are not expected to constrain the Court's decisions as much given the extraordinary majorities necessary to overturn such decisions.

To examine issue evolution, we use a measure devised by Pacelle (2003, 2009) that traces the development of an issue from its emergence through the creation of the landmark decision that defines the particular issue area, through second-generation cases that raise more difficult questions in a unidimensional issue space and finally through the "complex" stage when the specific issue may get tied to other issues, thus leaving the unidimensional space (Pacelle 2009; Pacelle, Marshall, and Curry 2007; Ulmer 1982; Wasby 1993).

The early attitudinal studies (Schubert 1965) and fact pattern analyses (Kort 1957) incorporated the difficulty of the case into the models. Segal (1986) and refined versions of the attitudinal model (Segal and Spaeth 2002) argued that the variation in case facts helped to explain the variation in decision patterns. The notion of issue evolution reflects the need to distinguish between cases. The measure combines aspects of precedent and case difficulty. It combines elements of the concepts of policy change developed by Wahlbeck (1997), the jurisprudential regimes of Richards and Kritzer (2002; Kritzer and Richards 2003, 2005), and the theories of minimalism and maximalism designed by Sunstein (1999). A jurisprudential regime is defined as "a key precedent, or a set of related precedents, that structures the way in which the Supreme Court justices evaluate key elements of cases in arriving at decisions in a particular legal area" (Richards and Kritzer 2002, 308). Jurisprudential regimes then highlight the relevant facts that justices consider when deciding a case. However, whereas the measures of case facts and jurisprudential regimes are confined to a single issue like free speech (Richards and Kritzer 2002), freedom of religion (Ignagni 1993, 1994), or search and seizure (Kritzer and Richards 2005; Segal 1984), the issue evolution measure has the advantage of permitting comparisons across policy areas.

In the first stage, doctrine is unstable as the Court, having little experience with the new issue, tries to find a doctrinal home in an existing area of law. For instance, early free exercise of religion cases led to instability in doctrine, and the Court tried to fit them into free speech doctrine. The second stage involves the cases that immediately precede and follow the landmark decision. In establishment litigation, the cases that led to *Lemon v. Kurtzman* (1971) and helped refine the Court-created test would be part of this stage. This is akin to Sunstein's notion of width. Sunstein (1999, 16–19) argues that decisions have width if they set a standard, are applicable to other cases in the specific issue area, and are governing principles for that area of law. In the third stage, cases get more difficult, causing support to decline. Government aid to religiously affiliated colleges and cases like *Wolman v. Walter* (1977) forced the Court to balance more difficult forms of public assistance (Pacelle 2009). The fourth stage is marked by a multidimensional issue space. In other words, the original issue is joined to a separate issue. Hate speech cases raise issues of free speech and civil rights and challenge the Court to find a doctrinal niche (Cleary 1994; Walker 1994). We expect issue evolution to be statistically significant and negatively related to liberal decisions. We expect issue evolution to be important regardless of whether the case is constitutional or salient.

The majority opinion allows the Court to justify its substantive decisions and serves as precedent to guide future justices, lower court judges, political actors, litigants, and the behavior of citizens (Epp 1998; Hettinger, Lindquist, and Martinek 2006; Spriggs and Hansford 2001). In normative terms, justices and analysts consider precedent an important component of a judicial decision. In addition to issue evolution, we utilize precedent as a proxy for a legal model variable. We seek to measure the impact of precedent, controlling for the collective position of the Court. We are interested in discovering whether precedent has an independent effect on the decisions of the Court.

Most assume the importance of precedent, but it is seldom modeled as a part of judicial decisions. The literature tends to have a dichotomous view of precedent. It is seen as either a determinant of decisions or a mere shroud for the sincere preferences of the justices. However, as Hansford and Spriggs (2006) argue, this dichotomy is too simplistic. If precedent were the sole factor, it would govern the preponderance of cases and be the only statistically significant determinant of Supreme Court decisions. Alternatively, if it were a mere cloak for naked preferences, we would expect to see the Court cite only precedents that supported the outcome the majority desired, with the attitudinal model the sole determinant. We argue that precedents influence decisions and structure the outcome or at least "remove certain arguments from the legal repertoire" (Sunstein 1999, 42).

In most cases, the controlling precedent in a case is easy to identify. The question is whether the Court is going to follow, distinguish, or overturn it. The Court may narrow or expand the reach of the existing precedent. In more than 40 percent of the civil rights and civil liberties decisions and 45 percent of the economic decisions, the majority opinion distinguished the case at hand or overturned the extant precedent. It appears, then, that it is not simply a cloak for naked preferences.

As a proxy for this legal factor, we code the ideological direction of the most important precedents cited in the syllabus of the case. The majority opinion author must approve the syllabus before the opinion can be released. Thus, Benesh and Spaeth (2001) argue that to cite a given opinion in the syllabus means that the opinion rests on or makes great use of the precedent in that case, and therefore that the controlling case is salient to the author and arguably to all of the justices in the majority opinion coalition.[8] If the Court follows the precedent, the decisions will be in the

---

[8] The syllabus is a summary of the majority opinion's holding in the case. Benesh and Spaeth (2001) consider the citation of a case in the syllabus to be a signal of the importance of that case to the majority opinion author. The reporter of decisions composes the syllabus, and a draft is sent to the chambers of the majority opinion author for editing and approval. Benesh and Spaeth (2001) prefer this measure to simply counting cases cited in the majority opinion because it eliminates the problem of string citations and the practice of citing precedent to back up any major argument. They found that the average number

same ideological direction. When the Court departs from the ideological position of the precedent, it is distinguishing the instant case from the existing precedent or, in some instances, overturning that precedent.[9] For example, in an attempt to circumvent *Brown v. Board of Education* (coded 1 as a pro–civil rights precedent), Southern states tried freedom of choice plans and closing the public schools. The Court, adhering to the *Brown* precedent, struck these state laws down.

In the wake of *Roth v. United States* (1957) and *Memoirs v. Massachusetts* (1966), the Court used these precedents to strike down state attempts to censor movies and books. However, in *Ginzburg v. United States* (1966), the Court adopted an exception for pandering, distinguishing the case from the standards laid out in *Roth* and *Memoirs* (each coded 1 as pro–civil liberties precedents). Ultimately, the Court changed the entire nature of doctrine in *Miller v. California* (1973) (coded –1 as a precedent limiting civil liberties) but had to distinguish cases like *Jenkins v. Georgia* (1974) from that precedent when local communities went too far in their restrictions.

The inclusion of this variable permits us to examine the decision in the instant case as a function of the direction of the precedent. If precedent is important, the Court should be constrained in its decision making. The variable is expected to be significant and positively related to the decision, controlling for the other variables. We think precedent will be important across the board, but it should be strongest in the less salient cases, where the Court is interested in standardizing the law, and weakest in the constitutional decisions.

In some of the decisions, the case before the Court is a direct reflection of a previous decision, and there is a precedent that is directly on point. On-point precedents typically refer to cases that are virtually identical to a recent decision. In most instances, the on-point case is a companion to the full decision. In the companion decision, the Court briefly refers to the basic decision without repeating all of the justifications laid out in the fuller opinion. In other circumstances, the on-point decisions occur in cases that follow the landmark decision by a year or two. This often

of citations in the syllabus of orally argued signed opinions handed down between the 1987 and 1998 terms was 1.30 citations per syllabus (2,062 citations in 1,583 decisions). Counting all cases cited in the opinion, rather than the syllabus, produced far more citations. They conclude that citing a case in the syllabus is more consequential (Benesh and Spaeth 2001).

[9] If there are multiple decisions cited in the syllabus, the precedent variable is coded as following precedent only when the Court claims it is following all of the precedents cited.

occurs just after the Court announces an important decision and then gets a series of cases that were percolating through the lower courts and raise very similar issues, but the lower court did not have the benefit of knowing the new precedent. Therefore, the Court's on-point decision would typically remand the case "in light of our recent decision." When the precedent is on point, the Court should be particularly constrained by the previous decision. The variable is expected to be strongly significant and positively related to the decision regardless of the type of case.[10]

Whereas on-point cases can occur in any field of law, in the period we examined there were a number of civil rights, internal security, and criminal cases that had significant abuses of defendants' rights. The Court had to step in and correct the lower court with a brief mention of the governing precedent. In total, such cases (coded 1 if on point, 0 otherwise) made up approximately 10 percent of the civil rights and civil liberties decisions. By contrast, fewer than 6 percent of the economic decisions in the 1953–2000 period were "on point."

A ROAD MAP FOR THE REST OF THE STUDY

Before we proceed to test our integrative model under the interactive conditions of issue salience and perceived levels of discretion and constraint, we use Chapter 4 to examine an aggregate model with all of the relevant variables and all of the cases. This will provide a first test of our hypothesis that decision making is more complicated than the attitudinal model or the legal model alone maintains. If our model fails the test, our job is done, and we will direct you to the appropriate chapter of Segal and Spaeth, *The Attitudinal Model Revisited,* and let them tell you the rest of the story. But here is a hint before you get your hopes up, we peeked ahead and you are not getting off that easy.

In Chapter 4, we examine three models. As noted, we look at all economic and civil liberties cases (1953–2000 terms) and measure decision making as a function of the ideological position of the Court, Congress, and the president as well as the evolution of the issue and the extant precedents. Then we move to the major research questions that animate this study: the grounds for the decision and the salience of the issue. We take our universe of cases and divide them in two different ways: First, we

---

[10] To create a directional measure of the on-point variable, a measure of how close the precedent is to the case at hand, we coded precedents that were directly relevant (1 = directly relevant) and multiplied that by precedent (-1 = conservative; 1 = liberal).

separate the constitutional decisions from the statutory to see if different factors have different impacts as a function of the type of case. Then we separate the civil rights and liberties cases from the economic cases and see if they are treated differently.

In Chapters 5 through 8, we refine our analysis and examine the interactive effects of case type and issue salience. There are four possible pairings: salient and unconstrained, salient and constrained, less salient and less constrained, and less salient and still constrained. When cases are salient (civil liberties and civil rights) and the Court is relatively free because the issues are constitutional in nature, we expect the attitudinal variable to be more prominent than the strategic and legal variables. However, we expect the strategic and legal variables to remain viable and to have a positive impact. This is our task in Chapter 5. When the issues are salient but the Court is more constrained (statutory civil rights and individual liberties), we still expect the attitudinal variable to be important, but we feel that the legal and strategic variables will have a comparable impact; certainly, we expect them to exert greater influence than in the constitutional cases. Chapter 6 determines if these hypotheses are confirmed.

Then we move to the economic cases, which we argue are less salient, in Chapters 7 and 8. In truth, such cases are less salient to scholars as well. For every study dealing with the Supreme Court's economic cases, there are ten or more dealing with civil rights and liberties. We cannot change that by ourselves, but we would like to do our part. Therefore, in Chapter 7 we examine the constitutional economic decisions to see if the relative impact of the various factors is different for the civil rights and individual liberties. We think it will be. It will be interesting to see if the attitudinal factor is still dominant or whether it is supplanted by the legal and strategic variables. Chapter 8 brings us to the cases everyone seems to ignore – the nonconstitutional economic decisions. We surmise that a constrained Court dealing with issues that are less interesting and exciting will be likelier to be deferential to Congress and to legal variables. We think the Court and the president just do not think these cases are sexy enough to warrant spending their precious and finite coin. But we could be wrong. Aren't you a little curious? I know we are.

4

Decision Making on the Modern Supreme Court

Examining the Influences

We started this project with a number of research questions. Despite the lure of the siren song of the attitudinal model, we were not seduced. Theories that are simple and elegant are openly embraced in the social and physical sciences. Yet reality is seldom simple and almost never easily compartmentalized. Sure policy predilections are important and likely the most compelling factor in explaining decision making. But are they the only explanation? It strains credulity. We start with this simple question: Is the attitudinal model the only factor that explains Supreme Court decision making? If so, this has important normative consequences. It suggests that the justices are simply legislators in robes who are free to impose their vision of the good society on the law and the public with impunity. They are the essence, then, of the Platonic guardians. And what makes the situation even worse is that the justices hide behind the pomp and circumstance of the institution and the velvet curtain that separates their bench from the public. They pretend to rely on the law, philosophy, neutral principles, and the Constitution, yet all the while they are simply exercising their sincere policy preferences (Segal, Spaeth, and Benesh 2005). Furthermore, they are beyond the reach of the public and cannot be removed from office (except in the case of very bad behavior).

For a few chapters, we have been setting up a theoretical model and an empirical one, and now we test those models to examine whether the decisions of the Supreme Court simply operate by the rule of five: Whoever has a majority can rewrite the Constitution.[1] We have argued that

---

[1] Justice Brennan was fond of saying that the number five ruled in the Supreme Court – whoever had five votes could, in essence, control the law. This sounds very attitudinal (Eisler 1993).

the framework of government, normative theories of governance, and the political process suggest a more nuanced view of judicial decision making. We believe the justices are trying to exercise their policy preferences but that they are constrained (Epstein and Knight 1998). They are influenced by the decisions of their predecessors (Hansford and Spriggs 2006). They take seriously their position at the pinnacle of the judicial system. They understand the constraints that the Framers imposed on them. They realize that no matter how much power they have accrued over the years, they still inhabit an institution that has limits to its physical and moral authority (Baum 1997). Finally, they know that there are powerful institutional rivals that care about many of the issues just as much as they do (Katzmann 1997; Scigliano 1971).

With that countervailing power and weakness in mind, we test an integrated model of Supreme Court decision making on all civil rights and civil liberties and economic cases from 1953 to the end of the twentieth century. The integrative model assesses the effects of the legal, attitudinal, and strategic frameworks on the important conditions we have outlined in Chapter 3. That is, there are certain key conditions that operate as constraints on the Court, whereas others offer opportunities. These include the statutory-versus-constitutional context of the case and issue area – whether there is a distinction in the Court's decision making on economic versus civil rights and civil liberties cases. In other words, the integrative model is designed to assess whether the impact of the legal, attitudinal, and strategic factors on judicial decisions differs across these conditions. By doing so, the integrative model provides valuable information on how and under what conditions these forces affect judicial decision making. Thus, we model the Court's decisions as a function of legal factors, the Court's ideological composition, and the ideological position of the president and Congress. In particular, the integrative model controls for legal considerations using three different variables – precedent, on-point precedent, and issue evolution. The model controls for the strategic impact of the ideological leanings of the House and Senate, as measured by the median member, and the president.

This span of time arguably represents the Supreme Court's historical pinnacle of power and influence. In 1937, in a moment of perhaps its greatest weakness since it opened its doors, the Court took one step backward before taking two steps forward. As we noted in Chapter 1, the Court was forced to reinvent itself. It had to rebuild its institutional legitimacy. Footnote Four was launched from the potential rubble, arguing for judicial deference to the elected branches in matters involving

economic policy but advocating judicial activism for civil rights and individual liberties. This was the so-called double standard: Civil rights and
civil liberties would be held in a "preferred position" (Pacelle 1991).
The Court was substituting one form of judicial activism for another. In
Brown and many subsequent cases, the Court did not confine its decision
to the four corners of the Constitution (a position often referred to as
noninterpretivism). Nor did the Court feel bound by the precedents of its
predecessors.

Footnote Four would change the Supreme Court and the nation in
significant ways. The Court ultimately validated its promise with the
Brown decision. The Court pushed these issues onto the center stage
of American politics. The issues became more salient to the Court, and
Congress and the president were forced to deal with them (Rosenberg
2008). These issues became the litmus tests for presidents in making
appointments and the basis for often-contentious confirmation battles
(Epstein and Segal 2005). The exercise of this new role as the protector of
individual rights and liberties expedited the process by which the Supreme
Court became a constitutional tribunal. This is the subject of Chapter 5.
When Congress and the president ultimately did begin to pass meaningful
civil rights acts, large portions of civil rights law became statutory. We
examine this in Chapter 6. Increasingly, economic cases became statutory
and less salient. We examine the implications of this in Chapters 7 and 8.

Brown is on the short list of major landmark decisions, but even
that seems to diminish its ubiquitous impact. Just confine the analysis of
Brown to civil rights, and it has an incredible scope. Ultimately, it helped
to desegregate the schools. The decision helped create the conditions for
attacking employment discrimination and paved the way for extraordinary remedies like busing and affirmative action (Greenberg 1994). But it
was so much more. The decision had important implications for federalism. The Court was requiring a change in education policy, traditionally
a state function.

The justices understood that *Brown* was announcing a social revolution and that they had to consider a full complement of protections for
African Americans. The Court altered doctrine in many other areas of
law, such as freedom of expression, freedom of association, search and
seizure, and procedural rights, to help protect minority rights (Pacelle
1991; Walker 1990). If few of these cases originated in the South, that
region was not far from the thoughts of the justices. To protect the civil
rights of African Americans, the Court revisited the process of selective
incorporation of the Bill of Rights (Cortner 1981).

Like most Supreme Court decisions, *Brown* was not self-executing. Indeed, it took over fifteen years for meaningful desegregation to occur. Ultimately, Congress and the president would, like the cavalry, come to the rescue. Congress finally passed civil rights legislation, although it took a decade to pass the monumental Civil Rights Act of 1964. Presidents narrowly complied with the Court's directives, but until Lyndon Johnson, they did the minimum. Ultimately, for a brief moment, the Court, Congress, and the president were a "triangle transformed." Working together, with favorable precedent to support them, they pushed the frontiers of civil rights and civil liberties (Wasby 1993).

The *Brown* decision also reflects the balance of factors that typically influence the Court. Judicial attitudes, congressional predilections, presidential priorities, existing precedent, and issue evolution in civil rights all played a role in the decision (Eskridge 1994; Pacelle, Marshall, and Curry 2007). Within five years, in another civil rights case, *Cooper v. Aaron* (1958), the Court asserted that it was the ultimate arbiter of constitutional questions (Powe 2000). And because the Court was also increasingly constitutionalizing the law, there were fewer constraints on its decision making.

In Chapter 3, we discussed four possible scenarios of Supreme Court decision making. In this chapter, we focus on the first two of those ideal type scenarios. Scenario 1 posits that the attitudinal model is the sole explanation for decision making and works to the exclusion of the other variables. Scenario 2 argues for the primacy of the legal model. As such, the legal variables, primarily precedent, would dominate decision making. If our data support either of these two scenarios, our integrated model will be called into serious question.

After we examine the universe of our cases to test the integrated model, we refine our analysis and look at two major questions: whether there is a difference between the relative impact of the different factors on constitutional and statutory cases and whether the Court treats economic cases differently from civil rights and civil liberties cases. This allows us to look at the other two scenarios: whether the Court is more constrained in statutory cases (Scenario 3) or in constitutional cases (Scenario 4). In Chapters 5 through 8, we refine our analysis even further. We pair our two dimensions to create four different conditions: salient constitutional, less salient constitutional, salient statutory, and less salient statutory. In those chapters, we discuss the models in the context of broad doctrinal trends in each of the four areas: constitutional civil rights and liberties,

TABLE 4.1. *Integrated Model of Supreme Court Decision Making: All Cases, 1953–2000 Terms*

	Model I	Change in Probability
Supreme Court	2.55**	.08
	(.29)	
President	.20*	.03
	(.09)	
House	.99**	.04
	(.28)	
Senate	−2.43	−.01
	(1.78)	
Precedent	.51**	.12
	(.04)	
On Point	.87**	.17
	(.10)	
Issue Evolution	−.27**	−.06
	(.05)	
Constant	.94**	
	(.13)	
Chi²	.00	
Log Likelihood	− 2,790.3	
N	4,494	

**$p < .01$. *$p < .05$.
Probabilities represent the growth (or decline) in the probability of a liberal decision for every one standard deviation change in the independent variable or from 0 to 1 for dummy variables, holding all the other independent variables at their respective means.

statutory rights and liberties, constitutional economic, and statutory economic cases.

THE INITIAL TEST OF THE INTEGRATED MODEL

Table 4.1 shows the results of the overall model using all civil rights, civil liberties, and economic cases, whether constitutional or statutory, in the 1953–2000 terms. In this aggregate analysis of the post-*Brown* period, attitudinal, legal, and strategic variables are all statistically significant. Moreover, every variable but the Senate is in the hypothesized direction and statistically significant. The third column of Table 4.1 illustrates the substantive effects of each variable on the probability of a liberal decision being rendered by the Court, with the attitudinal variable, the two precedent variables, and issue evolution having the largest individual influences. By contrast, the influence of the other branches on the Supreme Court's decision making is smaller, but statistically significant. As a result, we can reject Scenario 1's premise that decisions are strictly a function of sincere policy preferences – the naïve attitudinal model.

Precedent and on-point precedent have the largest impact. It is important to underline that on-point precedents occur in less than one in every ten cases. Still, the Court is clearly paying attention to its previous decisions. The facts of the case, as measured in our issue evolution variable, also have a statistically significant impact on decisions over the time period. As the facts of the case get more difficult, it is more difficult for the Court to issue a pro–civil rights, pro–civil liberties, or liberal economic decision. These legal factors play important independent roles in institutional decision making but clearly are not the sole factor, which means that we can also reject Scenario 2, the naïve legal model.

The House and the president, proxies for the strategic variables, also exert an influence on the Court's decisions, controlling for the other variables. The Senate does not appear to have a statistically significant impact on the Court's decisions. Of the institutional variables, it is not surprising that the attitudinal variable has the biggest impact on the decisions. The bottom line is that the attitudinal variable is not the only one that affects decision making. The simple explanations of decision making are not sufficient in and of themselves. Decision making by the Supreme Court is more complicated than either the legal or the attitudinal models maintain (Baum 1997).

Although the ideological position of the Court plays a significant role, the president and the House also exert some influence. The president's power of appointment, the SG, and authority over implementation are wedges that apparently influence the Court (Curry, Pacelle, and Marshall 2008). Congress also has a variety of weapons to use against the Court; thus, the justices do take at least the House into account (Katzmann 1997). The Court also pays attention to precedent in making its decisions (Hansford and Spriggs 2006). In addition, the probability of either a pro–civil rights and liberties decision or a liberal economic decision is negatively related to the stage of evolution of the particular issue (Pacelle 2009).

The preliminary results of this model confirm our suspicions and our basic hypothesis. In truth, we viewed these models as rather simplistic and easily challenged. The results paint an initial portrait of a Court that is influenced by a variety of factors and thus suggest a more nuanced model of judicial decision making than either the attitudinal or legal models alone can provide. However, Table 4.1 does not address whether the relative impact of these variables varies as a function of two dimensions – issue salience and the grounds for the decision.

Before we proceed, we wish to be clear that we are not arguing that each economic case is less important than each civil rights and liberties case, just that the typical civil rights and civil liberties case is more salient to the justices than the typical economic case (Pacelle 1991; Perry 1991). Alternatively, the modern Supreme Court has cared more about civil rights and individual liberties as a class of cases than it has about economic issues as a class of cases (McCloskey 1960). This is reflected in the growth of the proportion of the former on the Court's agenda and the shrinking percentage of the latter as well as the number of unanimous decisions in economic cases. Finally, it is important to acknowledge that there is some overlap between our two dimensions. Just 13 percent of the economics cases in our period were decided on constitutional grounds. By contrast, approximately 58 percent of the civil rights and individual liberties cases were decided on constitutional grounds. The constitutional cases tend to have broader scope and be more important than the statutory cases.

THE CONSTITUTIONAL SOLUTION?

The conventional wisdom holds that the Supreme Court will feel much more constrained in statutory cases. Because the veto point is a simple majority of Congress and the issues tend to be narrower, most analysts assume that the Court will be more deferential to the elected branches and likelier to follow precedent in nonconstitutional cases. We labeled this conventional wisdom Scenario 3. Andrew Martin (2006) makes the persuasive argument that the Court has much more to lose in a battle with the other branches over constitutional issues. The elected branches may be unable to effectuate a policy response to a constitutional decision they do not like, but they may respond with an institutional response. They can limit the Court's jurisdiction or attack the institution in other ways. If the Court were to lose such a showdown, the damage would be more severe than a mere policy reversal and potentially could have a long half-life. We presented this as Scenario 4.

We divide our analysis into constitutional and nonconstitutional cases to test Scenarios 3 and 4. Table 4.2 shows the results, comparing the impact of variables in constitutional and statutory cases. The results are rather striking. The attitudinal variable is significant in each subset of

TABLE 4.2. *Integrated Model of Supreme Court Decision Making: Constitutional vs. Nonconstitutional Cases*

	Constitutional Cases	Change in Probability	Nonconstitutional Cases	Change in Probability
Supreme Court	3.32**	.10	2.13**	.07
	(.47)		(.38)	
President	.16	.01	.20*	.05
	(.14)		(.10)	
House	.51	.01	1.18**	.06
	(.49)		(.35)	
Senate	−1.39	−.01	−4.26*	−.04
	(.99)		(1.97)	
Precedent	.17*	.04	.68**	.14
	(.06)		(.05)	
On Point	.91**	.20	1.93**	.28
	(.11)		(.27)	
Issue Evolution	−.46**	−.10	−.18**	−.05
	(.08)		(.05)	
Constant	1.40**		.74**	
	(.25)		(.16)	
Chi^2	.00		.00	
Log Likelihood	−1,082.1		−1,651.7	
N	1,747		2,747	

**$p < .01$. *$p < .05$.
Probabilities represent the growth (or decline) in the probability of a pro–civil liberties or pro–civil rights decision for every one standard deviation change in the independent variable or from 0 to 1 for dummy variables, holding all the other independent variables at their respective means.

cases, but the legal variables are, too. Precedent, on-point precedent, and issue evolution are all statistically significant, controlling for the other variables in both the constitutional and statutory decisions, though their relative impacts vary by the type of case. Issue evolution is more prominent in the constitutional than the statutory cases. Just the opposite is true for precedent, which exerts considerably more influence in the nonconstitutional cases. The on-point precedent variable has a large impact on both constitutional and statutory decisions but is operative in a relatively small percent of cases. None of the strategic variables is statistically significant in the constitutional cases, suggesting that the Court can keep the elected branches at arm's length in such cases.

Our results do not conclusively reject the idea that the Court is constrained by other institutions in constitutional cases, yet the comparison does suggest that the constraints are more operative in statutory cases than constitutional cases. Neither the president nor Congress appears to play a significant role in constitutional cases. Therefore, the Court has considerably more discretion and latitude in constitutional cases vis-à-vis the other branches. Our results suggest that the conventional wisdom about the constraints attendant to nonconstitutional cases is quite viable. The House and the executive branch are especially important elements for the Court to consider in nonconstitutional cases.[2] The House and the president have independent impacts on decisions that are only slightly less important than the attitudinal variable. Our data thus suggest that there is support for Scenario 3 but not for Scenario 4.

The attitudinal variable and issue evolution dominate the decision-making calculus in constitutional cases. With fewer constraints, the policy preferences of the Court and the facts of the case are the most influential factors, lending credence to the attitudinal model. Precedent has an impact, but it is decidedly weaker than the other two variables. The statutory cases provide an interesting contrast to the constitutional cases. The influence of the constraints is evident. Whereas the policy preferences of the Court remain important, they are tempered by the need to consider the House and the president and attend to precedent.

To return to Table 4.2, it is worth noting the juxtaposition of the attitudinal and precedent variables. The impact of the attitudinal variable is stronger in the constitutional than in the statutory cases. By contrast, the precedent variable is significant in each subset of cases but plays a much larger role in the statutory cases. Such cases tend to be narrower, and the Court may use fealty to precedent as a means of legitimating a decision and avoiding reprisal from the other branches. Gerhardt (2008, 84) argues that precedent has greater impact in statutory law. There is a decreased path dependency in constitutional cases. There is indeterminacy to constitutional law that permits the justices to distinguish current cases from existing precedent. The vague language coupled with the multiplicity of factual situations permit justices to migrate from existing precedent (Gerhardt 2008, 94–96).

The Court itself provides additional justification for the presumed differences, arguing that it is more important to follow precedent in statutory cases, in which the legislative branch can provide corrective measures if necessary. Alternatively, it is the Court that is responsible for correction

---

[2] Our results actually underestimate the real effects of the president and the House. We are using all statutory cases in this part of the analysis, but if we remove the state cases, the impact of the president and the House on the federal cases is even stronger (see Chapter 6).

in constitutional cases. In *Payne v. Tennessee* (1991, 827–828), Chief Justice Rehnquist wrote, "This Court has never felt constrained to follow precedent when governing decisions are unworkable or badly reasoned... particularly in constitutional cases, where correction through legislative action is practically impossible.... Considerations in favor of *stare decisis* are at their acme in cases involving property and contract rights, where reliance interests are involved; the opposite is true in cases such as the present one involving procedural and evidentiary rules."[3] Parenthetically, this quote forecasts our hypothesis for the next section – the difference between less salient (economic) and more salient (civil rights and civil liberties) cases.

The strategic factors seem to have little impact on the Court in constitutional cases. The lack of influence by the president is somewhat surprising given the role that the SG can play as a bridge between the administration and the Court. Like the Court, though, the SG has to balance the desires of the president with the need to attend to the law. Indeed, Pacelle (2006) shows that only in civil rights and civil liberties cases does the position of the SG closely align with that of the president. For instance, in 96 percent of the criminal procedure cases, the SG argued to keep the bad guys in jail. In internal revenue cases, the SG argued almost 80 percent of the cases for the agency and 84 percent of the federalism cases in favor of national power, regardless of which party held the White House. In statutory cases, the House and the president exert significant independent effects on decision making. The Senate variable was significant, but in the wrong direction. Also, perhaps as a consequence, the attitudinal variable has a considerably weaker influence on statutory decisions. But there is a potentially hidden effect as well. King (2007) argues that the Court has some control over the scope of the case and may choose to decide a case on constitutional rather than statutory grounds. This may be done to enhance the Court's discretion and make it less vulnerable to the other branches.[4]

In the end, this model shows that there is no real empirical support for the idea that the Court is more constrained in constitutional than in statutory cases. The consequences of executive or legislative retaliation may be considerably more profound in the constitutional context, but the Court

---

[3] A number of justices have made this very point in their opinions. Rehnquist reiterated the distinction between the impact of *stare decisis* on constitutional and statutory cases in *Seminole Tribe of Florida v. Florida* (1996). Even O'Connor, who made *stare decisis* the centerpiece of the joint opinion in *Planned Parenthood v. Casey*, stressed this point in her dissent in *City of Boerne v. Flores* (1997).

[4] Ulmer (1982) posits the idea of issue fluidity, whereby the Court can expand or contract the issues in a case, essentially changing the scope of the case.

apparently recognizes the diminished likelihood that such sanctions (akin to the so-called nuclear option) will be invoked. The attitudinal variable overwhelms the influence of the elected branches, suggesting that the extraordinary veto points necessary to overturn a constitutional decision give the Court discretion and leeway. But it is not the sole influence on decision making, even in this rather unconstrained environment.

The Salience of Issues

Not all issues are created equal. Whether we are talking about the American voter (Campbell et al. 1960), the president (Marshall and Pacelle 2005; Wildavsky 1975), members of Congress (Clausen 1973; Kingdon 1989), or Supreme Court justices, some issues are more salient than others. In general, we argue that on the modern Supreme Court, civil liberties and civil rights have occupied a higher ground – some have called it a "preferred position" – than economic issues (Pacelle 1991). If, as we argue, civil rights and individual liberties carry more weight with the Court, the attitudinal variable should gain primacy. It is possible that it will even be the sole significant variable, a return to Scenario 1. By contrast, if economic issues are less important to the justices, their attitudes may not dominate. They may defer to the elected branches or follow existing precedents. They may be more concerned with stabilizing the law and adopt what Perry (1991) called "the jurisprudential mode."

As we noted in Chapter 2, there is empirical evidence that rights and liberties cases are more salient than economic cases. First, the Court stated this very position in the famous Footnote Four, arguing that it would be deferential to Congress in economic matters. For civil rights and individual liberties, however, the Court would presume that a law restricting either was unconstitutional, and the burden would be on Congress (or the state) to justify the reason for the law. The government would have to meet a "paramount" or "compelling" interest in order to restrict rights or liberties. Therefore, civil rights and civil liberties would be held in a "preferred position" (Pacelle 1991).

Second, the Court issues far more unanimous decisions in economic cases than in civil rights and liberties cases. This is a clue that the attitudinal model is less prominent in the former than in the latter type of case.[5] This carries over to individual justices as well. Proponents of the

---

[5] Indeed, the attitudinal models typically drop all unanimous cases from the analysis. Not only do the economic cases scale less well, but many of them also are not even considered in the model.

attitudinal model use factor and dimensional analyses to demonstrate the impact of individual attitudes and values. The question is whether the cases will "scale" along that particular dimension. It turns out that civil rights and civil liberties cases scale much better than economic ones (Ducat and Dudley 1987; Dudley and Ducat 1986; Hagle and Spaeth 1992, 1993). This reflects the differences between the issues and the Court's treatment of them. Furthermore, if one looks at the reasons the Court grants *certiorari*, one sees some striking differences. The Court typically grants the petitions in civil rights and individual liberties cases to settle the important issue in the case. But when the Court accepts an economic case, the reason is much likelier to be to resolve a conflict between the lower courts (Pacelle 1991). The Court is likelier to expand the issues in a civil rights and liberties case and contract them in an economic case (Pacelle 1991; Ulmer 1982).

Table 4.3 permits us to examine the differences between the relative impacts of the factors in these very different types of cases. The results are suggestive but certainly not overwhelming. The attitudinal variable is a strong factor in each set of cases (and its impact is about the same in both subsets). Regardless of whether the case is economic or civil liberties, the ideological position of the Court is important. The strategic variables demonstrate an apparent trade-off. In the civil rights and civil liberties cases, the influence of the president is statistically significant, controlling for the other variables. Carmines and Stimson (1989) argue that race was, in essence, a realigning issue dividing the two parties, and for every president after Eisenhower, such issues were litmus tests for prospective nominees to the High Court. In addition, the role of the SG needs to be underlined. There is a long-standing notion that the SG, when filing an *amicus curiae* brief, will do the administration's bidding (Segal 1988; Salokar 1992). However, Pacelle (2006) has shown that this is true in only two areas of law: civil rights and individual liberties. Given that these are the two areas that are presumably salient to the Court and much likelier to be decided on constitutional grounds, it is not surprising that the presidential variable is statistically significant.

By contrast, Congress has no impact on the Court's decisions in rights and liberties cases. This is in keeping with the normative idea that the majority may not be well positioned to protect minority rights. Indeed, one of the major reasons civil rights groups found it necessary to use the courts prior to *Brown* was the intransigence of Congress toward such issues (Epp 1998; Wasby 1995). Part of the absence of congressional impact could be a function of the primacy of reelection for members of

TABLE 4.3. *Integrated Model of Supreme Court Decision Making: Civil Rights and Civil Liberties vs. Economic Cases*

	Civil Rights Cases	Change in Probability	Economic Cases	Change in Probability
Supreme Court	2.75**	.08	2.20**	.07
	(.38)		(.47)	
President	.25*	.05	.05	.01
	(.11)		(.14)	
House	.33	.01	1.13**	.05
	(.41)		(.41)	
Senate	− 1.17	− .01	− 4.06*	− .05
	(.81)		(1.86)	
Precedent	.23**	.05	.86**	.17
	(.06)		(.06)	
On Point	1.11**	.25	1.46**	.22
	(.10)		(.40)	
Issue Evolution	− .24**	− .05	− .32**	− .07
	(.06)		(.07)	
Constant	− .66**		1.30**	
	(.17)		(.21)	
Chi²	.00		.00	
Log Likelihood	− 1,627.9		− 1,089.1	
N	2627		1867	

**$p < .01$. *$p < .05$.
Probabilities represent the growth (or decline) in the probability of a pro–civil liberties or pro–civil rights decision for every one standard deviation change in the independent variable or from 0 to 1 for dummy variables, holding all the other independent variables at their respective means.

Congress (Mayhew 1974) and their ability to defuse controversial issues by leaving them to the Court (Silverstein 2009). Yet the House does play a role in economic cases. This is in keeping with the ideas advanced in Footnote Four: The Court would defer to the elected branches on economic issues. Members of Congress have greater interest in economic matters than do the president or the Court.

The president, however, does not have a statistically significant effect on the decisions in economic cases. To return again to the role of the SG, in the major economic areas – regulation, commerce clause, internal revenue cases, and federalism – the positions taken by solicitors general do not vary much by administration. Regardless of whether the president is a Democrat or a Republican, the SG traditionally argues for the ability of the federal government to regulate the economy, for upholding

internal revenue regulations, and for the authority of the central government (Pacelle 2006). Also, it is important to remember that when the
government is a party and the construction of a statute is involved, the
SG will be likelier to argue the case from the perspective of Congress than
that of the president (Pacelle 2003; Salokar 1992). Thus, the halo effect
of the SG can be transplanted to Congress.

The legal variables deserve a closer look because they may hold the
key to understanding whether issue salience plays a role in the Court's
decision making. Examining issue evolution is not particularly revealing.
The Court is influenced by the stage of evolution of the issue, regardless of
whether the case involves economic or civil rights and individual liberties
issues. Controlling for all other factors, the Court is less likely to make
a liberal economic decision or a pro–civil rights and liberties decision as
the cases get more difficult (Pacelle 2009).

The area where we do see the effects of a legal variable is precedent. At
first glance, there does not seem to be any real difference – precedent and
on-point precedent are both statistically significant regardless of the type
of issue. But if you move your eyes over one column, you will see a striking
difference. The impact of precedent on a decision is more than three times
greater in economic cases than in civil rights and individual liberties cases,
controlling for all other variables. We argue that this is evidence of issue
salience. The Court appears to be less interested in the economic cases, so
it narrows their scope. It is much likelier to decide them unanimously and
to defer to precedent because it wishes to limit its attention to such issues.
The Court would rather resolve these issues and introduce stability to
the law so that the lower courts can take over the role of supervising the
economic issues (Pacelle 1991). It is true that the Supreme Court will step
in to resolve a lower court dispute, but it is likely to confine its review to
that specific question. Remember the opinion of Chief Justice Rehnquist in
Payne, in which he argued that precedent is more important in property
and contract (economic) cases than in those involving procedural and
evidentiary rules (criminal procedure and civil liberties).

In the end, the evidence of important differential effects for salience is
not overwhelming. This fuels the contention of proponents of the attitudinal model that it is by far the most important factor. We do not dispute
this, but we believe we have shown that it is not the sole factor and does
not crowd out other influences. Others may well argue that salience is
all relative. Given the finite size of the Court's docket, every case is very
important; however, some are more important than others. We do not

dispute this, either. Ours is not the choice between salient and nonsalient cases but between more and less salient ones.

We have painted with a rather broad brush here and have found some consequential differences between constitutional and statutory cases. We believe that there are differences between the economic and civil rights and individual liberties cases, but they appear to be subtle. We want to examine this in some greater depth. We feel it is important to peel back another layer of the onion and refine our analysis a little further.

WHERE DO WE GO FROM HERE?

Maybe there is something about the interaction of these two dimensions that can help us understand decision making a little better. As we have discussed, whether issues are more or less salient and whether cases are constitutional or statutory are potential indications of the level of constraint on the Court. If we combine the two dimensions, we get four possibilities: more salient constitutional cases, less salient constitutional cases, more salient statutory cases, and less salient statutory cases. We argue that the opportunities for and constraints on the Court should differ across the four categories. Figure 3.1 (in Chapter 3) shows a matrix with the four possibilities. We argue that constitutional cases provide fewer constraints on the Court than statutory cases and that economic cases are less salient to the modern Supreme Court than civil liberties and civil rights cases.

By segmenting the data into these four categories, we can also compare the constitutional with the statutory cases. This may give us a richer picture of institutional decision making. We advanced four possible scenarios, and though they are ideal types – particularly those that argued that the attitudinal and legal variables were the sole determinants – it may be that under the conditions we examine, decision making approaches one of these types. For instance, the attitudinal variable may be important in each of the four types of cases, but it may be dominant relative to the other variables in the salient constitutional cases. The less salient statutory cases may see the dominance of the legal factors. We are curious about the areas in which precedent will be more or less important and in which the president and Congress might emerge as counterweights.

In Chapter 5, we use our basic model to examine constitutional civil rights cases, the more salient constitutional cases in our two-by-two matrix. These cases should also pose the fewest constraints, both external (the other branches) and internal (precedent) for the Court. But remember that Scenario 4 argued that the Court might feel more constrained because the weapons that the other branches could bring to a confrontation would be institutional in nature and could weaken the Court for a long period of time (Martin 2006). In Chapter 6, we stay with the more salient rights and liberties cases but move to the nonconstitutional realm. We hypothesize that these cases, as statutory ones, will meet Scenario 3: The Court will be cognizant of and influenced by the position of Congress and the president. Because the veto points are lower, any retaliation from the other branches is likely to be policy oriented and not directed to the Court as an institution. We also assume the legal factors will be prominent.

In Chapters 7 and 8, we move to the economic cases, which we argue are less salient to the justices. In Chapter 7, we take the constitutional, less salient cases. In Chapter 8, we examine the statutory economic cases. Because these cases are less salient and the constraints are more prevalent, we assume that there will be greater attention to the position of Congress and perhaps the president. In these less salient cases, we expect precedent to play a significant role in decision making. In each of these chapters, we enrich our empirical analysis with discussion of the major trends in decisional patterns in these areas of law.

5

Building a New Legacy

Constitutional Civil Liberties and Civil Rights

Brown launched the modern era of Supreme Court jurisprudence, but it did not emerge full-blown. Certainly, it was a product of the preferred position doctrine and part of a long-term process of doctrinal reconstruction (Wasby 1995). Before the *Brown* decision, the Court ordered Southern states to make their separate graduate and professional schools equal (or admit minority students to those all-white schools), forbade states from enforcing restrictive covenants, and banned the use of the all-white primary (Vose 1959; Wasby, D'Amato, and Metrailer 1977). The Legal Defense Fund of the NAACP pursued a litigation strategy that bore fruit in a series of cases that helped procure voting rights, housing, and education. That litigation strategy was predicated on attempts to build a nest of precedents favorable to civil rights. Eventually, presidents and Congresses would support these efforts through legislation, executive orders, implementation, and the work of the solicitor general (Pacelle 2003).

When we think of separation-of-powers models of policy making, we think of the Court as "the least dangerous branch of government." It is forced, by institutional circumstances and the design of the framers, to be in a reactive mode. Thus, strategic decision making posits that the Court will react to the other branches of government and temper its sincere collective preferences to avoid the various hammers that the president and Congress can use against it (Bergara, Richman, and Spiller 2003; Epstein, Knight, and Martin 2001; Sala and Spriggs 2004; Vanberg 2001). Better, the justices might reason, to retreat a bit and live to fight another day. But cases like *Brown* defy such characterizations. The Court was the aggressor – the proactive institution. It more or less forced the hand of the president and Congress (but see Rosenberg 2008).

Constitutional cases give the Court the potential to be a leader in setting policy. They give it the chance to be the first actor in this iterative game and to potentially have the last word as well. But there are risks attendant to this high-stakes game of policy making. If the Court bases its decision on its interpretation of the Constitution, it is difficult for the other branches to overturn it. There certainly are policy responses that can limit the scope of the decision, but to change a constitutional decision, the other branches need, in essence, to change the Constitution, which is not an easy task. Indeed, there have been few changes to the Constitution since the Bill of Rights was tacked onto the document. Of course, some amendments have been passed to overturn Supreme Court decisions. The post–Civil War amendments banning slavery, providing equal protection, and insuring voting rights were designed to overturn past Court decisions, as were amendments providing for an income tax and the eighteen-year-old vote. Yet the amendment process, by any measure, has disturbed only a tiny percentage of the constitutional decisions by the Court.

The Court understands that even though a policy response may be limited or unlikely, Congress and the president are not without other resources. Congress and the president can retaliate in ways that go beyond simple policy responses and threaten the institutional legitimacy of the Court itself. The ability to tamper with the Court's jurisdiction or to refuse to implement judicial directives can have more profound and longer-term consequences for the Court (Curry 2005; Pacelle, Marshall, and Curry 2007). Indeed, Martin (2006) posits that the Court may be more constrained in constitutional cases than in statutory decisions. Our initial test of this hypothesis did not find any support for the notion of additional constraints, but the idea is intriguing enough that we do not want to dismiss it without closer examination.

We have argued that civil rights and civil liberties are salient issues to the justices. Part of our justification for this assertion is that presidents have made such issues litmus tests for their nominees to the Court (Epstein and Segal 2005). Partially, as a result, confirmation politics have increasingly been contentious.[1] What does all of this mean? For one thing, the

---

[1] Epstein and Segal (2005) argue persuasively that this is not a new phenomenon. Periodically, the battles rage over nominees, particularly when there is divided government, a president is in or rapidly approaching an election or a lame duck period, and the Court is divided.

salience of these issues is hardly limited to the Court. Congress, the president, and important constituencies care deeply about such issues (Cheney 1998; Katzmann 1997; Pauley 2001). Therefore, when the Court makes a decision that favors civil rights or individual liberties, some will applaud; others will seek ways to limit or overturn the decision. The same goes for decisions limiting civil rights and civil liberties. Some groups and members of the other branches will have a response. One notable example was reproductive rights.

Roe v. Wade is not *Brown* in any number of ways, but it certainly ranks as one of the most important and controversial of the Court's decisions in the post-*Brown* era. It raises notions of noninterpretivism and judicial activism. Some have decried the decision as a return to the substantive due process that landed the Court in serious trouble in the pre– and early New Deal days (Bork 1996, 173–174).

Roe made reproductive rights a national political issue (Keynes with Miller 1989; O'Connor 1996). For sixteen of the next twenty years, Republicans dominated the White House, allowing them to place their imprint on the Supreme Court. The one Democrat to serve between 1969 and 1992, Jimmy Carter, was the only president since Reconstruction to be denied the opportunity to select a Supreme Court justice.[2] During the Reagan and Bush administrations, abortion was a litmus test for judicial nominees. Three of Ronald Reagan's selections, Sandra Day O'Connor, Antonin Scalia, and Anthony Kennedy, had supposedly been "right" on the issue. George H. W. Bush had the opportunity to nominate two justices, and it was widely assumed that David Souter and Clarence Thomas had passed similar litmus tests (Abraham 2008; C. Smith 1993).

Reagan and Bush also sent their solicitors general into the Supreme Court to argue that *Roe* should be overturned. For many years, the Court refused this invitation, and along the way, it even strengthened *Roe* (Pacelle 2003). But as the liberal members of the Court retired, the numbers were mounting in favor of the right-to-life position. It was no surprise that when the Supreme Court announced it would hear oral arguments in *Planned Parenthood of Southeastern Pennsylvania v. Casey*, pundits predicted the end of *Roe v. Wade*. A simple head count seemed to confirm the obvious: Chief Justice Rehnquist and Justice White had dissented from the original *Roe* decision and had opposed reproductive rights from the outset. Justice Scalia joined them in opposition. Justice O'Connor, though not as militant in her opposition, frequently held that

---

[2] Even James A. Garfield, who served just over six months, was able to appoint a justice.

Roe had been wrongly decided and often voted to permit state restrictions. In his first case on the issue, Justice Kennedy opposed reproductive rights. Justices Souter and Thomas had not yet faced an abortion rights case, but they had replaced liberal Justices Brennan and Marshall. Thus, there seemed to be at least five certain votes to overturn *Roe.*

A funny thing happened on the way to the demise of *Roe.* Justice Blackmun, the author of the original *Roe* decision, and Justice Stevens voted to uphold reproductive rights. As expected, Rehnquist, Scalia, Thomas, and White voted to strike the decision. The anti-*Roe* forces needed only one vote to constitute a majority. Both O'Connor and Kennedy were on record as opposing *Roe*, and at least one seemed certain to provide that vote. Yet in this case that seemed to be teed up for a reversal, O'Connor and Kennedy joined Souter to protect *Roe v. Wade* (Pacelle, Marshall, and Curry 2007).

The attitudinal model would predict one outcome (overturning *Roe*) and the legal model a completely different one (upholding *Roe*). The strategic model would probably urge the Court to be tempered in its response. In their joint opinion, O'Connor, Kennedy, and Souter, adopting a tone of judicial restraint, reaffirmed *Roe*, arguing that "principles of institutional integrity and the rule of *stare decisis*" mandated the holding. The three justices seemed to put aside their values and personal preferences, supporting existing precedent because it was settled law. Their opinion openly discussed the Court's legitimacy, its ultimate resource. The other justices appeared to resort to their values and attitudes in deciding the case (Baum 1997).

This is a single example, and of course an anecdote does not prove anything conclusively. But the case reminds us of the disconnect between the individual and institutional levels of analysis. Most of the justices voted on the basis of their sincere preferences, but the Court's decision did not appear to reflect those collective preferences. This is the enigma of understanding decision making: How is it possible that the individual justices vote largely on the basis of their sincere preferences, yet the Court seldom overturns precedents? We start to consider this by looking at the Court's constitutional civil liberties cases. We assume that attitudinal variables will emerge front and center as the main determinants of decision making in such cases. If any of our categories were to fit Scenario 1, the complete dominance of the attitudinal variable, this would be it. We assume that the Court will not be influenced much by Congress. The president presents an interesting puzzle. On the one hand, the extraordinary majority needed to overturn a constitutional decision suggests that the Court is relatively safe. On the other hand, the SG can bring the perspective of the president directly to the Court, and these are the very issues in which the position of the OSG reflects that of the president (Pacelle 2006).

Past attitudinal studies suggest that the facts of the case affect the propensity to make a pro–civil rights and individual liberties decision (Rohde and Spaeth 1976; Segal 1986). Therefore, we expect our issue evolution variable to help structure the decisions. Precedent is the key legal variable. Litigants cite precedents in their petitions. Justices refer to precedents in their decisions. Some argue that this is causal and done for legitimacy only. Others maintain that precedents are an important touchstone for lower courts and litigants and that justices seek to use legal reasoning to reach the correct results (Collins 2008). We hypothesize that precedent will have a significant impact on decision making in civil rights and individual liberties cases.

THE LEGAL ENVIRONMENT FOR CIVIL RIGHTS AND CIVIL LIBERTIES

Let's reiterate what we mean by constitutional civil rights and individual liberties cases. These are cases that are decided on constitutional grounds, mostly coming from the Bill of Rights and what some refer to as the Second Bill of Rights – the Thirteenth, Fourteenth, and Fifteenth Amendments. The substance of these cases varies from criminal procedure to freedom of expression and religion to claims of discrimination. Such cases claimed a relatively small percentage of the Court's decision agenda as our story opens. But *Brown*, decisions like *Mapp v. Ohio* and *Miranda v. Arizona*, and an expanded interpretation of the First Amendment created the conditions for more Court attention to rights and liberties (Pacelle 1991). Also, when the Burger and Rehnquist Courts decided to limit or reverse some of the policies of the Warren Court, the justices had to allocate further agenda space to continue the revised development of law. In the next section, we briefly examine the legal environment the Court faced on the eve of oral arguments in *Brown v. Board of Education* and how it changed during the next half century.

Legal Factors: Issue Evolution and Precedent

Issue evolution and precedent had been unsteady influences on constitutional civil liberties and rights jurisprudence in the years immediately prior to the Warren Court. With respect to issue evolution, many of these early cases were multidimensional in scope. That is to say, there were multiple issues in the cases. For example, the Court had to balance concerns about freedom of speech with security. This led to instability in doctrine, and such competing considerations proved particularly difficult to balance against the looming shadows of a world war (Murphy 1972). Regrettably, the Japanese internment cases would see the Court giving security precedence over civil rights (Irons 1993). In short, the Court needed multiple cases and "normal times" to impose some consistency and establish doctrinal equilibrium. Moreover, precedent did not exist in many areas, as the new cases were essentially opening new areas of law. Then, when the first few cases were decided, the narrowness of the decisions and the often-strange mix of facts did not lend themselves to the creation of stable doctrine or precedents that could easily be transplanted.

There are a number of areas that comprise civil rights and individual liberties. By way of illustration, we consider a few of these – freedom of expression, freedom of religion, criminal procedure, and race and gender discrimination – to provide some background on issue evolution and precedent. If there is one general statement that can be made about all of these issues, it is that there was initial flux followed by some stability and then the reintroduction of some flux. In general, the early cases were very fact intensive, arrived with no particular rhyme or reason, and were often multidimensional. The Court wrestled with them for a while and often was inconsistent in its early decisions. Later cases emerged more systematically as a result of the policy preferences of the justices, the growth of interest group activity, and the desire for stability of the law (Baird 2007; Pacelle 1991).

The existing evidence in doctrinal, institutional, and policy studies suggests that many of the factors we are using to explain decision making influenced the slow, unsteady development of doctrine prior to *Brown*. The attitudinal variable may not have been as influential in the wake of Footnote Four. None of the justices serving before *Brown* was selected because of his views on civil rights or individual liberties. Indeed, few of them had any prior judicial experience (Abraham 2008).[3] The political branches, faced with the impending clouds of war, were hardly disposed to protect rights and liberties. In any case, few decent precedents existed

---

[3] Indeed, the notion of the freshmen effect or newcomer effect seems time bound and connected to this era (Howard 1968). Pacelle and Pauly (1996) show that inconsistencies in the behavior of new justices do not occur much anymore. In part, this is because the issues are better established and new justices have experience before ascending to the Supreme Court.

to support rights and liberties. Issue evolution suggests that early cases would be "easier" to decide in a pro-rights and pro-liberties fashion, but that was not the case in this instance. They were set against a backdrop of war and presented the Court with little room for a measured consideration of rights.

First Amendment jurisprudence reflected many of these properties. The Jehovah's Witnesses were active in generating test cases (Konvitz 1966; Peters 2000), but the Court was conflating the religion and speech questions, thereby creating instability. The flag salute cases were emblematic of this difficulty (Bartee 1984). In the 1940s, the Court incorporated the free exercise and establishment clauses to the states. In the wake of *Brown*, the Court protected the rights of African Americans and civil rights protesters in the South. However, in seemingly parallel cases involving the free expression rights of alleged Communists, the Court was not so protective. In dissent, Black and Douglas wondered why "red" and "black" got different treatment (Ball and Cooper 1992).

Gradually, the Court expanded free speech, reaching a zenith in *Brandenburg v. Ohio* (1969). The Burger and Rehnquist Courts trimmed the sails a bit, but was the retreat a function of the more conservative nature of the Court or the result of issue evolution?[4] First Amendment litigation grew increasingly complex, evolving into libel and obscenity doctrine. By that time, the Court had worked through its initial problems and was able to impose some stability on doctrine. Of course, as the Court became more conservative, doctrine began to change. The Court chipped away at the protections under libel law and issued *Miller v. California* (1973), changing the direction of obscenity doctrine.

It is useful at this juncture to examine each of the major issue domains to see the influence of issue evolution and precedent on the macro level. We examine the general trends in freedom of expression, freedom of religion, criminal procedure, and civil rights jurisprudence. Obviously, we can only sketch the broad parameters of doctrinal development in these areas. We focus on important landmark decisions and changes in the direction of doctrine and judicial policy. In the next few sections, we highlight the major doctrinal developments to provide a context for the empirical results that come later in this chapter.

---

[4] The easy, and likely the correct, answer is the increased conservatism of the Court, but one should not be too quick to dismiss the notion of issue evolution. Consider the parabolic support for civil liberties of Black (Ulmer 1973) and Douglas (Ulmer 1979). The early reluctance to support civil liberties was a function of the novelty of the issues. The later decline in support was a function of the increased difficulty of the issues before the Court.

FIRST AMENDMENT DOCTRINE ON THE MODERN
SUPREME COURT

Freedom of Expression

The modern Court has developed a variety of tests or standards to guide
its First Amendment jurisprudence (Tedford and Herbeck 2009). In the
area of obscenity, it used the *Roth* test for about two decades and then
retreated to the *Miller* test. In libel, the Court created the *New York
Times v. Sullivan* (1964) test (Lewis 1991). The *O'Brien* test (*O'Brien
v. United States* [1968]) was applied when the Court was considering
a case that involved "symbolic speech," or speech plus conduct. *Central
Hudson* (*Central Hudson Gas and Electric Corporation v. Public Services
Commission of New York* [1980]) was the test the Court used when
it measured the value of commercial speech. In free exercise, the Court
adopted and then abandoned the *Sherbert* test, replacing it with the much
more forgiving *Smith* test (Long 2000). In establishment clause litigation,
the Court followed the *Lemon* test.[5]

The adoption of such standards and others (as in free speech with
"time, place, and manner restrictions") is the Court's way of animating
precedents to guide the lower courts and establish predictability in the
law. They are a guide for the justices and their successors as well as
for litigants, but mostly they serve the role of vertical precedent. These
tests represent the impact of the law and recognition that the Court must
balance difficult factual situations.

The interpretation and application of such tests can certainly be a
reflection of attitudes.[6] Justices who are ideologically inclined can interpret the *Lemon* test stringently to erect a high wall of separation between
church and state. Colleagues on the Court who are disposed to be
accommodating to religion could easily find that a government program passes the purpose and effect test. Similarly, one justice's public
figure is another's private citizen for purposes of libel law. These are not

---

[5] The adoption of the *Smith* test has been the bane of members of Congress, who tried
to force the Court to use the compelling interest standard, and of constitutional law
students who formerly had only to think of "Lemon Sherbert" to remember the dominant
standards in freedom of religion doctrine.

[6] Kobylka (1989) argues that Burger thought the *Lemon* test would be accommodating to
religion. For the most part, justices have used it as more of a device for separation of
church and state.

unambiguous standards, but it is also clear that such tests, regardless of how they are applied, are based on the notion that predictability in the law is desirable.

The Warren Court's initial foray into the realm of free speech came against the backdrop of the Red Scare. Three years prior to the beginning of Earl Warren's stewardship, the Court had decided *Dennis v. United States* (1951). That decision upheld the conviction of twelve individuals accused of violating the Smith Act, which made it a crime to advocate the overthrow of the U.S. government. Although the Court was not united in its reasoning, Chief Justice Vinson articulated a "clear and proba-ble danger" standard for considering such restrictions on free speech. That standard was relatively easy for the government to meet in limiting expression.

In 1957, a similar case, *Yates v. United States*, came to the Court. There, however, the Court cast its lot on the side of free speech. It effec-tively modified the *Dennis* standard, distinguishing between the advo-cacy of abstract doctrines and the advocacy of unlawful action. Thus, "although *Yates* did not advocate the preferred freedoms or absolutist approaches favored by Black and Douglas, it certainly liberalized free speech doctrine, making difficulties for Smith Act prosecutions" (Epstein and Walker 2007b, 238). In 1961, a slim majority of the Warren Court would uphold the Smith Act's ban on membership in subversive orga-nizations (*Scales v. United States*). However, by the mid-1960s, a clear majority of the Court seemed dissatisfied with governmental prohibitions of this sort (O'Brien 2008b, 425).

In *Brandenburg v. Ohio*, one of Chief Justice Warren's final cases, the Court struck down an Ohio law designed to punish the advocacy of illegal activities. In doing so, it held unanimously that such proscriptions could only be valid "where such advocacy is directed to inciting or producing imminent lawless action and is likely to incite or produce such action" (395 U.S. at 447). With this decision, the Court created a precedent that pushed free speech to its broadest expanse.

The progressivism on speech issues migrated to the printed word, other forms of expression, and other media. In *Chaplinsky v. New Hampshire* (1942), the Court ruled that libel, obscenity, and so-called fighting words were not protected speech. The Warren Court worked toward limiting the definition of obscenity and libel and pushing the frontiers of free expression. In a series of cases that began with *Roth v. United States* (1957) and culminated in *Memoirs v. Massachusetts* (1966), the Court ruled that material was obscene only if it was "utterly without redeeming social value." As a result, it became virtually impossible to get an obscenity conviction (McWhirter 1994).

In its landmark decision in *New York Times v. Sullivan* (1964), the Court liberalized libel law. Brennan's unanimous opinion in the case adopted the "actual malice" doctrine, elevating the burden of proof on public officials and making it difficult for them to win libel judgments (Lewis 1991). Then, in a series of decisions, the Court defined almost everyone as a public figure or public official, limiting their chances of recovering a libel judgment. The Warren Court's record on symbolic speech was more mixed. After it upheld the government's valid interest in preventing the burning of draft cards in 1968, the Court rejected a school district's policy of prohibiting students from wearing black armbands to protest the Vietnam War (Johnson 1997).

Though more conservative than its predecessor, the Burger Court did not radically reorient free speech and expression doctrine. Two of its decisions in 1971 reaffirmed the primacy of these constitutional protections in the face of attempted governmental suppression. In *Cohen v. California*, the justices held that, in the absence of violence or disruption, the government could not prohibit individuals from displaying offensive words in public. About three weeks later, the Court again ruled against the government, maintaining that the Nixon administration's attempt to prevent publication of the so-called "Pentagon Papers" was impermissible (Anastaplo 2007).

Ultimately, the Burger Court's free speech and expression jurisprudence would create a somewhat mixed legacy. In *Miller v. California* (1973), the Court narrowed the *Roth* test, the framework the Warren Court had produced for judging a work to be "obscene." In giving more regulatory authority to state and local governments in this area, the Court opened the doors to greater regulation of expression. The Burger Court also ultimately limited the defense for libel by holding that fewer and fewer people were public figures. As a consequence, they needed only to demonstrate that the published charges against them were false and caused harm.

Similarly, in *FCC v. Pacifica Foundation* (1978), the Court upheld the F.C.C.'s reprimand of a New York City radio station after the station aired George Carlin's "Filthy Words" monologue. However, a year earlier the Court had struck down an Arizona regulation that prohibited legal advertisements, stating that commercial speech was deserving of constitutional protection (*Bates v. State Bar of Arizona*) (Tedford and Herbeck 2009).

But perhaps the competing impulses that characterized much of the Burger Court's free speech jurisprudence were best encapsulated by its ruling in *Buckley v. Valeo* (1976). The justices held that limitations on campaign contributions and expenditures were effectively restrictions on candidates' free speech. Thus, the Court struck down a provision of the Federal Election Campaign Act of 1971 that limited campaign expenditures. Yet the Court upheld restrictions on campaign contributions, arguing that the governmental interest in reducing corruption in electoral politics was sufficiently important to override concern about protecting free speech (Anastaplo 2007).

Although the Supreme Court grew even more conservative under Rehnquist's leadership, his Court's first major free speech case did not indicate that rightward shift. In 1984, Gregory Johnson burned an American flag during the Republican National Convention in protest of the Reagan administration's policies. The Court's decision in *Texas v. Johnson* saw a coalition of liberals and conservatives vindicate Johnson's free speech rights, maintaining that his activity was protected by the First Amendment (Goldstein 2000).[7]

In 1992, the conservative Court again struck a blow on behalf of free speech, invalidating a St. Paul, Minnesota, ordinance that sought to regulate certain types of "hate speech" (Cleary 1994). In the Court's judgment, the law impermissibly singled out certain viewpoints. As Justice Scalia's majority opinion stated, "The First Amendment does not permit St. Paul to impose special prohibitions on those speakers who express views on disfavored subjects" (*R.A.V. v. City of St. Paul*, 505 at 391).

In many ways, the Rehnquist Court chose not to depart dramatically from the free speech precedents of prior courts. For example, in siding with Larry Flynt's *Hustler* Magazine in a libel dispute with Rev. Jerry Falwell (*Hustler Magazine v. Falwell* [1988]), the justices not only adhered to but pushed beyond the Warren Court's holding in *New York Times v. Sullivan* (Smolla 1990). The Court also upheld a Colorado law concerning speech by protestors at abortion clinics (*Hill v. Colorado* 2000). In doing so, the majority referred to the regulations as a time, place, and

---

[7] Scalia and Kennedy joined liberal justices Brennan, Marshall, and Blackmun to comprise a five-to-four majority in the case. Stevens, O'Connor, and Rehnquist dissented. Scalia would later say of the case, "If it was up to me, I would have thrown this bearded, sandal-wearing flag burner into jail, but it was not up to me."

manner restriction akin to ones previously upheld in other public contexts (e.g., *Ward v. Rock Against Racism* 1989) (Raskin and LeBlanc 2002).

With its decision in *Reno v. American Civil Liberties Union,* the Court's free speech jurisprudence transitioned into the twenty-first century. Faced with its first case regarding regulation of the Internet, the Court responded by declaring that provisions of the Communications Decency Act (CDA) of 1996 amounted to overbroad, content-based restrictions on free speech and were therefore unconstitutional. Although Congress has sought to revise the offending provisions of the CDA on multiple occasions in response to *Reno,* those efforts have, thus far, failed to satisfy the Court's First Amendment objections (see *Ashcroft v. American Civil Liberties Union* [2002, 2004]) (Axelrod-Contrada 2006).

The normal expectation for issue evolution is that cases will become more difficult over time, which indeed has been the case in most areas of First Amendment jurisprudence. The typical progression is toward multidimensional issues (Pacelle 2009). Hate speech cases, commercial speech, and cases that involved protests at abortion clinics all involved multiple issues. As expected in such cases, there were inconsistent patterns of individual decision making, as some justices found the free speech issue dominant and others thought the other issue should be the focal point of the decision. Some justices who were not typically strong advocates of free speech supported broader protection for expression that was commercial or shielded protesters at abortion clinics.

Freedom of Religion

Freedom of religion jurisprudence underwent significant changes over the period of our analysis. The Court had incorporated the Free Exercise and Establishment Clauses in 1940 and 1947, respectively. The Court wrestled with various fact situations before settling on a test. It was practically the judicial equivalent of the speed of light between the Court's decision in the Sunday closing laws cases and the compelling interest standard in *Sherbert v. Verner* (1963). For a generation, that was the dominant standard. The Court eventually reconsidered it in *Employment Division v. Smith* (1990). In dissent, O'Connor noted that the facts of the case – the use of peyote by drug counselors – did not require the Court to overturn the compelling interest standard (Long 2000).

In the Establishment realm, the Court grappled with two sets of questions – state aid to religious institutions (mainly parochaid cases) and attempts to put religious symbols and practices on public property.

In an early round of cases, the Court forbade school-initiated prayer and devotional readings before settling on the three-part *Lemon* test, which became the dominant standard for the parochaid cases (Dierenfield 2007). Despite arguments from O'Connor (favoring an endorsement test) and Scalia (supporting a coercion test), the Court has not overturned *Lemon*.

The cases that followed *Lemon v. Kurtzman* (1971) raised more difficult questions for the Court. On the same day that the Court decided *Lemon*, it ruled that aid to religious colleges and universities was permissible. *Wolman v. Walter* (1977) presented the Court with a multifaceted aid package. The Court upheld part of the package and rejected other provisions (Pacelle 2009). Later cases involved prayer in the locker room before an athletic event and prayer before a graduation.

The development of free exercise law followed the hypothetical path we laid out in the model of evolutionary change. Many of the recent cases were multidimensional in scope, involving different issues. A number of cases involved religious speech in schools (*Board of Education v. Mergens* [1990]) (Davis 2000), colleges (*Rosenberger v. University of Virginia* [1995]) (Shur 1995), and public property (*Lamb's Chapel v. Center Moriches Union Free District* [1993]) (Hoekstra 2003). What we see is that justices who are not typically strong supporters of free speech champion that freedom in cases where religious expression is implicated.

CIVIL RIGHTS FROM *BROWN*

We deliberately began our analysis with *Brown v. Board of Education* because it fulfilled the promise of Footnote Four and, in our view, fully launched the modern Supreme Court (see also Silverstein 2009). A landmark decision, by definition, alters the terrain of law in that specific era (Baird 2007; Pacelle 1991). *Brown*, of course, did that, but it did so much more. It shifted the landscape of both civil liberties and civil rights. Freedom of expression and association doctrine changed as a result of the Court's civil rights decisions (Bartee 1984). The Court also revised its criminal procedure doctrine, in no small part as a means of protecting African Americans (Cortner 1981; Pacelle 1991; Walker 1990). *Brown* was the super-precedent that spread its influence into all sorts of areas of law (Landes and Posner 1976; Sinclair 2007). In making its decision, the Court was committing future agenda resources to fleshing out civil rights doctrine (Pacelle 1991). Thus, *Brown* caused the Court to trim its attention to other issues.

In announcing its decision in *Brown*, the Court ruled that in the area of public education, separate but equal had no place. This began the process of overturning the existing precedent, *Plessy v. Ferguson* (1896). Yet segregation did not end on May 17, 1954.[8] The Court had to dismantle it piece by piece (Cottrol, Diamond, and Ware 2003). Southern states erected a number of barriers to desegregation. In terms of issue evolution, many of the post-*Brown* cases were relatively easy, and the Court unanimously razed them one at a time. After fifteen years, the Court finally ruled (in *Alexander v. Holmes County Board of Education* [1969]) that the South had dragged its feet long enough and that the time for all deliberate speed had passed (Patterson 2001).

Brown, abetted by the Civil Rights Act of 1964, pushed the Court into new frontiers of civil rights. The Court moved beyond education to secure equal access to accommodations, housing, employment, and personal relationships. The cases were becoming more difficult, but for more than a decade the Court did not retreat even as it got more conservative. The Court was anxious to redeem the promise of the CRA of 1964 and the Voting Rights Act of 1965. The justices sought to find a public nexus to private discrimination so that they could attack it under the Constitution (Wasby 1995). When race cases moved north, the Court had to deal with the differences between *de facto* and *de jure* segregation.

The Court would move from race to gender equality and then would tackle other forms of discrimination, but these cases would not emerge during the Warren Court. The initial cases tended to involve clear discrimination (e.g., *Reed v. Reed* [1971]). But soon the cases would present progressively more difficult issues such as government programs that discriminated on gender grounds but provided advantages to women. Indeed, groups pursuing gender equality carefully modeled their litigation strategies on those used by the NAACP to combat racial discrimination (Epp 1998; O'Connor 1980). The groups attacking gender discrimination were usually successful in winning their cases but ultimately failed to get the Court to use the strict scrutiny standard it applied in race discrimination cases (Epstein and Knight 1998). Certainly, part of this was due to the changes in the composition of the Court.

Ultimately, race discrimination cases would progress from ending discrimination to remedies, moving them further along the evolutionary scale. The Court had to deal with busing, affirmative action (Ball 2000; Urofsky 1997), minority set-asides, and racial redistricting (Thernstrom

---

[8] Or on May 31, 1955, the date of *Brown II*, the implementation decision.

1987). Initially, despite the difficulty of the cases, the Court supported the creation and extension of these remedies. For more than two decades, the Court followed precedent and expanded civil rights, even as the cases got more difficult and the Court got more conservative. But the Court would eventually begin to distinguish and overturn pro–civil rights precedents. The Burger and Rehnquist Courts would limit busing and affirmative action (Perry 2007) and, ultimately, in *Board of Education v. Dowell* (1991) would limit the reach of *Brown*.

CRIMINAL PROCEDURE

The Court's role in criminal procedure and the rights of the accused follows a similar pattern of doctrinal development. The Warren Court was clearly different from its predecessors or successors in dealing with these cases. The percentage of cases decided in favor of the accused was almost 55 percent during Warren's tenure. By comparison, the percentage was 40 percent for the Vinson Court, and fewer than a third of decisions were favorable to defendants for the Burger and Rehnquist Courts (Epstein et al. 2003, 230). In a series of highly publicized and controversial decisions, the Court began to support the rights of criminal defendants. *Mallory v. United States* was an unpopular decision that came on the heels of *Brown* and decisions that protected the rights of alleged Communists. These decisions sparked a furor in Congress and led to the introduction of a variety of Court-curbing bills (Murphy 1962, 194–196; Powe 2000).

As the Warren Court moved more forcefully into the area of criminal procedure, it had to uproot a great deal of precedent that would limit its designs (Graham 1970; Pye 1968). As far back as 1825, the Court had to deal with the issue of whether the Bill of Rights applied to the states. In *Barron v. Baltimore* (1833), Chief Justice Marshall, speaking for a unanimous Court, said that it did not (Newmyer 2001). Beginning in 1925, the Court began to undermine this holding one step at a time. First, the Court found that freedom of speech was protected against both federal and state restrictions. Yet it would be more than a dozen years before the Court extended that protection to free exercise of religion and two more decades before the establishment clause. The 1960s would see the Court sweep across the provisions of the Bill of Rights and incorporate most of them to the states, throwing out old precedents along the way (Cortner 1981).

In *Mapp v. Ohio* (1961), the Court took the judge-created exclusionary rule (a means of enforcing the Fourth Amendment) and incorporated it to the states. The case began as a test of the Ohio obscenity law (a First Amendment issue) but was transformed into a search and seizure case (Collins 2008; Long 2006). Within a few years, the Warren Court issued decisions in *Gideon v. Wainwright* (1963), *Escobedo v. Illinois* (1964), and *Miranda v. Arizona* (1966), selectively incorporating parts of the Fifth and Sixth Amendments (Baker 1983; Cortner 1981; Graham 1970; Lewis 1964).

The Court also wrestled with the legality of the death penalty. A majority held that the death penalty as constituted was cruel and unusual punishment in *Furman v. Georgia* (1972). However, the Court gave states the chance to redraw the provisions and found that a number of them satisfied the original objections (Epstein and Kobylka 1992; Latzer 1998; Walker 2008). Other cases raised questions concerning whether "three strikes and you're out" constituted cruel and unusual punishment (*Ewing v. California* [2003]) and whether excessive bail was a violation of the Eighth Amendment.

Over the subsequent decades, the justices would face a variety of factual situations, many asking the Court to draw finer lines, such as the differences between searches of automobiles and searches of houses. Technological changes, like wiretapping (*Katz v. United States* [1967]), pen registers (*Smith v. Maryland* [1979]), listening devices, thermal imaging (*Kyllo v. United States* [2001]), and aerial surveillance (*California v. Ciraolo* [1986]) also introduced new issues that the Court had to balance (Woessner and Sims 2003).

Although precedents such as *Mapp* and *Miranda* still exist, it would be a mistake to think that the Court has not undermined their vitality in significant ways. With a number of exceptions to the exclusionary rule (Pacelle 2004) and the *Miranda* warnings (Haynie 2004), the Court has chipped away at protections for the accused. Part of this is a function of the difficulty of the cases, but the lion's share is likely the result of changes in the composition of the Court. Nixon ran on a platform of law and order, and his nominees largely reflected his wishes in criminal procedure cases (Abraham 2008). Reagan and Bush completed the process of choosing justices who were likelier to side with the prosecution than with the defense. Even the last few selections in our time period (Clinton appointees Ginsburg and Breyer) have supported the rights of the accused less than 50 percent of the time (Epstein et al 2003, 495, 502). Regardless, given the opportunity to terminate *Miranda*, the Court demurred in *Dickerson v. United States* (2000) (Dripps 2001).

Like the civil rights and First Amendment cases, some criminal procedure cases also implicate other issues. It was not until the Warren Court that the practice of excluding blacks from juries was found suspect, and it was even later when women were given the right to serve. The use of preemptory challenges (*Batson v. Kentucky* [1986]) and claims that the death penalty is applied disproportionally to African Americans (*McCleskey v. Kemp* [1987]) involved civil rights (Kennedy 1997, 1988). A number of cases involved combinations of Sixth Amendment (right to a fair trial) and First Amendment (freedom of the press) concerns. *Sheppard v. Maxwell* (1966) was the most visible of these cases, though it did not settle the issue, and the Court was initially inconsistent in deciding whether the First Amendment took precedence over the Sixth (DeSario and Mason 2003).

Another multidimensional series of cases has combined elements from two disparate areas: due process (usually search and seizure) and economic issues or administrative matters. For example, the Court held that a warrant was required for housing and safety inspections (*Camara v. Municipal Court* [1967] and *See v. Seattle* [1967]) and inspections of mines (*Donovan v. Dewey* [1981]) but not for social workers (*Wyman v. James* [1971]). It also held that the Internal Revenue Service could issue "John Doe" summonses to banks (*United States v. Bisceglia* [1975]) (Rosenbloom and O'Leary 1997).

With this context in mind, we now return to our regularly scheduled programming – the macro-level analysis of our models. In this chapter, we examine decision making on the modern Supreme Court, a tribunal that claims hegemony in constitutional cases and has decided that civil liberties and civil rights require more exacting oversight than economic issues. We begin with the expectation that the influence of the political forces and precedent will be somewhat diminished. The attitudinal variable is expected to exert the greatest force. However, whereas these highly salient constitutional cases should provide the most favorable climate for judicial policy preferences to predominate, we do not expect that the attitudinal variable will overwhelm all other factors. We expect some of the legal and strategic factors to influence the Supreme Court's decision making in this area as well.

RESULTS

Table 5.1 contains the results of our model of Supreme Court decision making, as applied to the 1,512 civil rights and liberties cases decided on

TABLE 5.1. *Integrated Model of Supreme Court Decision Making: Constitutional Civil Rights and Liberties Cases, 1953–2000 Terms*

	Model	Change in Probability
Supreme Court	3.28**	.11
	(.50)	
President	.32*	.06
	(.15)	
House	.18	.01
	(.55)	
Senate	−.29	−.01
	(.99)	
Precedent	.13	.02
	(.08)	
On Point	.99**	.52
	(.12)	
Issue Evolution	−.55**	−.11
	(.09)	
Constant	−1.49**	
	(.58)	
Chi²	.00	
Log Likelihood	−913.9	
N	1,512	

** $p < .01$. * $p < .05$.
Probabilities represent the growth (or decline) in the probability of a pro–civil liberties or pro–civil rights decision for every one standard deviation change in the independent variable or from 0 to 1 for dummy variables, holding all the other independent variables at their respective means.

constitutional grounds between 1953 and 2000. As expected, the variable capturing the Court's collective policy position is positive and strongly significant. As the Court's median becomes more liberal, the institution becomes significantly likelier to issue a pro–civil liberties or pro–civil rights decision. We also anticipated, given the close connection between the executive and judicial branches (Curry, Pacelle, and Marshall 2008; Scigliano 1971) and the role of the SG (Pacelle 2003), that the presidential variable would exhibit statistical significance, and Table 5.1 bears out this expectation as well. Civil rights and individual liberties have been core concerns of the Court and the president since *Brown*. Indeed, they are said to be central to the so-called litmus tests that presidents have for their nominees. However, the Court does not appear to factor either house of Congress into its decision-making calculus in these cases. In some ways, this seems a little strange. Certainly, members of Congress (and their constituents) care deeply about such issues. However, Congress' collective action problems, its majoritarian impulses, and the extraordinary majorities needed to overturn a constitutional decision probably explain the lack of influence.

The results displayed in Table 5.1 are consistent with a number of basic conclusions. First, the overwhelming significance of the attitudinal variable underscores the overriding importance of civil rights and liberties cases to the justices. It also demonstrates that cases decided on constitutional grounds bestow the Court with an added measure of insulation from the pressures of other institutional actors. The results are particularly consistent with the conventional view that the Court is largely unconstrained by Congress in its constitutional decision making.

The presidential variable is the only strategic variable to attain statistical significance in this model. On the whole, the Court's constitutional civil rights and liberties decisions from 1953 to 2000 have generally mirrored presidential policy preferences. Though it issued *Brown* during the conservative Eisenhower presidency, the Warren Court's progressive decisions on issues including civil rights, school prayer, the right to privacy, and criminal procedure largely came against the backdrop of the liberal Kennedy and Johnson presidencies. Throughout much of the 1960s, then, the Court and the presidency were in sync. Though the Burger Court hardly constituted a "counter-revolution" (Blasi 1983; Schwartz 1998), its more conservative posture – particularly on "law and order" issues – closely reflected the views of President Nixon and future Republican presidents.

The role of the OSG is also evident and provides the potential for the president to have a more direct influence on the Court. Indeed, it is the case that the position argued by the SG most closely resembles the president in the areas of civil rights and civil liberties (Pacelle 2006). Because these are constitutional cases, the SG, like the Court, is a little freer from the strictures typically attendant to the office. Many of the cases involve state policies (like reproductive rights, criminal procedure, freedom of religion, or civil rights). The SG is free to file an *amicus* brief to reflect the position of the administration because the government has limited liability in that an adverse precedent will not have a great impact on the United States (Salokar 1992).

The effect of legal considerations on the Court's decision making in these cases is somewhat mixed. First, the results indicate that the Court is not constrained by precedent in constitutional civil liberties and rights cases. This finding is consistent with statements by the justices in Court opinions indicating that they feel less constrained by precedent in constitutional cases (Gerhardt 2008). The lack of significance of precedent is also historically intuitive, given the Court's high-profile rejection of established precedent in *Brown* and, later, in criminal procedure cases such as *Mapp* and in legislative reapportionment decisions (*Baker v. Carr* [1962]; *Reynolds v. Sims* [1964]; *Wesberry v. Sanders* [1964]) (Cortner 1970).

On-point precedent exerts a statistically significant effect on these decisions, but it is important not to overestimate the substantive importance of this finding: On-point precedents were only relevant to a small percentage of the cases during the time period encompassed by the analysis. For example, after the decision in *Gideon*, the Court continued to review a number of cases concerning the right to counsel in state proceedings. After *Gideon*, the Court typically used *per curiam* decisions to vacate and remand such cases for reconsideration in light of that landmark decision (e.g., *Huggins v. Raines* [1963]; *Pickelsimer v. Wainwright* [1963]).

Thus, the Court only appears to be constrained by precedent in constitutional civil liberties and rights cases when it is directly on point. This is a setback for the legal model because it suggests that the justices are not overly constrained in their decision making unless the instant case is very similar to the existing precedent. Absent a direct precedent, attitudinal considerations presumably occupy a larger role.

The legal consideration that appears to have the greatest influence on the Court's constitutional civil rights and liberties decisions is issue evolution. As these cases grew more difficult, it became harder for the Court to issue pro–civil rights and liberties decisions. A number of cases that came on the heels of the *Mapp* and *Miranda* decisions illustrate this finding. The Court extended the exclusionary rule's applicability to the states in 1961, but over time the Court grew reluctant to push *Mapp* to its limits. Instead, it carved out multiple exceptions to the warrant requirement in the years following *Mapp. Terry v. Ohio* (1968) permitted warrantless stop-and-frisk searches in the interests of public safety. Tellingly, in *Terry*, only one of the four justices still on the Court who had voted to extend the exclusionary rule in *Mapp* was prepared to rule in favor of defendant John Terry.[9] In *Nix v. Williams* (1984), the Court refused to

---

[9] Douglas was the lone dissenter in *Terry*. Warren, Black, and Brennan had voted in favor of Dollree Mapp in 1961 but voted in a conservative direction in *Terry*.

exclude evidence seized without a warrant because its discovery would have been inevitable. In the same term, the Court recognized a good-faith (*United States v. Leon*) exception to the exclusionary rule and reiterated its commitment to the independent source exception (*Segura v. United States*) (Pacelle 2004).

The Court's treatment of self-incrimination issues followed a similar pattern. *Miranda v. Arizona* announced a seemingly bright-line rule with respect to suspect self-incrimination. However, the Court soon created an exception to the warnings in the interests of public safety (*New York v. Quarles* [1984]). And in *Illinois v. Perkins* (1990), the justices refused to extend *Miranda* to prohibit the introduction of incriminating evidence obtained from suspects by undercover police officers (Haynie 2004). Consistent with the results presented in Table 5.1, these progressively more complex fact patterns saw the Court grow less willing to vote in a liberal direction.

Why are attitudes so important, yet the impact of precedent appears to be so muted? First, these results should not be surprising. Most analysts agree that the attitudinal variable is the most important factor in decision making. In addition, the cases isolated for this analysis are the most amenable to the sincere preferences of the justices. Pacelle (1991) and Perry (1991) argue that civil liberties and civil rights cases are among the most important parts of the Court's volitional agenda – they are the cases the justices care the most about.

By contrast, the impact of legal considerations is difficult to discern because the law seldom lies conclusively on one side or the other. The legal ambiguity of such cases makes it difficult to follow precedents and frees the Court to rely on its collective preferences. In addition, by using only full decisions and not memoranda and *per curiam* decisions, we underestimate the impact of precedent (Songer and Lindquist 1996).

The Supreme Court has undergone some profound changes over the last half century. Maybe the biggest one inaugurated our study period – *Brown v. Board of Education*. It continued a revolution in federalism, overturned precedent, was wanton judicial activism, and initiated a dramatic change in civil rights and individual liberties. It was the most visible manifestation of the preferred position doctrine (Pacelle 1991). That philosophy would dominate the Court for the next generation. It provided a super-precedent that structured decision making. Indeed, even as proponents of the preferred position doctrine were exiting the Court and being replaced by justices who rejected its tenets, the standard remained in force. Ultimately, though, as the last holdouts left the Court, a new theory or doctrine began to emerge (Tushnet 2003), the result of presidential appointments that alter the ideological balance of the Court. The advent of a new guiding principle means a destabilization of precedent in the short term. But as soon as the new theory gains majority support, the goal is to build an interrelated edifice of precedents that will sustain it for a generation or more.

Precedent, issue evolution, and the attitudinal variable were linked in civil rights and criminal procedure cases throughout the period we examine. As noted, during the Warren Court, the justices almost split the criminal procedure cases in half. Slightly more than 52 percent of the decisions were in favor of the defendant. That percentage was cut significantly in the Burger and Rehnquist Courts, as they decided about 29 percent in favor of the defendant. Similarly, although at much higher levels, support from the Warren Court for civil rights (almost 93 percent) was reduced during the Burger and Rehnquist years (56 percent). As the Court got more conservative, it issued decisions that were likelier to favor the prosecution and limit civil rights. This was partly due to issue evolution, with cases becoming more difficult as time went on. The *de jure* segregation cases of the 1950s gave way to remedies like busing and affirmative action, forcing more difficult decisions. Race questions were reformulated as gender issues and groups sought the heightened levels of protection afforded race. A similar process unfolded in criminal procedure. As soon as the Warren Court embarked on these areas, it sought to build consistency into its decisions. The Burger Court undermined some of those precedents and, together with the Rehnquist Court, built a new series of precedents to support its decisions.

The one area of civil liberties that did not change dramatically was the Court's First Amendment jurisprudence. The support levels were remarkably consistent across the time period. The Warren Court decided about 40 percent of First Amendment and related cases in favor of civil liberties claimants. This would decline to 35 percent under the tenures of Burger and Rehnquist. This was partly a function of the early free speech cases that the Warren Court wrestled with against the backdrop of the Cold War. Its decisions became progressively more supportive of speech and expression. The Burger Court pushed these frontiers for a while before it began to retreat in libel and obscenity cases. Both the Burger and Rehnquist Courts reformulated the basic tests in these areas and in freedom of religion and speech (moving to balancing tests like the time, place, and manner restrictions).

A DIFFERENT INTERPRETATION OF THE RESULTS?

There is a different possible interpretation of the results. Attitudinalists could argue that the results do not disprove the attitudinal model or support the legal and strategic models. Those proponents could argue that the causal arrows could be reversed. Segal and Spaeth (1996a, 1996b; Brenner and Spaeth 1995) are among those who argue that justices reach their decisions and then search for precedents that support their preferences. Furthermore, it might be argued that the apparent impact of the president represents the strategic activity of the SG rather than the strategic response of the Court. Indeed, the congruence between the SG and the Court may be a result of the SG "playing the odds" and responding to the Court, not the reverse (McGuire 1998).

This raises the question of whether the impact of precedent is normative or empirical (Brisbin 1996). Is precedent a viable factor in judicial decision making, or is it merely a normative construct that shrouds the dominance of the attitudinal model? As noted, the impact of *stare decisis* is difficult to gauge because precedent is seldom clear. The cases before the Supreme Court raise different questions than those settled in the precedents. The lower courts can take care of those cases that are just like the precedent. Legal ambiguity frees justices to rely on their policy preferences.

In our model, precedent did not have a statistically significant effect on the Court's constitutional civil liberties and rights decisions between 1953 and 2000. However, there is reason to suspect that precedent's influence in this area may be more nuanced. Overruling a number of key precedents in areas such as civil rights, criminal procedure, and voting rights constituted a major component of the Warren Court's jurisprudence in this area of constitutional law. Another cut at the data may help to unravel the impact of precedent. In addition, perhaps precedent is more important in some issue areas than in others. We test this idea in Chapters 7 and 8.

Another possibility is that precedent has a greater impact at some stages of issue development than at others. In addition, precedent may be time dependent. Perhaps the Court has changed as an institution such that precedent played a significant role during one time period but not so much during other periods. We test these two propositions. In effect, it may be the case that precedent exerts no global effect on the constitutional civil liberties decisions but may be an important determinant of decision making in different eras. It is also possible that precedent's influence is dependent, in part, on the difficulty of the case at hand. To test

TABLE 5.2. *The Impact of Different Factors Across Time,*
1953–1969 and 1970–2000 Terms

	1953–1969 Terms	1970–2000 Terms
Supreme Court	X	X
President		X
House		
Senate		
Precedent		X
On Point	X	X
Issue Evolution	X	X

X represents a positive, statistically significant relationship with the
decisions of the Court.

these propositions, we present two auxiliary analyses. The first tests the
possibility that precedent's influence may be time dependent; the second
examines the relevance of precedent to decisions at each stage of issue
evolution.

We use 1969 as a dividing point to assess this first possibility. The
nomination of Thurgood Marshall, followed a few years later by the
election of Richard Nixon and the retirement of Earl Warren, represents
a potential change in the Court (Abraham 2008). Until the mid- to late
1960s, few justices were chosen because of their views on civil rights and
individual liberties. Previous civil libertarians such as Douglas, Black,
and Brennan were selected because of their views on economic regulation
(Abraham 2008), to embarrass the Supreme Court (McKenna 2002), and
to help Republicans make inroads into the Catholic vote (Powe 2000). In
short, civil rights and liberties issues were not litmus tests for nominations
to the Court. By contrast, Nixon made the judiciary a campaign issue,
pledged to nominate "strict constructionists" to the High Court, and
soon had the opportunity to replace Warren with conservative Chief
Justice Burger.

There does appear to be a temporal effect for precedent, as summarized
in Table 5.2. The attitudinal variable remains statistically significant and
is in the hypothesized direction for both periods. The variable for the
president is not statistically significant prior to 1970 but subsequently
emerged as a strong factor. Is this a statistical anomaly, or are there
good reasons for these apparent changes? In the 1953–1969 period, the
Court began its first significant foray into civil rights and civil liberties
(McCloskey 1960). Despite the fact that these issues were new and there

was some individual-level inconsistency in decision making, the impact of the attitudinal variable remains strong.

The results of the empirical analysis confirm notions of doctrinal development in civil rights and civil liberties. On the broadest level, we see that the attitudinal variable is statistically significant. This is to be expected, as these have been the so-called litmus test issues for nominees to the Court since at least the Kennedy administration (Epstein and Segal 2005). Many of the holdovers from the Roosevelt period, like Douglas, Black, and Frankfurter, were not selected for their views on civil liberties and civil rights but for their stances on economic regulation. As a result, there was a great deal of inconsistency in decision making in these areas prior to 1953. This was partly a function of the novelty of the issues and the fact that many of the justices had no prior judicial experience (Pacelle 1991). By 1953, these issues were becoming regular staples of the agenda, and justices were developing consistent patterns of behavior.

The impact of the president similarly is not surprising. The president can affect the Supreme Court through his nominations and through the OSG. Pacelle (2006) shows that civil rights and civil liberties are the only issues on which the position of the SG will reflect that of the president. A closer examination of Table 5.2 shows that presidential impact varied over time. In the 1953–1969 period, the impact of the president was not apparent from our model results. This may be partly ascribed to the "mistakes" Eisenhower made in choosing liberal justices Warren and Brennan. They helped tip the balance on a Court that already had been packed by Democratic presidents. In the early period of our study, solicitors general, regardless of party, supported civil rights claimants (Pacelle 2003). For the 1970–2000 period, the ideology of the president has a statistically significant impact on decisions. Republican presidents had the chance to exert a major influence on the Court, and they made the most of their chances. As a result, the views of the president were faithfully represented on the Court.

The impact of Congress is not evident in the model. Once again, this supports the general notion of congressional decision making over time. In the early period of our study, Congress was a graveyard for civil rights legislation. Congress and the Court had pitched battles over civil rights, criminal procedure, and communism (Murphy 1962). Ironically, as the Court got less supportive of civil rights and civil liberties, Congress moved in the opposite direction. As Simon (1995, 81) has noted, "For more than three decades, the modern Supreme Court has served as the crucial national institution that had encouraged the civil rights movement by broadly interpreting the Constitution and federal laws to protect racial minorities. The 1988 Court term . . . marked the end of that historic judicial era. With the advent of the conservative Rehnquist Court majority, Congress, not the Court became the channel for civil rights activism."

The legal variables had differential effects. Issue evolution played a strong role, whereas precedent appeared to be absent in our aggregate analysis of civil rights and liberties decisions. We expected support for civil rights and individual liberties to decline as cases got more difficult, and that is what occurred. Free speech for alleged Communists raised more difficult issues than free speech for civil rights protestors. After the Court made its decision in *New York Times v. Sullivan*, there were a number of "hard" cases involving whether the aggrieved party was a public figure. In civil rights, cases moved from *de jure* to *de facto* discrimination and to controversial remedies like busing, affirmative action, and minority business enterprises. In criminal procedure, cases moved from overt violations of defendant rights like the denial of counsel or failure to read rights to grayer areas like searches of automobiles and whether harsher sentences for crack cocaine than powder cocaine are a form of racial discrimination and from the mandatory exclusion of blacks from juries to whether preemptory challenges could be used to exclude blacks from a jury.

As we have noted, the Warren Court was rewriting constitutional law in civil liberties and civil rights, which might explain why precedent had no discernible impact during these years (Belknap 2005). After 1970, the exodus of liberal justices and a shift to the right marked the change from the Warren to the Burger Courts. Still, the Burger Court did not initiate a constitutional counterrevolution (Maltz 2000, 264–266). Even the Rehnquist Court failed to overturn many of the Warren Court precedents (Yarbrough 2000, 267–268). The presidential variable emerges as significant in this period. This is not surprising, as the parties split decisively on civil rights and individual liberties issues (Pacelle forthcoming), which became litmus tests for new nominees (Curry, Pacelle, and Marshall 2008).

Precedent's lack of impact also fits with notions of doctrinal development. In many decisions, the Court wrote on a blank slate, overturned old precedents, or distinguished new cases from existing precedents. Table 5.2 reveals a more nuanced view of precedent. Precedent appears to have played no significant role during the Warren Court, and the analyses of the period show that it did not respect precedent in many areas of civil rights and civil liberties. The Court overturned *Plessy v. Ferguson*

TABLE 5.3. *Reexamining Precedent: The Influence of Issue Evolution*

Variable	Stage			
	I	II	III	IV
Court Ideology		X	X	
President			X	
House				
Senate				
Precedent		X		
On Point	X		X	

X = significant and in the hypothesized direction.

(1896) in the area of equal protection. In criminal procedure, the Court began an incremental process of incorporating provisions of the Bill of Rights to the states. With each decision, the Court flushed another old precedent. Various studies consider the Warren Court an activist super-legislature that created a constitutional revolution (Powe 2000; Schwartz 1983).

Precedent does play a statistically significant role in the Burger and Rehnquist Courts, more so in the former than in the latter. Again, this is consistent with studies maintaining that the Burger Court did not initiate a new constitutional revolution. The Burger Court did not start overturning precedents. Indeed, the Burger Court often expanded on the decisions of the Warren Court, supporting affirmative action and reproductive rights (Blasi 1983). The Rehnquist Court has been described as the most activist in history (Keck 2004), but we only see a little evidence of this in civil rights and individual liberties. The Rehnquist Court was certainly less respecting of precedent than its predecessor, but its most visible activism occurred outside these areas.

To test whether the impact of precedent is dependent on various stages of evolutionary development, Table 5.3 presents the results obtained when our integrated model is applied to each stage of issue evolution. At the initial stage, on-point precedent is the only variable to attain statistical significance. This is not surprising, given that cases during this stage of development arise in an unsystematic fashion. Doctrine is unstable, as the Court attempts to make jurisprudential sense of an issue. During the second stage of issue evolution, when the issue emerges, precedent is statistically significant. Not surprisingly, the attitudinal variable is statistically significant as well. With a chance to stamp its imprimatur on the new issue, preferences crystallize. In addition, the Court pays attention to precedent as it attempts to build coherent policy.

Doctrinal construction continues in the third stage of issue evolution. In this stage, the cases typically raise more difficult issues but remain in a unidimensional policy space. At this stage of development, the Court must decide whether to apply existing precedent and, if so, how far that precedent will be extended. The Court often distinguishes its decision in these more difficult cases from the extant landmark; therefore, it is not surprising that there is no relationship between precedent and decisions at this stage of development. During this third stage, the attitudinal variable, the presidential variable, and on-point precedent are statistically significant. Because cases at this stage of development are more difficult, the collective attitude of the Court (measured by the median justice) emerges as a dominant determinant of decisions. The significant influence of the president is probably a result of the SG, who typically does not participate in the early stages of issue evolution unless invited (Pacelle 2003). Rather, the SG waits for the Court to define the issue and its parameters and only then assists the Court in filling in doctrinal gaps.

In the fourth and final stage of issue evolution, none of the variables of interest is statistically significant. This fourth stage is the point at which the current issue becomes multidimensional and attracts other issues (Pacelle 2009). Because some justices view one issue as dominant and other justices view another as primary, there is an absence of consensus on the Court, and no precedent is controlling.

In the end, then, precedent's impact appears to be a function of both temporal factors and the evolution of issues. It generally appears to be unimportant in constitutional civil rights and individual liberties cases, but we hesitate to say that it has no impact. Though precedent failed to exert an across-the-board effect in these cases, it appears that it has had a conditional impact on the Court's decision making within constitutional civil rights and liberties jurisprudence.

CONCLUSION

The results of this chapter indicate that the Supreme Court's collective policy preferences, when the Court is confronted with highly salient cases and few institutional constraints, represent the overriding factor in its decision making. However, even within this subset of cases, where we would expect the attitudinal variable to be strong, neither strategic nor legal influences were completely irrelevant to the Court's decisions. Indeed, we uncovered evidence that the influence of these variables is even more nuanced. As we have seen, the importance of several variables is dependent on the evolution of the particular legal issue. There also appears to be a temporal effect in the Court's treatment of civil liberties and rights cases decided on constitutional grounds, with the precedent variable vanishing from importance during the Warren Court era but reasserting itself in the Burger and Rehnquist years.

The two most important factors were the attitudinal variable – the ideology of the Court as measured by the median justice – and issue evolution – the difficulty of the case on the docket relative to other cases in that issue area. Most impressively, each is statistically significant controlling for the other. The influence of the president is also a factor and likely speaks to his ability to speak with one voice and influence both the composition of the Court through the appointment process and the construction of precedent through the OSG. Congress did not have a discernible impact. This may be partly due to the collective action problems that Congress faces (Mann and Ornstein 2006). Anther reason may be the majoritarian impulses that guide the legislative branch and are juxtaposed with the nature of civil liberties and civil rights (Eskridge 1991b; Krehbiel 1998). The Court's very rationale for the preferred position doctrine was to protect the rights of insular minorities and unpopular ideas. The lack of a statistically significant relationship is also consistent with our notions of the ideological trends in both institutions. Congress was antithetical to civil rights during the most liberal period of the Supreme Court. Then, as the Court got increasingly conservative, Congress was becoming more supportive of civil rights (Simon 1995). As a result, we find no support for Martin's (2006) hypothesis that the Court is more constrained in constitutional cases.

The results of the model also confirm the historical and doctrinal trends that others have identified. They also are very consistent with the ideological trends on the Court over the last half century. We chose *Brown* as the starting point because we feel that it ushered in the modern era on the Supreme Court. If the concept of a super-precedent has any validity, it certainly reflects decisions like *Brown*. The Court, in seeking to protect African Americans, made important changes in free expression and criminal procedure doctrine. Indeed, it would not be an exaggeration to say that *Brown* structured judicial decision making (as well as American politics and policy) for more than a generation (and likely two) (Pacelle 1991).

This leaves us with a puzzling, almost ironic juxtaposition. As the Warren Court was tearing up precedents in civil rights (like *Plessy*), free speech, and criminal procedure (like *Betts v. Brady* [1942]), it was formulating a consistent macro-precedent structure. As soon as the Court committed to the protection of civil rights, it had to ensure it by strengthening voting rights; freedom of association, speech, and the press; and incorporating almost all of the Bill of Rights to the states (Cortner 1981). Of course, in our analysis, it looks like the Warren Court ignored precedent. But it ignored old precedents with larger, coherent goals in mind.

The *Brown* decision also ushered in, or more precisely animated, the process by which cases get to the Court, decisions are made, and subsequent cases find their way up the judicial hierarchy. With many groups following the model set out by the LDF of the NAACP, the process became more predictable. A group litigant would sponsor a case, get the help of a number of *amici*, read the Court's decision, and plan the next step in its litigation strategy (Wasby 1995).[10] For a while, liberal groups seemed to hold sway, but as a defensive strategy; later, because the Court turned to the right, conservative groups took their causes into the courts (L. Epstein 1985). This was partly attitudinal in scope. Ideological repeat players were carefully watching the decisions of their fellow travelers on the Court. What was their overriding goal in doing so? It was to accumulate victories, not just for some impressive batting average, but to shape the law. The ultimate goal was to build a web of precedents that would serve both vertically and horizontally to make the law reflect their sincere preferences and to endure.

The influence of the attitudinal variable was expected to be particularly strong in this subset of cases. They are the most salient for the justices, and because they are constitutional, the sanctions the other branches can bring to bear are relatively limited. In addition, just after its decision in *Brown*, the Court boldly proclaimed that it was the final arbiter of the Constitution, serving notice to its institutional rivals.

As a super-precedent, *Brown*'s impact went even further. Eventually, Congress and the president would support broad legislative measures to support *Brown* and extend the range of civil rights protections (Branch 1998). The litigation battles took a familiar form. Provisions of the CRA of 1964 (and subsequent acts) and the VRA of 1965 would be challenged

---

[10] Although the LDF gets the credit for blazing the paths that every other group followed, it is important to remember that the NAACP followed the Jehovah's Witnesses, who were one of the first strategic organized litigants (Konvitz 1966; Peters 2000)

on constitutional grounds. As soon as the Court verified that they were indeed constitutional, the battlegrounds shifted to statutory grounds. That story plays out in Chapter 6 as we examine the interpretation of statutory provisions in civil rights and individual liberties.

Just when you think that *Brown* could not have even more influence, we turn to the economic cases. One of the hidden impacts of a landmark precedent is the promises the Court makes in issuing it. Most landmark decisions open new areas of law and some close them. If the Court decides on the latter, it has agenda resources to contribute to other areas. But if the Court opts for the former, the situation is more problematic. When the Court decided it was going to support equal protection, it was clearly committing agenda resources to future civil rights cases. Where would the Court get these agenda resources? It needed to carve out agenda space to fulfill its promise of equal protection and civil liberties. The ledger would be balanced on the economic cases – the Court had to sacrifice agenda space (Pacelle 1991). This is one of the reasons we argue that economic issues are less salient to the Court (Perry 1991). How those patterns of decision making vary are the subjects of Chapters 7 and 8.

6

Sharing the Protection of Minorities

Statutory Civil Rights and Individual Liberties

In this chapter, we continue our examination of civil rights and individual liberties but shift our focus to the nonconstitutional decisions. These decisions would be based on a state or federal statute (we concentrate on the latter) rather than constitutional grounds. These cases are salient to the justices, but we argue that the constraints on the Court are much greater. Because these cases are based on statutory grounds, Congress can flip a decision it does not like with a simple majority of both houses. In the last chapter, we saw that the attitudinal variable, issue evolution, and the president were the dominant influences on constitutional civil rights and civil liberties decisions. Precedent did not have an across-the-board impact. Whereas the issues will be similar in content, we expect some significant differences between the constitutional and statutory cases. The latter should be contested on narrower grounds, which should enhance the influence of Congress and precedent. Of course, it is important to remember that the Court has some control over the scope of the issue – it can sometimes decide the case on the grounds it chooses (King 2007). The Court can simply say it is deciding the case on constitutional grounds. Conversely, it can take a case that is being litigated on constitutional ground and redefine it as statutory.

We expect the attitudinal variable to remain important, to be sure, but precedent should emerge as an important factor. A number of justices have commented that the Court pays more attention to precedent in statutory than constitutional cases (Gerhardt 2008). Institutional constraints suggest the impact of the strategic variables. We expect both the president and Congress to remain important factors. This should be the closest to what we labeled Scenario 3, which holds that the constraints on the Court will cause it to temper its sincere preferences.

The Supreme Court has become a constitutional tribunal. When the Court gained discretion over its agenda, it could concentrate on the cases it wanted (Pacelle 1991). By jettisoning economic issues and putting civil rights and individual liberties issues in a preferred position, the Court concentrated on issues that raised constitutional questions. Congressional involvement in issues like civil rights, however, meant that there would be a number of statutory provisions to interpret. There is also a notion that the Court should decide issues on the narrowest grounds and avoid, if possible, the constitutional issues (see *Ashwander v. Tennessee Valley Authority* [1936]).

The normal process of lawmaking in Congress lends itself to vagueness and the need for judicial and administrative interpretation. With regard to the maze that is the legislative process, it is not surprising that legislation is going to need outside interpretation. To pass all the veto points in the process (subcommittee and committee votes, the Rules Committee in the House, the floor, the other body, and the president's veto), legislation is typically painted in broad strokes (Quirk 1989; Sinclair 2007). This passes the task of interpretation along to unelected judges and bureaucrats.

There is a certain aura of inevitably to the vagueness inherent in legislation. However, Michael Bamberger (2000) argues that occasionally a more sinister process is in place. He maintains that Congress will pass "reckless" legislation that is obviously unconstitutional to pander to the public and pass the buck to the Court. For instance, with the blessing of President Bill Clinton, Congress passed the Communications Decency Act (CDA) during an election year. In the view of many legal analysts, it was obviously constitutionally suspect, and the Court's ultimate decision seemed inevitable.

Of course, the Court does not often exercise the power of judicial review. Most decisions involve the interpretation of statutory or constitutional provisions. For major legislation, there is a familiar pattern to litigation. Opponents (and sometimes supporters) seek a vehicle to test the constitutionality of the statute in question. If the Court upholds the constitutionality of the statute, the cases then move to statutory grounds and the interpretation of the law's provisions. Civil rights followed this pattern. The Court quickly and decisively removed any doubts that the Civil Rights Act of 1964 and the Voting Rights Act of 1965 were constitutional.

Particularly for the latter, the Court was proactive in expediting review (Pacelle 2006).

The civil rights and individual liberties cases tend to be more coherent than the economic cases in their development. There are two reasons for this. First, the Court cares more about the former than the latter cases (we examine the economic cases in Chapters 7 and 8). They are, in a word, more "salient." As a consequence, there are many more of them, making it easier to construct doctrine. Second, the process of building doctrine is shared between the Court and organized litigants who read the entrails of current decisions and bring the next round of litigation (Collins 2008; Epp 1998; Pacelle 1991). Groups like the NAACP (Greenberg 1994), the American Civil Liberties Union (ACLU) (Walker 1990), and conservative groups like the Washington Legal Foundation (L. Epstein 1985; Teles 2008) carefully monitor litigation, policy, and judicial decisions. They bring cases or file *amicus curiae* briefs to continue the process of developing doctrine. The SG is the most important and ubiquitous of these repeat players. Pacelle (1991) and Baird (2007) have shown that the Court sends signals and then depends on repeat player litigants to receive those signals and react to them. Collins (2008) demonstrates that justices pay attention to *amici* briefs, and Johnson (2004) shows that the oral arguments in these cases play a major role at least in the language of the opinions. This process of doctrinal construction may be a little more complicated in statutory cases because of the impact of Congress.

As noted, the primary repeat player is the SG. The role of the SG can be evident in all areas of law, but the OSG plays a particularly important role in individual liberties and civil rights. Pacelle (2006) shows that civil rights and civil liberties are the only areas that really separate the parties. In all other areas of law, it does not matter who controls the White House, as the SG will argue consistently. For example, in federalism and regulation cases, the SG argues for the authority of the central government (Pacelle 2006). There are differences between the roles that the SG plays in constitutional and statutory cases. There is greater discretion in constitutional cases, because they often involve the states and there is limited liability for the government when it files *amicus* briefs. If the SG backs the losing side, the precedent does not adversely affect the national government. Thus, the SG is free to argue the policy position of the president. It is not surprising, then, that our model in Chapter 5 finds an impact for the president.

In the statutory cases, however, the government tends to be a party in the dispute. As such, the precedent emerging from the case will have important consequences for the government. Therefore, the OSG will need to be more strategic in filing briefs and taking positions. Because the office is defending the government and a statute is typically involved, the SG may not be the agent of the president who selected him or her,[1] but the agent of Congress. This is part of the reason we expect Congress to play a role in the Court's deliberations and decisions. We examine the role of the various legal, strategic, and attitudinal factors after we set the context for the civil rights and individual liberties cases decided during the 1953–2000 terms. Before we turn to that, however, let's use an illustration to demonstrate some of the features of these cases.

GRIGGS V. DUKE POWER: THE *BROWN* OF EMPLOYMENT DOCTRINE

One of the features of civil rights and civil liberties litigation, whether constitutional or statutory, has been the personal aspect of the cases (Irons 2006). The NAACP often wanted to immerse the justices in the human elements of the cases on the docket.[2] *Brown* was not just a case involving school segregation; it was the story of little Linda Brown. Similarly, we know the stories of Allan Bakke, Ernesto Miranda, and Clarence Earl Gideon. But most people do not know who Willie Griggs was. *Griggs v. Duke Power Co.* is arguably the most important statutory decision of the twentieth century. The others were involved in noted constitutional cases that every schoolchild (or at least college student) studies.

In 1955, Duke Power Company instituted a policy of requiring a high school education for the initial assignment (hiring) to any department except Labor, which largely performed janitorial services throughout the plant. In addition, a high school degree was required for promotion or transfer from Labor or Coal Handling to any of the "inside" departments – Operations, Maintenance, and Laboratory.[3] In response to Title VII of the Civil Rights Act of 1964, which forbade employers

---

[1] We used to be able to say "he" to describe all solicitors general. But President Barack Obama changed that with his selection of Elena Kagan, who soon moved to the Supreme Court.

[2] Although this was a staple of groups like the NAACP and the ACLU, conservative groups have adopted this tactic as well.

[3] These "inside jobs" required the ability to read and understand manuals. The Operations Department had to operate the generating equipment and handle interconnections between the various power stations that the Company owned. Maintenance was charged with maintaining and repairing the equipment. Technicians in the Laboratory Department analyzed water and coal samples and needed to calibrate instruments and gauges.

from limiting, segregating, or classifying employees in any way that would deprive them of employment opportunities because of race, color, religion, gender, or national origin, the company began to require high school graduation as a condition of transfer and promotion.

As of July 2, 1965, the date Title VII became effective, Duke Power added another requirement for new employees: To qualify for a position in any department except Labor, applicants had to have a high school degree or receive satisfactory scores on two standardized tests to measure general intelligence (the Wonderlic Personnel Test and Bennett Mechanical Comprehension Test). Neither test was designed to measure the ability to perform specific jobs in the plant. The required scores for employment or transfer would be based on the national median for high school graduates.[4]

The company created a grandfather clause to exclude those who had been employed prior to the introduction of the new requirements. Thus, if an employee had been with Duke Power prior to the new requirements, completion of high school alone was sufficient for transfer to the desirable departments. In addition, those in the operating departments, who were all white, did not need to have a diploma or pass the examinations if they were performing their jobs adequately (Greenberg 1994, 418).

African American workers in the company historically had been limited to the lowest-paying jobs, particularly in the Labor Department. Indeed, prior to 1966, no black employee had held any position in the company outside the Labor Department. The *Griggs* case arose from the Company's Dan River Steam Station in Draper, North Carolina. There were ninety-five employees at the Station, fourteen of whom were African Americans. Thirteen of the fourteen joined the class-action suit that spawned this case. Like Linda Brown, Willie Griggs was the named plaintiff carrying the banner for a number of similarly affected individuals.[5]

African American employees were less likely to have a high school degree than their white counterparts. In addition, white employees were much likelier to get satisfactory scores on the standardized intelligence tests than were African American employees. Fifty-eight percent of the white employees got satisfactory scores on the examinations, whereas

---

[4] The facts of the case come from the Court of Appeals and Supreme Court opinions (*Griggs v. Duke Power Company* 420 F. 2d 1225 (1970) and *Griggs v. Duke Power Company* 401 U.S. 424 (1971)).

[5] Ironically, according to Robert Belton, who helped argue the case, Willie Griggs was more or less indifferent about the case. Other plaintiffs were more engaged.

only 6 percent of the African American employees passed.[6] Thus, the burden of the two requirements fell disproportionately on African Americans (Maltz 2000, 191).

Title VII of the CRA of 1964 made it an unlawful employment practice for an employer to limit, segregate, or classify employees on the basis of race, color, education, sex, or national origin. Title VII authorized the use of ability tests, provided that such tests were not designed, intended, or used to discriminate. In this case, Griggs and other African American workers in the plant sought transfer to become coal handlers. They challenged the requirement that a diploma or a satisfactory score on an aptitude test was necessary to perform the duties of the new department.

The question for the Court was whether Title VII prohibits an employer from requiring a high school education or a passing grade on a standardized examination as a condition of employment, transfer, or promotion when a) neither requirement is significantly related to successful job performance; b) both requirements operate to disqualify African Americans at a substantially higher rate than whites; and c) the jobs in question had only been filled by white employees as the result of a longstanding practice of giving preferences to whites.

Consider the cluster of factors – legal, attitudinal, and strategic – that we think influences Supreme Court decision making. There was no direct precedent governing the *Griggs* case. Rather, this was a case of first impression. Certainly, the Supreme Court had created a battery of precedents favorable to civil rights. In education, housing, voting, and even intimate relations, the Court struck repeated blows for equal protection (Wasby 1995). The *Griggs* case was a little more difficult in terms of issue evolution than many of the previous civil rights cases. Private discrimination was not actionable under the Constitution. The CRA sought to change that. At the same time, the Court that was about to decide *Griggs* was somewhat more conservative than the Court that had made the previous pronouncements. Strategically, President Nixon and the SG supported the extension of employment discrimination protections (Pacelle 2003).[7] The CRA of 1964 seemed to be at odds with the position that the government and attorneys for Griggs were advocating, but it is true

---

[6] The company considered a score of 20 on the Wonderlic and 39 on the Bennett satisfactory.

[7] John Skrentny (1996) argued that it was the genius of Nixon's plan that he supported equal employment opportunity, disparate impact, and affirmative action as a means of driving a wedge between organized labor and African Americans and breaking up the Democratic coalition.

that the Congress that was sitting in 1971 was relatively liberal (Eskridge 1994).

The Supreme Court decided unanimously that the company's program violated Title VII. Maybe most importantly, the plaintiffs did not need to demonstrate that the employers had an intent to discriminate. Rather than focus on the explicit provisions of the law, the Court argued that the objective of Congress in passing Title VII was clear: to achieve equality of employment opportunities and remove barriers. Tests could be used only if they were a reasonable measure of job performance. Had that been the bottom line, the unanimous decision would not have been so surprising, and *Griggs* would have been an important decision, but far from a landmark. However, Chief Justice Burger, writing for the Court, added a paragraph that had the effect of making *Griggs* the *Brown* of employment law (Eskridge 1994, 24–37), stating, "Congress directed the thrust of the Act to the *consequences* of employment practices, not simply the motivation" (*Griggs v. Duke Power Co.*, 401 at 432).

In effect, the Court had opted for a "disparate impact" standard, rather than an intent standard, for evaluating discrimination. Disparate impact meant that the plaintiffs needed only to demonstrate the consequences of the employment practices. If the result of the practices and policies appeared to be discriminatory, the plaintiffs might well have a cause of action. It was a relatively easy standard to meet. The intent standard would have required the plaintiff to demonstrate that the employers took affirmative steps to discriminate and clearly intended to do so. It would be an onerous task for the plaintiff to demonstrate this (Blumrosen 1993).

Griggs is important in many respects. In addition to being a landmark decision, it created the conditions that made affirmative action all but inevitable. The decision was considered surprising in many senses. The case occurred just seven years after the passage of Title VII. The legislation seemed rather clear that the alleged victims of employment discrimination would need to show intent to make their case (Graham 1990). Because the Court's decision appeared to be so far beyond the provisions of the CRA of 1964, one could argue that the Court was not paying attention to the intent of the Congress that passed the Act. Thus, on one level, it appears that the Court did not act in a particularly strategic manner. William Eskridge (1994) argues that the Court did act strategically, but in a different way. He maintains that the Court's decision was a reaction not to the Congress that passed the law in 1964, but to the Congress that was sitting in 1971. After all, it was the latter that would be responding to the

Court's decision. Furthermore, a Republican administration supported an expansive view of Title VII.

Wasby (1995, 186) argues, "The Title VII campaign was probably larger in scope than the *Brown* campaign, but it received less attention because it had to compete for attention with many other litigation efforts and did not lead to a single Supreme Court ruling of *Brown*'s stature, although *Griggs v. Duke Power Co.* was very important." The decision in *Griggs* "paralleled *Brown* in its importance in its area of law." Congress, with a chance to revisit and reverse the decision, demurred. The Court felt that the silence of Congress spoke volumes and continued to develop and expand doctrine in employment law (Eskridge 1994).

For the purposes of this study, we want to unpeel one more layer of the proverbial onion. Not long after the *Griggs* decision, a similar case, *Washington v. Davis* (1976), appeared on the Court's docket. In this case, a verbal test required of prospective firefighters disqualified more African Americans than whites. The case seemed to be similar enough to *Griggs* that that precedent should govern. Instead, the Court ruled that the plaintiffs needed to show intent. Why the difference? To be sure, the Court was more conservative, but *Griggs* was unanimous, and there were not enough membership changes to suggest that as the only reason for the change. Precedent now existed, and this was not a much more difficult case than *Griggs*. The president and the SG supported continuing the disparate impact standard (Pacelle 2003). Congress, by its quiet assent, did so as well. Where does this leave us? The answer is tied to our thesis that the Court operates differently under different conditions.

The difference here was the grounds of the case, which was constitutional (the Fifth Amendment). *Griggs*, on the other hand, was a statutory case. During oral argument, Justice Powell raised the issue of whether the standard in constitutional cases, like this one, should be equivalent to statutory grounds under Title VII. Ultimately, the Court claimed that there had to be intent to discriminate and that the rigorous statutory standard of Title VII involved a more probing judicial review and less deference to the acts of administrators than is appropriate under the Constitution. In this case, the Court ruled that there was an apparent racial impact, but no discriminatory purpose had been claimed.

In a statutory case such as *Griggs*, Congress could overturn a decision relatively easily. A simple majority of both houses could pass legislation to overrule the Court's decision. Thus, the theory is that the Court will temper its sincere preferences and act strategically to avoid congressional retaliation. Yet in the constitutional cases, the override numbers are pro-hibitive for Congress. To overrule a constitutional decision, a two-thirds majority is required in each house. Here was an example of the differences played out with real-world consequences. The juxtaposition of these cases is central to the questions that animate our study. In this instance, the Court treated similar cases differently as a function of the grounds of the case. Is this differential treatment a symptom of the difference between constitutional and statutory cases? Chapter 5 examined the former. Now we proceed to the latter.

ISSUE EVOLUTION AND PRECEDENT

In Chapter 5, we examined issue evolution and precedent as part of the context for decision making in constitutional civil rights and individual liberties cases. Those decisions and the development of doctrine also pro-vide the context for the nonconstitutional cases. The early Warren Court took a while to exert its influence, particularly in civil liberties. It was ten-tative in dealing with the cases involving freedom of expression among alleged Communists. It also struggled, albeit for a short time, with free exercise cases, issuing the conflicting Sunday closing law and *Sherbert v. Verner* decisions within two years (Pacelle 2009). In civil rights and due process cases, the Warren Court pushed the frontiers dramatically and engendered hostility from Congress and, at the end, President Nixon.

The Burger Court stemmed the tide in areas like criminal procedure. But in other areas like individual liberties and civil rights, the Burger Court built on the foundation its predecessor had started and even expanded that foundation in areas like reproductive rights and remedies like busing and affirmative action. Issue evolution was making the cases more difficult, which certainly played a role in criminal procedure jurisprudence but did not spur a major retreat.

The Rehnquist Court represented the significant break in continuity. The accumulation of membership changes, coupled with the exodus of super-liberals Brennan and Marshall, pushed the Court median to the right. The cases got more difficult at the outset and, paradoxically, easier as time went on. After the Rehnquist Court reversed some of the prece-dents, easier cases reached the justices as groups hoped the Court would continue its retrenchment. In fact, the Court felt compelled to make some pro-defendant decisions and lectured the lower courts that they were misinterpreting the trend of decisions. The Rehnquist Court retreated on reproductive rights, free exercise, civil rights, and civil rights remedies (Savage 1992; Yarbrough 2000).

The ideology of the Court certainly was the major factor influencing decision making after *Brown*. Issue evolution and the president also affected decision making in the constitutional cases. On-point precedents played a significant role, although they were not found in a large number of cases. We argue that precedent, which does not appear to have an impact over the entire period, had at least a time-bound effect. Congress did not have an impact in the constitutional cases. In this chapter, we see if that will change. We are interested in seeing whether precedent has a stronger influence on statutory cases than on constitutional decisions. As we continue our consideration of issue evolution and precedent, we expand the context to consider the major legislation that was the subject of the statutory Supreme Court cases in the 1953–2000 terms. Did Congress assist, hinder, or even influence the evolution of doctrine?

Half of the nonconstitutional federal decisions were in criminal law or criminal procedure cases. Many came to the Court under *habeas corpus*, the Federal Rules of Criminal Procedure, the Omnibus Crime Control and Safe Streets Act of 1968, or the interpretation of individual criminal statutes. Other statutes that were responsible for more than two dozen decisions include the Civil Rights Act of 1964, the Voting Rights Act of 1965, section 1983 of the CRA of 1871, the Freedom of Information Act of 1966, and various incarnations of the Immigration and Naturalization Act. As a condition of their original passage, the CRA and VRA required periodic extensions. The extensions and amendments of these and other statutes define strategic interaction between the president, Congress, and the Court. When Congress passes legislation, which the president might introduce or lobby for, does it overturn the Court's most recent decisions or extend them?

THE CONSTRUCTION OF POLICY AND DOCTRINE

In this section, we consider several major pieces of legislation that spawned a large number of cases and show a range of different relationships between the elected branches and the Supreme Court. We examine the CRA of 1964 and the VRA of 1965 as well as a number of their extensions, Habeas Corpus Acts, and the Immigration and Naturalization Acts. We also consider a variety of other statutes to illustrate some of the results from the aggregate analysis.

The civics book notion is that the Supreme Court is a passive institution that must wait for the proper case that has standing to make its determinations, but students of the Court know that this is not completely accurate (Horowitz 1977). The Court can signal its intent to the many anxious litigants who sequence litigation (Baird 2007; Epp 1998; Pacelle 1991). It can use issue fluidity to broaden or narrow the scope of its review (McGuire and Palmer 1995; Pacelle 1991; Ulmer 1984), and this reflects the differences we examine. In the civil rights and individual liberties cases, the Court often expands the case before it. In the economic cases, the Court often confines the case at hand to one narrow issue, usually to resolve a circuit conflict (Perry 1991). As we have previously noted, the Court may expand a case to make it a constitutional issue, thereby enhancing its discretion, or narrow it to statutory grounds (King 2007). If the Court turns a case into a constitutional issue, it becomes that much more difficult for the elected branches to overrule the decision.

In some areas, the Court's role seems to be more proactive. In taking the lead in civil rights, the Court eventually forced the president and Congress to respond. In addition, the Court's decisions fueled the litigation process and encouraged the next round of cases. In criminal procedure, the Warren Court did two things that changed the nature of litigation: First, the decisions, which were supportive of defendant rights encouraged groups like the ACLU to redouble their efforts. In tandem with its other criminal law decisions, the effect of *Fay v. Noia* (1963) (and other cases that term regarding *habeas corpus* access) was to expand significantly the ability of federal courts to review state prisoners' claims (Harriger 1997, 8). Second, the Court opened and then shut access to its own docket. In expanding the definition of *habeas corpus*, the Warren Court threw open its doors to invited litigants. The Burger Court, and later the Rehnquist Court, would narrow that definition and limit access to its agenda. In other areas such as immigration, the Court did not seem to lead or respond to changes in the law.

MAJOR LEGISLATION AND THE SUPREME COURT

Legislation can create certain rights or contract them. When civil rights and liberties are involved in a statute, the Supreme Court and the Constitution are imposing backdrops and most often serve as a constraint on Congress. Provisions in such legislation can animate litigants to bring successive rounds of litigation and help the Court construct doctrine. Typically, initial cases test the constitutionality of the statute. If it survives, then a flurry of statutory challenges will ensue. The modern Court has considered itself to be the final arbiter of the Constitution and announced that it was placing rights and liberties in a preferred position. These were signals that Congress needed to tread carefully. But the post-Depression and post–World War II period not only empowered the Court, it also strengthened the presidency and forced Congress to adopt a more national perspective (Dodd 1986).

In some of the following examples, Congress followed the Court's lead. In other areas, it was Congress that took the lead and the Court that reacted. We have described these issues as salient to the justices. But that salience means that presidents use such issues as litmus tests for their judicial nominations. And if it is salient to the president and the Court, there will be groups who find such issues salient and will not be reluctant to tell Congress (McCubbins and Schwartz 1984). It is important to remember that not every reactive congressional provision or Supreme Court decision is designed to retaliate against the other branch (Pickerill 2004; Sager 2004). The Court and Congress often work together to smooth out problems in judicial decisions or statutory provisions (Hausegger and Baum 1999).

Civil Rights Act of 1964 and the Voting Rights Act of 1965

The Court's decision in *Brown* prodded a reluctant president and Congress to support equal protection. Congress passed the CRA of 1957, but a number of subsequent bills could not survive the legislative labyrinth. The eventual assistance for the Court came in the form of the CRA of 1964. With the help of Senator Everett Dirksen, a coalition of Northern Democrats and Republicans broke an eighty-two day filibuster to create the "greatest liberal achievement of the decade" (Graham 1990, 152).

For all its benefits, the CRA did not eliminate voting problems. Litigation, the primary existing remedy, was a slow process. There were three available alternatives: a Constitutional amendment, legislation taking federal control of voting, or legislation to empower a federal agency to monitor voting. With a large congressional majority and weakened conservative coalition, the administration decided to pursue the third alternative, despite concerns about its constitutionality – indeed, similar legislation had been struck down after Reconstruction (Pacelle 2003). With the legislative majority intact, Congress passed the Voting Rights Act of 1965.

The CRA and the VRA provided significant authority for the Justice Department and Congress. They also changed the nature of the SG's work. Rather than being a passive agent that had to wait for cases to be brought to the Court and enter them as *amicus*, which meant a lack of control, the Justice Department could sequence litigation. The CRA and VRA gave the government the statutory authority to bring litigation as a party. The VRA gave the attorney general the power to suspend literacy tests, bring suits, require preclearance for changes in election law, disallow problematic changes (Walton 1988, 140–141), and dispatch federal authorities to enfranchise voters (Graham 1990, 163–170).

Section 5 of the VRA shifted the burden of proof to state governments that had a history of discrimination. These "covered jurisdictions" had to preclear changes in voting procedures with the attorney general or the Federal District Court in Washington, D.C. Section 2 prohibited discrimination in voting in states not covered by section 5 and applied to discriminatory procedures instituted before 1965 (Thompson 1984, 2–3). The VRA had the potential to restructure the social and political fabric of the South and to change national politics (Matthews and Prothro 1966, 475).

Support in Congress was important because the CRA and VRA were subjected to a number of challenges regarding both their constitutionality and statutory interpretation. Having strong congressional support reinforced the SG and the Court in these challenges. In 1964, in *Heart of Atlanta Motel v. United States* and *Katzenbach v. McClung*, the government argued that the Fourteenth Amendment should not be construed as a limit on congressional power under the Commerce Clause (Cortner 2001; Wasby, D'Amato, and Metrailer 1977, 330). Solicitor General Archibald Cox felt that "*Wickard v. Filburn* provided the basis for this" (Pacelle 2003, 100). The Court upheld this view in *Heart of Atlanta Motel*, arguing that Congress had the power under the Commerce and Necessary and Proper Clauses to regulate local activities that had "a close and substantial relation to commerce" to foster and promote commerce or relieve burdens and obstructions on commerce. The Court accepted the government's view that racial discrimination burdened commerce; thus, prohibiting discrimination was a legitimate exercise of power (Wasby, D'Amato, and Metrailer 1977, 326–327). The Court would expand this authority even further in *Katzenbach v. McClung*, a case involving a restaurant that refused to serve African Americans (Cortner 2001).

Attorney General Katzenbach argued in *South Carolina v. Katzenbach* (1966) that the VRA was a legitimate exercise of the Fifteenth

Amendment. The brief departed from typical procedure: Rather than wait for individual violations to create cases that might take years to litigate, the government asked the Court to consider a range of questions concerning the VRA. The Court ruled that Congress was not limited by its expressed powers merely to allow the courts negative authority to strike down state laws in violation of the Amendment, but that Congress could take positive action as well. The Court unanimously dismissed South Carolina's contention that the act was unconstitutional, ruling that Congress had not usurped the reserved powers of states (Bland 1993, 139; Davis and Clark 1992, 259). For the Court, Warren claimed that the "burden of time and inertia" should be shifted to the states and supported the act's relatively automatic remedies (Claude 1970, 112). According to Stephen Pollak, then a deputy in the Civil Rights Division, "*South Carolina v. Katzenbach* was the most important vindication of voting rights" (Pacelle 2003, 104).

Other Civil Rights Acts

In *United States v. Guest* (1966) and *United States v. Price* (1966), Solicitor General Thurgood Marshall argued for a broad view of section 1983 of the Reconstruction-era civil rights acts. Section 2 of the 1870 Act (18 USC section 241) forbade private interference with the rights of citizens as provided within the privileges and immunities clause of the Fourteenth Amendment. Under Section 17 (18 USC section 242), a state officer who interfered with the rights of citizens could be punished for denying privileges and immunities and violating the due process and equal protection clauses of the Fourteenth Amendment (Bland 1993, 133–134).

Price and *Guest* gave the government the chance to test the scope of those statutory provisions. These were important cases involving provisions that had been ignored for decades. The Justice Department wanted to know the extent of its power to implement civil rights initiatives. The government tried to link Reconstruction statutes to the CRA of 1964. Marshall claimed that section 241 could be used against those who conspired to deprive others of rights created by Title II of the CRA. The Court needed to act in a way that was consistent with congressional intent yet would not mitigate the need for additional legislation. The department did not feel that it could press Congress for new legislative authority until existing judicial remedies were exhausted. The Court confined its decision to statutory grounds, thus avoiding constitutional interpretation.

The Court accepted the government's position that the actions of private citizens took place under the color of state law (Pacelle 2003).

In *Jones v. Alfred Mayer* (1968), the government argued for a broad construction of past civil rights acts and for defining the private/public distinction in housing discrimination. The case was an extension of *Shelley v. Kraemer* but involved exclusion from an entire community rather than a single dwelling. According to Pollak, who signed the brief, "The arguments in *Jones* were hard to make because of past Supreme Court decisions. The Solicitor General must respond to Court precedents and the precedents were negative. The decision in *Jones* was a great victory and not expected at all. . . . It was a radical decision" (Pacelle 2003, 105).

According to Hugh Davis Graham (1990, 375), the decision "signaled the intention of the mature Warren Court to read into legislative history the policy preferences of the Court's majority." The opinion by Justice Potter Stewart was "a revolutionary reading of the statute" (Bell 1980, 498). The Court ruled that the 1866 Civil Rights Act barred private discrimination in housing. Unlike the other decisions, though, the authority stemmed from the Thirteenth Amendment, which banned slavery and provided Congress with positive authority to enforce it. The Court ruled that the amendment was also designed to remove "the badges and servitudes of slavery." Stewart provided a broad reading of the amendment to include "the freedom to buy whatever a white man can buy, the right to live wherever a white man can live. If Congress cannot say this much, then the Thirteenth Amendment made a promise the Nation cannot keep" (Pritchett 1984, 279). According to Pollak, "*Jones* was a very significant interpretation of section 1982. The Court breathed new life into the dormant provision" (Pacelle 2003, 105). Congress would pass the Civil Rights Act of 1968 (dealing with fair housing), but in effect, the decision in *Jones* made it unnecessary.

Support for civil rights declined over time, but the dimensions were different from those of criminal and substantive rights cases. There were only eleven statutory civil rights cases during the Warren Court, and ten were decided in favor of civil rights claimants. Support during the Burger and Rehnquist Courts declined precipitously but remained at more than 60 percent. Through most of the half century, the legislation coming from Congress was supportive of civil rights. Most presidents supported civil rights as well, with the government arguing for *Brown* and *Griggs* during Republican administrations (Pacelle forthcoming). The decline can be attributed to issue evolution and changes in the composition of the

Court, but the overall continued support for civil rights was a function of following precedent.

Later civil rights legislation was a result of congressional reaction to litigation and presidential priorities. The Civil Rights Act of 1991 was passed to reinforce the CRA of 1866 and Title VII of the CRA of 1964 and to reverse a number of Supreme Court decisions. President George H. W. Bush vetoed the bill initially but signed a second version when his opposition proved politically untenable. The CRA of 1991 overturned a series of Supreme Court decisions including *Patterson v. McLean Credit Union* (1989), which limited an employee's recourse if he or she faced racial or sexual harassment on the job, and *Ward's Cove Packing Co. v. Atonio* (1989), which changed the disparate impact standard to an intent standard (Pacelle 2003). In some issue areas, the relationship between Congress and the Court was not antagonistic. Rather, they worked together to find evolving solutions that would satisfy each institution (Barnes 2004; Sager 2004). But in this instance, there was a clear agenda for the Court and a clear response from Congress.

Habeas Corpus Act

In a series of cases beginning with *Brown v. Allen* in 1953, the Supreme Court expanded access to federal *habeas* review for state prisoners. This trend reached its zenith in 1963 in *Fay v. Noia* and *Townsend v. Sain*, *habeas* cases issued to aid in the implementation of Court decisions such as *Gideon v. Wainwright*, which was issued on the same day (Patchel 1991). The Warren Court viewed access to federal review as a matter of fundamental right (Harriger 1997, 6).

In 1967, the Congress amended the Federal Habeas Corpus Act in an effort to ease the tension between the judicial systems by limiting the abuse of federal *habeas corpus* by state prisoners and encouraging the states to adopt adequate fact-finding procedures. These changes were adopted in the wake of the flood of *habeas* petitions that followed the Court's loosening of its access rules. Within a decade, the number of *habeas* petitions in the federal courts increased by more than tenfold (Harriger 1997; Patchel 1991).

The changes Congress adopted had little impact on the flow of petitions, in part because they closely followed the decisions of the Court. The amendments were largely deferential to the courts, allowing federal judges to determine whether petitioners had deliberately abused the writ. Rather than opposing the developments in legal doctrine, Congress appeared to be taking its cues from the Court, adopting the deliberate-bypass standard into statutory law and accepting the Court's assumption about the inadequacy of state proceedings (Yarbrough 2000, 71–73).

Less than a decade after these new *habeas* decisions were announced, they were severely limited by the Burger Court in *Stone v. Powell* (1974) and have been consistently limited since (Patchel 1991). In *Wainwright v. Sykes* (1977), Justice Rehnquist argued in conference and in a draft opinion that the history of federal *habeas corpus* doctrine "suggests that *stare decisis* has been something less than the cardinal principle which has guided the Court in this area." This would leave the Supreme Court, he claimed, "feeling less constrained in deciding this case by the principle of *stare decisis* than we would if we were dealing with a different statute and a less volatile course of decisional law" (Harriger 1997, 11).[8] A pair of decisions, *Murray v. Carrier* and *Smith v. Murray* (1986), further narrowed access to *habeas corpus*.

Over the course of two decades, the Court gradually whittled away at Warren Court precedents that expanded access to federal review as a matter of individual right. It was not until 1996 that Congress acted to change the federal *habeas corpus* statute to limit the ability of state prisoners to have their claims heard in federal court. This occurred with the Antiterrorism and Effective Death Penalty Act of 1996, once again embracing the changes already wrought by the Supreme Court (Harriger 1997, 18). As Katy Harriger (1997, 20) noted, "The Supreme Court unanimously upheld this act (*Felker v. Turpin* 1996)....In endorsing the statute, the U.S. Supreme Court did little more than endorse its own actions of the last several decades. After years of debate, Congress had endorsed the lead taken by the Supreme Court and long advocated by the states. The 'dialogue' was a long one, but the various discussants appeared to understand each other throughout the process." The Court has reframed *habeas corpus* as a federalism issue instead of a rights issue. Therefore, the central question for the Court is now about the relationship between the federal and state judiciaries, not the relationship between a defendant and the criminal justice system (Harriger 1997, 4).

The Supreme Court's treatment of criminal procedure and criminal law cases reflects the pattern of legislation. Court support for defendants' rights in nonconstitutional cases declined from 57 percent during the Warren Court to 33 percent after. This certainly can be partly attributed

---

[8] Over the strong objections of Justice Stevens and others, Rehnquist toned down the language.

to the ideological changes in the Court, but issue evolution played a part as well. Although Congress was never supportive of defendants' rights, legislation grew more restrictive over time. The pattern here seems to reflect the influence of all of the variables, whether attitudinal, legal, or strategic.

Freedom of Information Act

The Freedom of Information Act (FOIA) provides a particularly useful illustration of the institutional pressures that often characterize the development of statutory law. Passed in 1966, FOIA's central purpose was to facilitate greater public access to governmental documents (Lowe 1994, 1282). Though FOIA contains a number of exceptions, its overall message is that governmental agencies generally must make information available to the public (Waples 1974, 896–897).[9] Most notably, FOIA provides for judicial review whenever disputes arise about the nature of the governmental compliance required in a given situation. In effect, "[b]y transferring decisional power to the courts from the document's custodian, Congress acted to ensure that disposition of information requests would turn on public, rather than self-serving agency values" (Waples 1974, 899).

FOIA's judicial review provision immediately impacted the federal district courts, as approximately two hundred cases were brought under the act between 1967 and 1974 (Clark 1975, 741). The Supreme Court's role in demarking FOIA's parameters has been extensive as well. As a general matter, the Court has tended to favor governmental secrecy over public openness. As Foerstel (1999, 174) has concluded, "From the beginning, the courts have offered timid support for the FOIA, deferring to government demands for secrecy on virtually all matters relating to law enforcement and national security." This has been particularly evident in the Supreme Court's FOIA decisions.

In the first case it heard regarding FOIA, *E.P.A. v. Mink* (1973), the Court held that documents that had been classified by an official pursuant

---

[9] According to 5 U.S.C. Section 552(b), the nine exemptions from the FOIA include 1) Classified information; 2) internal agency personnel rules; 3) information that has been specifically exempted from FOIA by statute; 4) trade secrets or personal financial information; 5) interagency or intra-agency communications that are privileged; 6) personnel and medical files, the disclosure of which would constitute a clearly unwarranted invasion of personal privacy; 7) investigatory files compiled for law enforcement purposes; 8) agency reports on the regulation of financial institutions; and 9) geologic information related to oil wells.

to an executive order were exempted from disclosure under FOIA. The ruling even dismissed the idea of *in camera* judicial review of those executive decisions, meaning that courts would be barred from second-guessing the "classified" status of such documents (Clark 1975, 753). At the same time, in *Mink*, the Court expressed "open exasperation with the FOIA" and urged Congress to improve its draftsmanship (Foerstel 1999, 46). In 1974, Congress took up the Court's invitation and passed a series of amendments to FOIA over President Ford's veto (Note 1976, 401). The amendments directly repudiated *Mink*, authorizing district courts to "'examine the contents of such agency records in camera' to see whether they are covered by 'any of the [nine FOIA] exemptions'" (Clark 1975, 753).

Despite Congress's amendments to FOIA – in 1974 and, more recently, 1976, 1986, 1996, 2002, and 2007 – many contend that a number of the Supreme Court's statutory decisions in this area have not been faithful to congressional intent. Giving particular emphasis to the FOIA's relevance to the Central Intelligence Agency (CIA) and the Federal Bureau of Investigation (FBI), Foerstel (1999, 175) argues that the Court "has gone beyond expansive interpretations of the FOIA's exemptions to the point of creating new exemptions unsupported by the statute." One plausible explanation that has been advanced is that, as judicial conservatives such as Rehnquist, Scalia, and Thomas have ascended to the High Court, those justices have reflected conservative disdain for both the underpinnings and consequences of the FOIA's adoption. Indeed, Scalia has been quite critical of FOIA, referring to it as " . . . the Taj Mahal of Unanticipated Consequences, the Sistine Chapel of Cost-Benefit Analysis Ignored" (Scalia 1982, 14–15).

Two years after the Court's first foray into FOIA in *Mink*, the Court issued its decision in *Federal Aviation Administration v. Robertson* (1975), which effectively broadened the category of statutes that agencies could rely on to justify the withholding of documents from the public. Much as it had done in the aftermath of *Mink*, Congress again amended the FOIA in order to overrule *Robertson* in 1976 (Berner 1976, 1030).

The Court issued additional rulings during the late 1970s and early 1980s, virtually all of which held in favor of the government. The Court was particularly active in interpreting FOIA in 1980, issuing four decisions related to that portion of the U.S. Code. Two rulings in particular – *Forsham v. Harris* (1980) and *Kissinger v. Reporters Committee for Freedom of the Press* (1980) – saw the Court define the term "agency records" in such a way as to exempt numerous items from FOIA's reach. These rulings, in combination with various lower court decisions guided by those rulings, "show[ed] a trend toward restricting disclosure under the Act" (Peacock 1981, 338–339). They also served as signals of decisions to come. For example, in *F.B.I. v. Abramson* (1982), a narrowly divided Court concluded that records compiled as part of an investigation remain exempt from the FOIA even if those records are revised and used for other purposes. In 1985, the Court provided "a virtual blanket exemption for all CIA files by way of FOIA Exemption 3" (Foerstel 1999, 175).

Congress amended FOIA again in 1986 – but this time in a direction favorable to governmental agencies. These changes broadened FOIA's law enforcement exemption and made it easier for agencies to keep information from the public (Beesley and Glover 1987, 521). At the same time, these amendments spawned no immediate uptick in FOIA litigation before the Supreme Court (Benecki 1988, 567–568). During the next several years, the Court would interpret those amendments to restrict document access. By all indications, Congress and the Reagan administration supported such a posture. Attorney General Meese lauded these developments, calling them "a long overdue correction of a federal information policy that he believed had tilted too far towards liberal disclosure" (Waldron and Israel 1989, 687–688). In this instance, interbranch discussions of FOIA appeared cooperative, rather than confrontational.

In 1996, Congress passed a series of FOIA amendments designed to update the legislation in light of growth in electronic record keeping. In 2002, the law was amended to further restrict certain access to U.S. intelligence agency records in response to the September 11, 2001, terrorist attacks (Pack 2004, 822–823). The Court's involvement in FOIA cases has ebbed in recent times, as it heard only one FOIA case between 1989 and 2000 (and just three cases between 1989 and 2007).

More broadly, Court support declined across time in substantive rights cases. During the Warren Court, support for such liberties registered slightly less than 70 percent. This declined to less than 30 percent for the Burger and Rehnquist Courts. As with the criminal cases, the reasons for the decline are varied and include changes in the composition of the Court and issue evolution. The reduced support also tracks the trend in presidential prerogatives. At the same time, support in Congress seemed to run in the opposite direction. The early period was marked by restrictive legislation like the Smith Act, whereas more supportive legislation was passed as the Court drew in the reins. But Congress would also swing back to adopt a more restrictive position.

Immigration and Naturalization Act

The 1952 immigration law abolished racial restrictions but kept some quotas that favored western Europeans. The Immigration and Nationality Act of 1965 (Hart-Cellar Act), passed in the wake of the CRA and VRA, brought quotas based on national origin to an end. Indeed, the law was passed and signed as part of the momentum coming from the CRA and consciously reflected some of the same goals. Major amendments were passed in the late 1970s, and the legislation continued to recalibrate the numbers and change the status of immigrants from various nations (Karst 1989).

Judicial behavior in immigration cases at the Supreme Court is characterized by a "remarkable stasis" (Law 2003). The Court has systematically deferred to Congress on immigration matters and has "declined to review federal immigration statutes for compliance with substantive constitutional constraints" (Legomsky 1985, 255; Schuck 1984). Thus, there has been no real dialogue between the Court and Congress, as we have seen in the CRA, FOIA, or *Habeas Corpus* (Motomura 1990). The Court's deference and faithfulness to congressional designs has meant few victories for the individuals (Legomsky 1995; Tichenor 2002). Indeed, support for restrictions on immigration stayed at consistent levels throughout the 1953–2000 period. Fewer than 40 percent of the cases were decided in favor of the individuals, which remained steady regardless of time period, administration, Congress, Court ideology, or issue evolution. The Court typically justifies its decisions on the grounds of congressional plenary power in the area of immigration law as well as concern for national sovereignty (Aleinikoff 2002; Shanks 2001). What has been missing from the equation, critics charge, is a concern for procedural rights (Motomura 1992).

There has been an explosion in the number of immigration cases that end up in the federal courts in the last two decades, stimulated in large part by the passage of several key pieces of legislation: the Refugee Act of 1980 and the Immigration Reform and Control Act of 1986, the Immigration Act of 1990, the Anti-Terrorism and Effective Death Penalty Act, and the Illegal Immigration Reform and Immigrant Responsibility Act (Schuck and Wang 1992). Congress sought to excise layers of judicial review and eliminate access to *habeas corpus* for certain classes of aliens (Neuman 1996, 1998). This was consistent with the general limitations on *habeas corpus*. The increase in immigration cases appealed to the Courts of Appeals was a function of tougher enforcement of immigration laws and a new, streamlined approach to cases at the Bureau of Immigrant Affairs (BIA), which left individuals feeling like they were short-circuited in the administrative process (Aleinikoff 2002; Neuman 2002). Reforms in the BIA for the purposes of cutting its caseload have created a plethora of cases being appealed to the Courts of Appeals, particularly in the Fifth and Ninth Circuits. Because the Supreme Court can review only a handful of cases in each term, the Courts of Appeals have effectively become the courts of last resort for aliens fighting to enter or remain in the country. The growing caseloads, in part, may have had the unintentional consequence of encouraging some Courts of Appeals to shirk precedent and congressional intent and engage in creative noncompliance practices (Law 2003; Loue 1985).

Attempts to restrict judicial review of immigration matters raised questions about judicial independence. Did Congress have the right to shield federal authorities from judicial review for removal procedures of certain classes of aliens? The federal courts were being stripped of their traditional power to review challenges to exclusion or detention, animating separation-of-power issues (Neuman 1998). This was a clear intrusion on the turf of the federal courts. As Anna Law (2003) asked, "Is the Supreme Court living up to its self-designated role of protecting 'discrete and insular' minorities, acting to check Executive and congressional overreach or abuse of discretion?"

RESULTS

These brief summaries provide us with glimpses of strategic decision making in civil rights, criminal procedure, and substantive rights. They provide a mixed picture of the influences on the Court's decisions. In each area, the changes in decision-making patterns seem to reflect changes in the ideology of the Court. In some areas, the influence of Congress appears to be significant; in others, less so. In civil rights, for example, the Court and Congress seemed to move in opposite directions for much of the post-*Brown* period. All of this begs a more systematic analysis, so we reprise our integrated model for the federal, nonconstitutional rights and liberties cases. We are interested in the interplay between the salience of the issues and additional constraints that face the Court in statutory cases.

Table 6.1 contains the results of our analysis of the statutory civil rights and civil liberties decisions. As was the case in our global analysis of civil rights and liberties decisions (Chapter 4) as well as the cluster

TABLE 6.1. *Integrated Model of Supreme Court Decision Making: Nonconstitutional Federal Civil Liberties and Civil Rights Cases*

	Model	Change in Probability
Supreme Court	2.22**	.08
	(.79)	
President	.60*	.07
	(.23)	
House	1.76*	.07
	(.85)	
Senate	− 3.68	− .03
	(2.21)	
Precedent	.39**	.10
	(.10)	
On Point	2.46**	.46
	(.48)	
Issue Evolution	− .19	− .04
	(.11)	
Constant	− .42	
	(.36)	
Chi²	.00	
Log Likelihood	− 356.3	
N	605	

$** \ p < .01. \ * \ p < .05.$

Probabilities represent the growth (or decline) in the probability of a pro–civil liberties or pro–civil rights decision for every one standard deviation change in the independent variable or from 0 to 1 for dummy variables, holding all the other independent variables at their respective means.

of those cases decided on constitutional grounds (Chapter 5), the attitudinal variable is statistically significant. This finding is not surprising, given the relatively high salience of civil rights and liberties issues to members of the Supreme Court (Pacelle 1991; Perry 1991; Rohde and Spaeth 1976). These are the issues that the contemporary Court cares most about, and they are the primary questions around which confirmation hearings revolve; thus, it should come as no surprise that, regardless of whether the case is decided on constitutional or nonconstitutional grounds, the Court's collective policy preferences, as reflected in the institution's median justice, are an important determinant of its civil rights and individual liberties decisions. Even controlling for the other variables and despite the notion that the Court is thought to be more constrained in nonconstitutional cases, the attitudinal variable's influence remains strong.

Similarly, the variable representing the president's ideological position is a positive and statistically significant predictor of the Court's statutory civil rights and liberties decisions as well. In fact, its impact is just slightly less than that of the attitudinal variable. As we have suggested elsewhere (Curry, Pacelle, and Marshall 2008), executive influence over judicial decision making in these nonconstitutional cases can occur via several routes. Perhaps the most fundamental of these routes involves the SG – the president's point person before the Court who serves as a credible legal source for the justices. The SG can shape the Court's decision making by influencing its agenda. In a more direct fashion, the SG represents the U.S. government when it is a party before the Court. The SG may also advocate the administration's legal positions to the justices during oral argument or at the merits stage, injecting presidential influence into judicial decisions (Bailey, Kamoie, and Maltzman 2005; Johnson 2004).

Although the SG is the attorney for the government and must pay attention to the Court and Congress, it is clear that the president's appointee will carry water for the administration on the most important issues of the day – most notably, civil rights and individual liberties issues. It is also noteworthy that, in the estimation of many observers, the OSG has become much more closely aligned with the president since the early 1980s (Caplan 1987; Pacelle 2003; Salokar 1992). But it is also important to remember that in many of the statutory cases, the government is a party to the case. In such circumstances, the OSG may need to advocate a position that is more in line with Congress than the president. Still, controlling for all of the other factors, the variable representing the president has a statistically significant impact on the Court's decisions. Beyond the synergy between the president and the SG, of course, the president has the ability to influence the implementation of Court directives. It is conceivable that the Court also considers these notions of executive compliance when formulating its decisions.

However, several important differences between the results obtained in this analysis and the findings presented in Chapter 5 do appear. Specifically, in contrast to our model of the constitutional civil rights and liberties decisions, strategic considerations move to the fore in the statutory cases. The House variable is statistically significant and in the correct direction. However the variable representing the Senate's collective policy preferences does not reach statistical significance. As with the presidential variable, the impact of the House is only slightly less than the impact

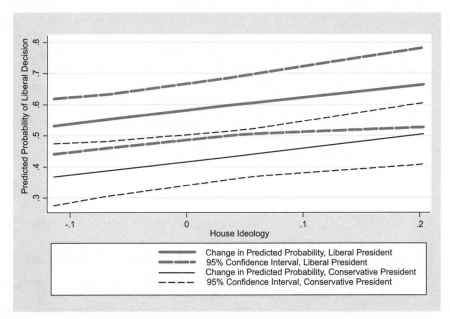

FIGURE 6.1. Effects of House Ideology on Statutory Decisions, by Presidential Ideology

of the attitudinal variable. Taken with the presidential variable's significance, the results suggest that the Court does take the other branches into account in deciding nonconstitutional civil rights and liberties cases. This is not surprising, given that the cases are decided on statutory grounds and the Court has to interpret the meaning of legislative provisions. It also lends some credence to the notion of Eskridge (1994) that in interpreting statutes, the Court pays attention not to the intent of the Congress that passed the legislation, but to the sitting Congress that can overturn or modify the decision. Comparing the results from this chapter with those from the previous chapter does provide us with considerable leverage in understanding the effects of case context – whether the basis of the decision is constitutional or statutory. The effects of the elected branches, particularly those of Congress, were absent in constitutional cases but significant in the statutory cases. This highlights the theoretical importance of strategic considerations. The Court does appear to anticipate how the House will react to its decisions, and the case context reflects a key conditioning factor, as evidenced by the differences we find between the two types of cases.

Figure 6.1 illustrates the significant influence of the other branches on the Court's statutory civil liberties and rights decisions in graphical form. First, the baseline probability of the Court issuing a liberal decision is greater when the president is liberal, represented by the thick black line, than when the president is conservative, as evidenced by the thin black line.[10] Second, irrespective of presidential ideology, as the median ideology of the House grows more liberal, so, too, does the probability that the Court will issue a decision favoring civil liberties and rights.

The fact that our findings reflect differences between the chambers is certainly consistent with the bicameral nature of Congress. We see two distinct institutions that uniquely structure decision making and outcomes within each chamber but also shape how the Court responds to each. The House tends to be more responsive and sensitive to concerns rising from members' districts. Not only do representatives have to run for election more often, but individual districts also tend to be more homogenous than the larger, more populous states that senators represent (Fenno 1973; Kingdon 1989; Mayhew 1974). Thus, there are important electoral incentives that explain why senators tend to be characterized more as policy generalists, but their House counterparts develop as narrower specialists. In addition, differences in size and procedural rules tend to favor more rapid and frequent legislative activism and oversight in the House than in the Senate (Smith 1989). There exists, then, a greater risk of political confrontations with the Court that could damage its institutional legitimacy. Because of these differences, the Court may be sensitive to the House. Therefore, the Court's decisions may be conditioned more heavily on the House than on the Senate.

The legal variables are a different matter. In contrast to our findings in the constitutional cases, here the precedent variable is statistically significant and positively related to the Court's decisions. In fact, the impact of precedent, controlling for the other factors, exerts a stronger impact than the attitudinal variable. This is in keeping with the Court's frequent admonitions that precedent should be especially dispositive in nonconstitutional cases (Gerhardt 2008). On those limited occasions when the Court does overrule statutory precedents, those precedents are often quite dated and have been supplanted by subsequent congressional legislation (Eskridge 1990, 2456). For example, in *Oncale v. Sundowner Offshore Services, Inc.* (1998), in which the Supreme Court unanimously held that

---

[10] All other variables were held at their mean values or, in the case of dichotomous variables, their modes. We used the ideological value of President Kennedy to represent the effects of a liberal president and the value for President Reagan for the effects of a conservative president, as Kennedy and Reagan were, respectively, the most liberal and most conservative presidents in our data set.

Title VII of the CRA of 1964 permits causes of action regarding claims of sexual harassment by members of the same sex, it unambiguously justified that decision in light of prior precedent. Specifically, it pointed to *Meritor Savings Bank FSB v. Vinson* (1986), which held that Title VII prohibits sexual harassment that creates a hostile work environment. Justice Scalia's majority opinion in *Oncale* also noted that, in light of decisions such as *Newport News Shipbuilding & Dry Dock Co. v. EEOC* (1983) and relying on broader principles from *Castaneda v. Partida* (1977), "nothing in Title VII necessarily bars a claim of discrimination 'because of . . . sex' merely because the plaintiff and the defendant . . . are of the same sex."

Precedent is particularly central to decision making in these statutory cases when precedents exist that are directly on point – although such cases comprised a very small proportion of the cases in this data set. By contrast, the issue evolution variable, though strongly significant in both the full model of civil rights and liberties cases and the constitutional subset, does not have a statistically significant influence on decision making in these nonconstitutional cases at the .05 level (it just misses, however, surviving the .10 cutoff).

What accounts for issue evolution's lack of explanatory power in federal statutory cases? Congress appears to be partially responsible, because the intermittent passage of legislation can interrupt the normal development of issues before the Court. The Court may be building doctrine in a particular issue area, only to have Congress interrupt and either advance or retard its evolutionary development. Consider the Court's 1984 decision in *Grove City College v. Bell*. In interpreting Title IX of the Education Amendments of 1972, the justices held that only discriminatory programs – not institutions as a whole – could be sanctioned for violating Title IX by discriminating against women. Three years later, Congress overruled that decision when it passed the Civil Rights Restoration Act of 1987 over President Reagan's veto. Consistent with strategic considerations, the Court adapted its decisions to those changes regardless of case difficulty.

The Freedom of Information Act provides another example. After the Court urged Congress to revise the FOIA in *Mink*, Congress did just that in the following year. After overruling the Court's statutory interpretation in *Mink*, Congress then overruled a second FOIA decision with a series of 1976 amendments (Berner 1976, 1030). In effect, that legislative activity reshuffled the statutory deck and prevented the natural evolution of FOIA issues before the Court.

Similarly, Eskridge (1991b, 623) notes a host of occasions when Congress interrupted the Court's doctrinal construction in statutory civil rights cases by overriding its decisions. Although the relationship between the Court and the elected branches was characterized by cooperation during the 1960s, he contends that "[t]he most important development during [the 1970s and 1980s] was the gradual rightward drift of the Presidency and the Supreme Court, relative to Congress." That period, which extended into the 1990s, saw Congress interrupting the natural evolution of issues before the Court with legislation designed to "reset" the unfolding statutory doctrine.

Issue evolution's lack of impact may also be a function of the attitudinal variable. When the Court reverses field by overturning an existing precedent, it revisits the original landmark decision. In doing so, it is inviting future litigation, and it is logical that the groups that are buoyed by the Court's reversal will want to bring more cases to see if they can induce a majority to continue to build doctrine in the new direction. This means that the cases may get easier.

The lack of impact of issue evolution appears to be an artifact of a peculiar situation. As in Chapter 5, we want to refine our analysis one step further. Without the fifty-one immigration cases, there is a significant change in the results – a statistically significant change.[11] We see the new analysis in Table 6.2. The issue evolution variable, which was not quite statistically significant in the total sample (it was significant at the .10 level but not the .05 level), has a significant impact when the immigration cases are excluded. In addition, it has a relatively strong impact, controlling for the other variables. The rest of the variables (except the Senate) remain statistically significant and in the correct direction. In fact, when we consider the immigration cases alone, we find that none of the variables, whether attitudinal, legal, or strategic, is statistically significant.

This model better reflects our initial hypotheses that the strategic variables and the legal variables would influence decision making. As with

---

[11] We opted to exclude the immigration cases in this auxiliary investigation of issue evolution because, as previously noted, there is a good deal of scholarship indicating that the Court almost always defers to Congress on such matters (e.g., Aleinikoff 2002; Law 2003; Legomsky 1985; Motomura 1990, 1992; Shanks 2001; Schuck 1984; Tichenor 2002). In light of this research, inclusion of these fifty-one immigration cases in the aggregate analysis likely operated to understate the effect of issue evolution in the aggregate model of statutory civil rights and liberties cases – if the modern Court has indeed made the conscious decision to defer to Congress on immigration matters, this would virtually ensure the outlier status of these cases in terms of the issue evolution variable.

TABLE 6.2. *Nonconstitutional Federal Civil Liberties and Civil Rights Cases Minus Immigration Cases*

	Model	Change in Probability
Supreme Court	2.39**	.09
	(.86)	
President	.53*	.06
	(.25)	
House	1.86	.08
	(1.03)	
Senate	−4.26	−.03
	(2.74)	
Precedent	.39**	.11
	(.11)	
On Point	2.41**	.41
	(.53)	
Issue Evolution	−.37*	−.08
	(.14)	
Constant	−.96*	
	(.42)	
Chi²	.00	
Log Likelihood	−289.9	
N	554	

** $p < .01$. * $p < .05$.
Probabilities represent the growth (or decline) in the probability of a pro–civil liberties or pro–civil rights decision for every one standard deviation change in the independent variable or from 0 to 1 for dummy variables, holding all the other independent variables at their respective means.

the constitutional civil rights and individual liberties cases, the attitudinal variable is statistically significant. But whereas it was the most important variable (with issue evolution), now it shares top billing with a number of other factors – most notably, precedent. Congress – at least the House – has an effect on decision making, controlling for all of the other variables (see Table 6.1). The general conclusion we can draw is that these issues are indeed salient to the justices. Because the Court is more constrained, there are more factors it must balance in making its decisions.

In analyzing this subset of statutory cases, then, we have demonstrated that precedent plays a major role in structuring the Court's decisions and that issue evolution does when we add a qualification. Thus, it appears that *stare decisis* provides at least a "gravitational effect" on the Court (Clayton and Gillman 1999; Segal, Spaeth, and Benesh 2005, 29).

Still, this does not fully explain why precedent has variable effects when the issues are basically the same except for their foundation. Statutory cases do tend to be narrower and less important substantively. Because they are narrower, they may be more easily covered by existing precedent than constitutional issues. This finding is consistent with a study by Spriggs and Hansford (2001). It is also consistent with the public statements of justices who openly admit that they pay closer attention to precedents in statutory cases than in constitutional cases (Gerhardt 2008).

CONCLUSION

The results suggest that the Court feels some level of constraint in statutory cases, even for the salient issues. This matches Scenario 3, which predicts that the Court will act strategically under conditions of constraint. It appears to respond to the president, Congress (the House at least), and precedent. Therefore, decision making in nonconstitutional cases is a complicated mix of attitudinal, legal, and strategic variables. In the constitutional cases, by contrast, the attitudinal variable was clearly the strongest factor.

In analyzing the determinants of decision making in constitutional and nonconstitutional civil rights and liberties cases, we have uncovered significant variation in the importance of strategic and legal considerations contingent on the grounds on which those cases were decided. At the same time, the Court's collective policy preferences have remained central to decision making, regardless of the grounds. This reflects the salience of the issues and the primacy of this independent variable.

Some proponents of the attitudinal variable argue that the policy values of the justices are the only factor that really influences decisions. We argue that the results of this chapter suggest that the simple, elegant theory that the Court is composed of single-minded policy entrepreneurs pursuing their sincere preferences is exaggerated. The results do not argue that attitudinal considerations are not important. Quite the contrary, they are likely the dominant factor, but they are not the sole element in decision making. We look at the process of institutional decision making and the broader construction of public policy not as a soliloquy by the Supreme Court, but as a colloquy consisting of a series of actors operating in contexts that shift based on the salience of the issue and the grounds of the decision.

The results suggest that the strategic model of decision making is the best explanation for the Court's actions in nonconstitutional liberties and civil rights cases. Thus, the collective policy preferences of the Court are filtered through the constraints the institution faces (Congress and the president) as well as the norms and rules of the judicial system (precedent and issue evolution). The Court may have to temper its sincere preferences to avoid retaliation. We caution, though, that to view this iterative process as a classical dialectic struggle between the Court and the other branches is not always accurate. There is significant interbranch cooperation and a desire to "get it right." Of course, to the extent that conflict does ensue or animate the "separation of powers game," it is likelier to occur in salient cases when the Court is constrained.

This chapter shows that under conditions of issue salience and institutional constraints, legal as well as strategic factors share influence over the Court's decision making. Once again, we argue that our results are valid because they reflect the narratives of statutory decision making in civil rights and liberties cases. In civil rights, the Court and Congress were taking turns leading in an elaborate, long-term dance. In criminal procedure, the Court ultimately responded to Congress. In free speech and substantive rights cases, the Warren Court was responsive to Congress and slow to protect individual liberties. The Burger and Rehnquist Courts drew in the reins in part because they were ideologically wired to do so, but also in response to a more conservative Congress.

To generate a more comprehensive picture of the determinants of Supreme Court decision making, however, we must consider whether the differential influence of attitudinal, strategic, and legal factors remains robust beyond the realm of these highly salient civil liberties and rights cases. To that end, Chapter 7 begins our two-chapter investigation into the determinants of decision making in economic cases – which are thought to be less salient to the Court, Congress, and the president than the cases we have examined thus far. Chapter 7 begins by summarizing the modern Court's decision making in economic cases decided on constitutional grounds. In our final empirical chapter, Chapter 8, we extend that analysis to encompass the Court's collective decision making with respect to nonconstitutional economic cases.

7

Avoiding Another Self-Inflicted Wound

Constitutional Economic Cases

By including Footnote Four in the *Carolene Products* decision, the Supreme Court was, in essence, admitting that it had overreached. It was also trying to salvage some of its institutional integrity. Loathe to repeat its jurisprudence of the recent past in which it had struck down numerous New Deal programs as unconstitutional, it set out to chart a different course. Rather than write its own views on economic policy matters into constitutional law, the Court would presume such legislation to be constitutional (Miller 1968). It was retreating from the wanton judicial activism of substantive due process that occasionally marked its economic jurisprudence. As we noted in Chapters 5 and 6, this change in orientation allowed the Court to pivot to a greater emphasis on individual rights and liberties issues. The effect of this new posture was to bring relative stability to its constitutional economic decisions for decades to come. By clearing out the constitutional underbrush, the Court could begin to address and resolve the narrower statutory economic cases that are the subject of Chapter 8. Therefore, in articulating the Court's legal standard for assessing the constitutionality of economic cases, Footnote Four brought stability to the law and enabled the institution to turn its focus to what it considered more pressing issues.

Although even the most seasoned observers would be hard-pressed to generate a list of the Warren Court's economic cases decided on constitutional grounds, the cases it did hear reflected this new deference toward governmental action in the economic realm. For example, in 1954, the Court assessed the constitutionality of the District of Columbia Redevelopment Act of 1945 in *Berman v. Parker*. Prior to this decision, it was considered "a perversion of the public use doctrine to acquire land by condemnation for [redevelopment] purposes" (R. Epstein 1985, 178). In *Berman*, however, the Court unanimously upheld a governmental program that utilized the government's eminent domain power to redevelop slum areas of Washington, D.C. Part of that program permitted the reselling of government-acquired property to different private owners, provided their use of that property would be consistent with the general land-use plan (Hensley, Hale, and Snook 2006, 210). The issue in *Berman* was whether reselling this government-acquired property to private individuals could be reconciled with the Constitution's "public use" requirement.

In passing the District of Columbia Redevelopment Act, Congress determined that it would be necessary to utilize the power of eminent domain to eliminate slum housing conditions in certain parts of the Washington, D.C., metro area.[1] Pursuant to the act, the National Capital Planning Commission formulated a plan to redevelop an area known as "Project Area B" in Southwest Washington. Located just more than a mile from the U.S. Supreme Court, Project Area B was, by any measure, a public health nightmare: 64.3 percent of the area's dwellings were beyond repair, and nearly 58 percent had no indoor toilets. Nearly 30 percent lacked electricity, and more than 80 percent of the area had no central heating, washbasins, or laundry tubs. In addition, of the area's five thousand residents, more than 97 percent were African American.

Max Morris owned a small department store that was in satisfactory condition on Fourth Street, then the commercial heart of southwest Washington (Allen 2005). Indeed, approximately 17 percent of the area's structures met acceptable health and safety standards. Morris objected to the government's effort to take his property because it was not slum housing (Epstein and Walker 2007a, 672). Upon Morris's death, his executor, Sam Berman, sought to keep the government from seizing the property. Although a three-judge District Court did express reservations about the scope of the program, it ultimately upheld the Redevelopment Act's constitutionality. The Supreme Court then granted review. Perhaps reflecting the ease with which the decision was made, just thirty-four days passed between oral argument and the Court's decision in the case.

In his majority opinion, Justice Douglas made it clear that the Court would defer to the elected branches on Takings Clause issues:

> The definition [of this police power] is essentially the product of legislative determinations addressed to the purposes of government, purposes neither abstractly nor historically capable of complete definition.... Subject to

[1] Unless otherwise noted, all case facts come from *Berman v. Parker* 348 U.S. 26 (1954).

specific constitutional limitations, when the legislature has spoken, the public interest has been declared in terms well-nigh conclusive. In such cases, the legislature, not the judiciary, is the main guardian of the public needs to be served by social legislation.... This principle admits of no exception merely because the power of eminent domain is involved. *The role of the judiciary in determining whether that power is being exercised for a public purpose is an extremely narrow one* (emphasis added).

In *Berman*, the Court thus affirmed the rational basis test, requiring the minimum of judicial oversight as the governing standard in takings cases (Hensley, Hale, and Snook 2006, 211).[2]

In many ways, *Berman* is the anti-*Brown*. It is a case of judicial restraint, whereas *Brown* represented judicial activism. *Brown* was meant to open doors both literally and figuratively, whereas *Berman* was designed to close the courthouse door. *Brown* was the Court's investment of agenda resources for the future and a portent of greater protection for rights and liberties. *Berman* was the Court's announcement that its debts had been paid and a sign that litigants seeking redress of such issues should look elsewhere. In one way, though, *Berman* and *Brown* were the same. In both instances, the Court cleared away a precedent it no longer found viable.

In its following term in *Williamson v. Lee Optical*, the Warren Court rebuffed an attack on the constitutionality of a state regulation that made it "'unlawful for any person ... to fit, adjust, adapt, or to apply ... lenses, frames ... or any other optical appliances to the face' unless that person was a licensed ophthalmologist ... or an optometrist.'" According to the Oklahoma statute, opticians could not fit lenses without a written prescription issued by an ophthalmologist or optometrist (Epstein and Walker 2007a, 645). Lee Optical Company challenged this law as an unreasonable exercise of state authority, but the Supreme Court unanimously disagreed. Writing for his colleagues, Justice Douglas served notice that "the day is gone when this Court uses the Due Process Clause of the Fourteenth Amendment to strike down state laws, regulatory of

---

[2] Additionally, the Supreme Court modified the District Court's ruling to underscore the fact that maximum discretion should be afforded to the elected branches with respect to policy choices of this sort. To wit, "The District Court below suggested that, if such a broad scope were intended for the statute, the standards contained in the Act would not be sufficiently definite to sustain the delegation of authority.... We do not agree. We think the standards prescribed were adequate for executing the plan to eliminate not only the slums as narrowly defined by the District Court but also the blighted areas that tend to produce slums" (348 U.S. at 35).

business and industrial conditions, because they may be unwise, improvident, or out of harmony with a particular school of thought" (348 U.S. at 488).

Chief Justice Burger's Supreme Court, more conservative than Warren's in some respects, essentially adhered to its predecessor's views with regard to these types of economic cases. As Justice O'Connor wrote in a 1984 Takings Clause case, "When the legislature's purpose is legitimate and its means are not irrational, our cases make clear that empirical debates over the wisdom of takings – no less than debates over the wisdom of other kinds of socioeconomic legislation – are not to be carried out in federal courts" (467 U.S. at 243).

However, soon after William Rehnquist ascended to the Court's center chair in 1986, he and his fellow conservatives – most notably, Justice Scalia – began to shun certain aspects of the Court's economic jurisprudence. The first glimpse of the Court's shift was manifested in its reassertion of limitations on governmental activity under the Takings Clause (Brisbin 1997). The Rehnquist Court's activism in the economic sphere was by no means confined to property rights cases (Keck 2004), but it was this area where the Court first signaled its willingness to restore certain categories of economic claims to a more prominent position on its agenda. Witness *Nollan v. California Coastal Commission* (1987).

James and Marilyn Nollan owned a beachfront lot in Ventura County, California. A small, broken-down bungalow stood on the lot, and the Nollans decided to rebuild the structure. To do so, they were legally required to secure a coastal development permit from the California Coastal Commission. An ocean-side beach and a public recreation area were located just north of the property, and another public beach was located just south of their lot. The Coastal Commission approved the Nollans' application, but that approval was subject to a contingency – the Nollans would be required to set aside a public easement on their property allowing access between the two public beaches (Peterson 1989; Tushnet 2005).

In its five-to-four decision in the case, the Supreme Court held that the state of California could only require the Nollans to construct an easement across their property if it paid for it. In other words, it was unlawful for the Commission to condition the granting of the building permit on the building of an easement across the property. The dissenters, led by Justice Brennan, felt that the decision significantly departed from the spirit of détente that had characterized this legal area for more than thirty years. Brennan's dissent called the decision "inconsistent with our standard for reviewing the rationality of a State's exercise of its police power for the welfare of its citizens" (483 U.S. at 842–843). Furthermore, he excoriated the majority for "overruling an eminently reasonable exercise of an expert state agency's judgment, substituting its own narrow view of how this balance [between private development and public access] should be struck" (483 U.S. at 864).

In *Nollan*, then, the Court broadened its view of the types of governmental regulations that would constitute a taking. As detailed later in this chapter, the Court soon moved beyond *Nollan* and continued to breathe new life into the Takings Clause. The Rehnquist Court's willingness to police governmental activities for violations of the Takings Clause represented a substantial break with the Court's governing practice in constitutional economic cases generally (Schultz and Smith 1996, 6–10). With specific regard to eminent domain issues, in the decades before *Nollan*, the Court had been deferential to the reasonable exercise of state police power and was reluctant to invalidate such actions under the Takings Clause. But as the Court grew more conservative during the Reagan and Bush years and the justices sought to stanch the institution's sympathy toward civil liberties and rights claims, certain types of economic cases became more important to the justices, and the Court approached them with an increasingly critical eye. Whereas the Warren and Burger Courts adopted deferential standards of review in order to move these economic cases off the agenda, under Rehnquist the Court became more deferential toward many of the civil liberties issues that had pushed economic cases to the margins. As a consequence, the Court's civil liberties docket shrunk, economic cases began to fill that void, and increasingly conservative judicial preferences created a more activist atmosphere in which getting certain types of economic cases "right" became more important than continuing stability in the law. In effect, the signs were visible that the Court was standing the double standard on its head. Some argued that the Court was increasingly deferential to the government in individual liberties and civil rights while putting economic issues in a preferred position (Keck 2004; Yarbrough 2000).

Judicial attitudes have played a role in reopening the agenda to such issues, and the Court might reestablish its influence in these areas. Such a move would make the Court even more of a constitutional tribunal and would have spillover effects for statutory economic cases as well as civil rights and liberties issues. If the Court were bent on revisiting its past jurisprudence and being less deferential, it would require agenda resources that would presumably be borrowed from civil rights and civil liberties

(Pacelle 1995). To whatever extent the Court destabilizes constitutional law in the economic area, it has substantive effects on the statutory cases as well.

As soon as these constitutional issues made their way onto the agenda, issue evolution and precedent would begin to play a significant role. The Court wrestled with the interpretations, taking tentative steps forward and then retreating a bit. Part of this was a function of issue evolution. As newer, more difficult issues arose, the Court would step back. But part of it is also attributable to the need to attend to precedent. At this point, precedent was tenuous. There were decisions on the books, but the Court seemed to be moving away from them. There was the uncertainty that often occurs when the Court is deciding whether existing standards have continued viability.

THE EVOLUTION OF CONSTITUTIONAL ECONOMIC DOCTRINE

In the decade and a half before Earl Warren became its chief justice in October 1953, the Supreme Court had been in transition. As soon as the Court resigned itself to the New Deal, Chief Justice Hughes retired and Harlan F. Stone replaced him. Stone sought to stake out a new role for the Court, but as a holdover appointee from the 1920s, he remained a transitional figure (Mason 1956; Urofsky 1998). Fred Vinson, his successor, had neither the skill nor the inclination to be an effective leader on the Court, and his death on the eve of the term that will forever be associated with *Brown v. Board of Education* is symbolic of his transitory status.[3]

Yet this succession of chief justices did not represent the Supreme Court's only transition. These years also signaled a shift in its approach to economic cases decided on constitutional grounds. Since the late eighteenth century, the Court had relied on the doctrine of substantive due process, strict notions of federalism, and a cramped reading of the Commerce Clause to invalidate regulations prohibiting child labor (*Hammer v. Dagenhart* [1918]; *Bailey v. Drexel Furniture Co.* [1922]), the minimum wage (*Adkins v. Children's Hospital* [1923]), and various portions of the New Deal (*A.L.A. Schechter Poultry Corp. v. United States* [1935]; *Carter v. Carter Coal Company* [1936]; *United States v. Butler* [1936]), to name but a few. By 1938, the Court seemed to have cast aside such rigid approaches, but it remained to be seen how it would navigate the

---

[3] Vinson's death occasioned Justice Frankfurter's quip, "This is the first indication I have ever had that there is a God" (Abraham 2008).

future. Under Chief Justice Warren's leadership, the Court's new priorities became abundantly clear (Ely 1992; McKenna 2002).

A cursory look at any major constitutional law textbook tells the story. The Warren Court made few memorable decisions involving the Commerce Clause, federalism, the Contract Clause, eminent domain, or substantive due process issues, and the notable constitutional economic decisions it did issue can almost be counted on one hand.[4] From the 1950s to the 1980s, the Court trained its focus on civil rights and liberties and largely placed its constitutional economic case law in a holding pattern.

Commerce Clause Cases

In *N.L.R.B. v. Jones & Laughlin Steel* (1937), the Supreme Court upheld the constitutionality of the National Labor Relations Act, New Deal legislation that had been challenged as a violation of the Commerce Clause. That decision "announced a break from the past and ushered in a new era in the constitutional relationship between the government and the economy" (Epstein and Walker 2007a, 453). Five years later, the Court unanimously affirmed the Agricultural Adjustment Act (AAA) on similar grounds. With its decision in that case, *Wickard v. Filburn* (1942), the Supreme Court gave Congress a virtual blank check with respect to its regulatory power under the Commerce Clause. The scope of *Wickard* was sweeping because, although the case did deal with economic activity, in no way did the activities at issue directly implicate "interstate" commerce. The decision seemed to articulate the clear message that the Court was going to be deferential to congressional exercise of authority under the Commerce Clause.

Roscoe Filburn, a farmer living outside Dayton, Ohio, exceeded the quota of wheat he was allowed to grow under the AAA and was fined by the secretary of agriculture (Chen 2003). Filburn refused to pay the fine, arguing that Congress had no constitutional authority to regulate wheat grown on his farm for purely on-farm consumption. The Court disagreed, writing, "Congress may properly have considered that [the regulation in question] would have a substantial effect" on interstate commerce (317 U.S. at 128–129). More than a half century would elapse before the Court

---

[4] Epstein and Walker's (2007a) undergraduate constitutional law text excerpts opinions from *Berman Parker* (1954), *Williamson v. Lee Optical Company* (1955), and a Commerce Clause challenge to the 1964 Civil Rights Act (*Heart of Atlanta Motel v. United States* [1964]).

would impose any significant limitations on Congress's ability to regulate interstate commerce.

Indeed, "the Warren Court's Commerce Clause jurisprudence rates among that era's least innovative – and consequently, its most secure – doctrinal developments" (Chen 2003, 1745). To the extent that the Warren Court addressed the Commerce Clause, on several occasions it did so to extend the promise of racial equality embodied in *Brown v. Board of Education*. In *Heart of Atlanta Motel v. United States* (1964) and *Katzenbach v. McClung* (1964), the Court held that the interstate Commerce Clause provided Congress with the authority to prohibit race discrimination in hotels and restaurants (Cortner 2001). Similarly, in *Daniel v. Paul* (1969), eight justices held that, although there was no evidence that any interstate traveler had ever used a particular out-of-the-way recreational facility in rural Arkansas, it would nevertheless be forced to comply with the Civil Rights Act of 1964 because it operated in interstate commerce (Epstein and Walker 2007a, 464).[5]

More generally, the Warren Court remained responsive to arguments that the Commerce Clause provided a broad constitutional basis for governmental action with respect to economic issues (Benson 1970). In *Maryland v. Wirtz* (1968), the Court held that the Commerce Clause gave Congress the constitutional authority to extend the Fair Labor Standards Act to employees of hospitals and public schools. Punctuating the seemingly definitive nature of the Court's views on such matters, Justice Harlan's opinion in the case read, "The contention that in Commerce Clause cases, the courts have power to excise, as trivial, individual instances falling within a rationally defined class of activities has been put entirely to rest" (392 U.S. at 192–193). The Court seemed to pass Congress another blank check. The Burger Court's approach to the Commerce Clause followed a similar trajectory. In 1971, eight members of the Court upheld the constitutionality of the Consumer Credit Protection Act against an accused loan shark who, like Roscoe Filburn, argued that any potentially illegal transactions were purely local in character (Chen 2003, 1747).

Significant changes in the Commerce Clause jurisprudence did not come until the 1990s. In *United States v. Lopez* (1995), a sharply divided Court invalidated the Gun Free School Zones Act of 1990, marking the

---

[5] The Court reasoned that the club operated in interstate commerce because 1) it advertised in publications known to be read by some interstate travelers; 2) it leased several paddle boats from an Oklahoma company; 3) it owned a jukebox and records that had been manufactured out of state; and 4) three items sold at the snack bar contained ingredients from out of state (Epstein and Walker 2007a, 464).

first time since the Roosevelt years that it had struck down legislation for exceeding Congress's power to regulate interstate commerce. In that case, the justices held that possessing a weapon on school grounds did not implicate issues of interstate commerce (Tushnet 2005, 258–261). Moreover, Chief Justice Rehnquist's opinion faulted Congress for failing to provide any hint of a relationship between gun violence and interstate commerce when it passed the legislation.

When the Court struck down the Violence Against Women Act of 1994 in *United States v. Morrison* (2000), it was apparent that the truce that had characterized the Court's activity in this area since the 1940s had begun to unravel. In *Morrison*, Christy Brzonkala alleged that Antonio Morrison had raped her and filed a civil suit against him as authorized in the Violence Against Women Act (Tushnet 2005, 261–264). Though Congress had relied on its power to regulate interstate commerce in passing the Act, the Court "reject[ed] the argument that Congress may regulate noneconomic, violent criminal conduct based solely on that conduct's aggregate effect on interstate commerce."

In 2001, the Court was asked to recognize a series of small ponds on a Chicago-area development site as instruments of interstate commerce. Specifically, because the ponds served as habitats for migratory birds that crossed state lines, the Army Corps of Engineers claimed that the development project implicated interstate commerce and consequently had to meet with its approval. Here again, however, a majority of the Court refused to extend the federal government's regulatory oversight on those grounds (*Solid Waste Agency of Northern Cook County v. Army Corps of Engineers* [2001]). Even so, the current state of the Commerce Clause jurisprudence remains mixed. That is particularly true in light of decisions such as *Gonzalez v. Raich* (2005), in which the Court upheld the federal government's authority under the Commerce Clause to regulate the use of locally grown marijuana by two California women for medicinal purposes.

Economic Substantive Due Process

The modern Supreme Court's approach to economic substantive due process issues has followed the general pattern evidenced in its Commerce Clause cases – there was a lengthy initial period of deference to the government, and there has been a slight reassertion of certain limitations of late. After it rejected the concept of economic substantive due process in *West Coast Hotel v. Parrish* (1937), in which it upheld the constitutionality of minimum wage legislation, the Court coalesced around a rational basis test that presumed that such economic regulations were constitutional (Epstein and Walker 2007a, 644). That, of course, stood in stark contrast to cases such as *Lochner v. New York* (1905) and *Adkins v. Children's Hospital* (1923), in which the Court found itself articulating a substantive right against "unreasonable, unnecessary, and arbitrary" governmental influence in the marketplace (*Lochner v. New York*, 198 U.S. at 56) (Gillman 1993).

The Court would apply that standard in a number of subsequent cases, with *Williamson v. Lee Optical Company* (1955) the Warren Court's first major foray into the realm of economic due process. There, as we have noted, the Court essentially shut the door to such constitutional challenges. Occasionally, however, cases raising questions of economic due process did make their way to the Court's steps. In 1963, the Court continued its deference on these economic matters in *Ferguson v. Skrupa*, in which it upheld the constitutionality of a Kansas statute that made it a misdemeanor for non-lawyers to engage in "debt-adjusting." Frank Skrupa was a "credit advisor" who engaged in the practice and believed that the state regulation was an unreasonable restriction on his business. The Supreme Court unanimously disagreed and reiterated its "abandonment of the use of the 'vague contours' of the Due Process Clause to nullify laws which a majority of the Court believed to be economically unwise" (372 U.S. at 731). Further punctuating its lack of interest in such matters, Justice Black's opinion concluded, "Whether the legislature takes for its textbook Adam Smith, Herbert Spencer, Lord Keynes, or some other is no concern of ours" (372 U.S. at 732). The Court would reserve its judicial activism and gambols into substantive due process for laws that restricted civil liberties and civil rights (Dunne 1977, 385).

In sum, the Court has been consistent in deferring to most legislative determinations with respect to the "reasonableness" of economic policies. For example, in 1988, the justices refused to invalidate a municipal rent-control scheme on substantive due process grounds (*Pennell v. San Jose* [1988]). At the same time, the Court has indicated its receptiveness to substantive due process when weighing the reasonableness of punitive damages awards in certain civil cases. Prior to 1996, the Supreme Court did not invalidate punitive damages as unreasonable or excessive, but it did acknowledge that particularly arbitrary damage amounts could violate notions of substantive due process (e.g., *TXO Production Corp. v. Alliance Resources Corp.* [1993]; *Pacific Mutual Life Insurance Co. v. Haslip* [1991]).

In 1996, however, the Court did invalidate a civil judgment of $4 million in punitive damages (compared to just $4,000 in actual damages) against the BMW Corporation, saying that ratio between punitive and compensatory damages was so excessive as to "transcend the constitutional limit." In effect, then, the Court held that what it considered to be "excessive awards" violated notions of fairness embodied in the Fourteenth Amendment's Due Process Clause (see *BMW Corporation of North America v. Gore* [1996]). With echoes from an earlier era, the dissenting justices all but accused the majority of reading its economic views into constitutional law. Nevertheless, the Rehnquist and Roberts Courts have remained willing to declare certain jury awards excessive, thereby violating the Constitution (e.g., *Cooper Industries v. Leatherman Tool Group* [2001]; *State Farm Mutual Automobile Insurance Co. v. Campbell* [2003]; *Exxon Shipping Co. v. Baker* [2008]).

Epstein and Walker (2007a, 650) have noted that "these decisions are confined to a single area and do not represent a return to the thinking of *Lochner* and *Adkins*. Indeed, aside from *BMW v. Gore*, more than seventy years had elapsed since the Court struck down a law on economic substantive due process grounds." Moreover, somewhat paradoxically, even the Court's recent willingness to assert itself in the area of punitive damages is ultimately a testament to the Court's overarching goal in stabilizing the law in these less salient areas of economic case law. First, the Court's two most recent Republican appointees, Chief Justice Roberts and Justice Alito, have not championed a retreat from recent precedents in this area. To the contrary, whereas their conservative judicial philosophies might have led some to speculate otherwise (see Kmiec 2007), both Roberts and Alito voted in favor of limitations on punitive damages in *Philip Morris USA v. Williams* (2006) and *Exxon Shipping Co. v. Baker* (2008).

Even more surprisingly, despite their avowed disagreement with the Court's precedents limiting the scope of punitive damages in the aforementioned cases, Justices Scalia and Thomas grudgingly abided by those precedents in *Exxon Shipping* (e.g., Mauro 2008). Scalia's concurring opinion, joined by Thomas, seems to represent a clear exposition of precedent's value – even when a justice believes that precedent to be misguided: "I join the opinion of the Court, including the portions that refer to constitutional limits that prior opinions have imposed upon punitive damages. While I agree with the argumentation based upon those prior holdings, I continue to believe the holdings were in error" (*Exxon Shipping Co. v. Baker* [2008]). The apparent willingness of Scalia and Thomas to reconcile themselves to these precedents stands in sharp contrast to their continued disdain for precedent in areas of arguably greater salience, most notably abortion rights.

The Contract Clause

The Contract Clause, described as "perhaps the strongest single constitutional check on state legislation during our early years as a Nation," became a virtual dead letter as a result of the Court's 1934 decision in *Home Building & Loan Association v. Blaisdell* (*Allied Structural Steel Co. v. Spannaus* [1978], 438 U.S. at 241). Until the 1970s, the Court's appraisal of the Contract Clause followed its trajectory in the more general area of substantive due process claims – the justices simply were not going to rely on the Contract Clause to strike down state legislation, and state and local policy makers would be afforded maximum discretion in economic matters (e.g., *El Paso v. Simmons* [1965]). Therefore, far from the heady days when Chief Justice John Marshall's Court enforced the prominence of Contract Clause protections, *Blaisdell* and succeeding cases largely sapped the clause of its previous strength. The fact that the Court entertained no Contract Clause cases between 1965 and 1977 further testifies to the provision's ebbing significance.

As the Court grew more conservative during the 1970s, however, the Contract Clause began to merit closer attention. In *United States Trust Company v. New Jersey* (1977), a plurality of the Court held that the repeal of an agreement regarding mass transit in the New York metropolitan area violated the Contract Clause. As Justice Brennan's dissent observed, the decision threatened to upend this legal area. Noting that the Court's recent decisions had elevated the exercise of state police power over contractual rights, he contended, "Today's decision . . . rejects this previous understanding and remolds the Contract Clause into a potent instrument for overseeing important policy determinations of the state legislature. . . . [It] substantially distorts modern constitutional jurisprudence governing regulation of private economic interests" (431 U.S. at 33).

In the very next term, the Court continued to enforce the Contract Clause, holding that Minnesota had run afoul of the constitutional command after it "substantially altered" previously negotiated pension agreements between a company and its employees (*Allied Structural Steel Co. v. Spannaus* [1978]). Yet this awakening did not signal a fundamental shift in the Court's appraisal of contract disputes. In 1983, the

Burger Court unanimously upheld the constitutionality of state energy legislation that had been challenged under the Contract Clause (*Energy Reserves Group, Inc. v. Kansas Power and Light Company*). Writing for a five-member majority in *Keystone Bituminous Coal Association v. DeBenedictis* (1987), Justice Stevens wrote that "it is well settled that the prohibition against impairing the obligation of contracts is not to be read literally" (480 U.S. at 502). Furthermore, he put forward a narrow construction of the Clause, arguing that it was intended to deal with state debt relief in the wake of American independence. Taken together, "[t]he clause is a weak protection for property rights and not destined to recover to pre-*Blaisdell* days. However, the Contract Clause is not dead and the Supreme Court does not appear ready to bury it permanently" (Schultz 1992, 49).

Governmental Taxation and Spending

In state taxation cases, the Warren Court pursued the path of least resistance. Just prior to Warren's ascension to the Court, in *Spector Motor Service v. O'Connor* (1951), the justices held that state taxes on the "privilege of doing business" were per se unconstitutional as applied to entities operating in interstate commerce. In other words, state attempts to tax aspects of wholly interstate commercial activity were invalid. With that decision, the Court underscored that the national government's power to tax interstate commerce was exclusive and thereby removed itself from the business of policing state tax arrangements on a case-by-case basis. Indeed, relatively few taxation cases with constitutional dimensions were decided during the Warren Court's tenure.

Perhaps more than anything else, the Court's treatment of tax-related constitutional issues under Burger and Rehnquist was characterized by significant intracourt legal and philosophical agreement. During the 1970s, the Court upheld the constitutionality of a state ad valorem tax on imported French and Canadian goods being stored in a Georgia warehouse for later distribution. It thus rejected the argument that these materials, housed in their original containers, were exempt from state taxation (*Michelin Tire Corp v. Wages* [1976]). In doing so, it overruled a 104-year-old precedent, but it did so unanimously, arguing that time had proven it to be unworkable (Pritchett 1984).

In the following term, the Court was also united in upholding the validity of a Mississippi "privilege of doing business tax" in the face of a Commerce Clause challenge. Specifically, it discarded the absolutism that the Warren Court adopted from *Spector Motor Service* and enunciated a four-pronged test against which to judge state taxation of interstate commerce (*Complete Auto Transit v. Brady* [1977]). More recently, the Court has invoked this framework as a way to balance states' rights against national power on a case-by-case basis (see *Wardair Canada v. Florida Department of Revenue* [1986]; *Goldberg v. Sweet* [1989]; *Oklahoma Tax Commission v. Jefferson Lines* [1995]). These decisions were consistent with the changing and emerging jurisprudence in federalism, suggesting the impact of the preferences of the majority or the coalescence around a constrained and integrated judicial philosophy.

Although the Rehnquist Court issued several notable taxation decisions during the 1980s and 1990s, none of them proved exceptionally controversial. The Court would frequently uphold taxation programs and occasionally invalidate them. When it did invalidate tax arrangements, however, this tended to result from what the Court believed to be particularly clear violations of specific constitutional commands or legal doctrines. For example, eight members of the Court voted to invalidate a North Dakota use tax as applied to an office supply retailer with no physical presence in the state (*Quill Corp. v. North Dakota* [1992]). In doing so, the Court referenced a key precedent, *National Bellas Hess, Inc. v. Department of Revenue of Illinois* (1967), which held that state attempts to tax corporations with no physical presence within that state represented an unconstitutional restraint on interstate commerce. Similarly, relying on the Export Clause of the Constitution,[6] the Court invalidated the imposition of export taxes in *United States v. IBM* (1996) by a seven-to-two vote and *United States v. United States Shoe Corp.* (1998) in a nine-to-zero decision. The results reflect the impact of issue evolution: As the cases got easier or more difficult, the Court reacted in the predicted direction.

In other cases, however, the Court deferred to governmental revenue collection and distribution programs. In *South Dakota v. Dole* (1987), seven members of the Court found no constitutional violation in the federal government's conditioning the availability of highway funds on states establishing a minimum drinking age of twenty-one. In *South Carolina v. Baker* (1988), with only Justice O'Connor dissenting, the Court ruled that federal legislation had not violated the principle of intergovernmental tax immunity.

---

[6] According to Article I, Section 9, of the Constitution, "No Tax or Duty shall be laid on Articles exported from any state."

The Takings Clause

The Takings Clause represents the final major component of the Supreme Court's constitutional economic decisions since the mid-1950s. Again, the Court was largely deferential toward governmental actions in this area until the late 1980s. As previously noted, the Warren Court, exercising judicial restraint, unanimously deferred to Congress on how to interpret the Constitution's mandate on taking private property for "public use" in *Berman v. Parker*. The Burger Court extended that same deference to state legislatures in *Hawaii Housing Authority v. Midkiff* (1984). In an effort to break up land monopolies that had long plagued the islands, the state of Hawaii implemented a wide-ranging land reform program. In essence, the state program was to accomplish the goal of redistributing land ownership by, first, condemning parcels of residential real estate and compensating the owners and, second, reselling the property to those who had been leasing it. When this arrangement was challenged as violating the constitutional command that eminent domain powers be confined to "public use," the Court concluded that the state program was permissible because it furthered "a legitimate public *purpose*" (467 U.S. at 245; Coyne 1985). The Court would show the same deference to local governments in the more contentious case of *Kelo v. City of New London* (2005).

The Court has shown an unbroken history of deference to legislative interpretations of the Fifth Amendment's public use requirement. With the notable exception of *Kelo*, such cases have been decided unanimously and have occupied relatively little of the modern Supreme Court's attention. The settled nature of questions regarding the scope of "public use" has enabled the modern Supreme Court to concentrate its energies elsewhere.

By contrast, the Court's treatment of questions surrounding the types of governmental regulations that constitute takings requiring just compensation has been more uneven. Prior to the Rehnquist era, the Court generally engaged in "essentially ad hoc, factual inquiries" (*Penn Central Transportation Company v. City of New York* [1978], 438 U.S. at 124) that gave governments considerable latitude in pursuing regulation. For example, although the Court occasionally declared governmental activities to be takings (e.g., *Armstrong v. United States* [1960]; *Griggs v. Allegheny County* [1962]), the Warren (e.g., *United States v. Central Eureka Mining Co.* [1958]; *Goldblatt v. Hempstead* [1962]; *United States v. Caltex* [1952]; *YMCA v. United States* [1969]) and Burger

(see *Penn Central Transportation Company v. City of New York* [1978])
Courts typically gave governments wide latitude in pursuing regulatory
policies.

Not until the Rehnquist years did this deference toward governmental
policies begin to erode. That erosion was visible and swift. Its first evidence came in 1987 with the Court's decision in *First English Evangelical
Lutheran Church v. County of Los Angeles,* in which six justices held that
a regulatory ordinance deprived a church of its property in violation of
the Fifth Amendment. However, as discussed at the outset of this chapter, the Court's decision in *Nollan v. California Coastal Commission*
in the following term was a clearer indication of the more conservative Court's willingness to give greater attention to these property rights
matters.

Five years later, *Lucas v. South Carolina Coastal Council* demonstrated that *Nollan* had been no jurisprudential fluke. After a developer
purchased property on one of South Carolina's barrier islands, the state
passed an environmental regulation that ultimately prohibited him from
developing that property – which had been his intent at the time of purchase (Epstein 1993; Sax 1993). The Supreme Court agreed that the
Takings Clause required the state to compensate the developer, writing,
"When the owner of real property has been called upon to sacrifice *all*
economically beneficial uses in the name of the common good, that is, to
leave his property economically idle, he has suffered a taking" (O'Brien
2008a, 1056).

However, not all of the Rehnquist Court's takings decisions favored
property rights. In *Tahoe-Sierra Preservation Council v. Tahoe Regional
Planning Agency* (2002), a majority of the justices embraced the view that
a temporary moratorium on development did not represent a constitutional taking. That decision notwithstanding, the Rehnquist Court's overall orientation toward property rights issues did represent some modifica-
tion of previous Court holdings. Ultimately, that revised attitude toward
the Takings Clause was perhaps best articulated by the chief justice himself, writing for the majority in a 1994 case:[7] "We see no reason why
the Takings Clause of the Fifth Amendment, as much a part of the Bill
of Rights as the First Amendment or Fourth Amendment, should be relegated to the status of a poor relation in these comparable circumstances"
(*Dolan v. City of Tigard,* 512 U.S. at 392).

---

[7] That case, *Dolan v. City of Tigard,* held that a city's attempt to attach certain land use
conditions to a building permit without providing compensation was unconstitutional.

MODELING THE CONSTITUTIONAL ECONOMIC CASES

When we first empirically tested the applicability of our integrated model of Supreme Court decision making in Chapter 4, we noted several things. For one, with respect to our universe of constitutional decisions, none of the variables representing the policy preferences of the other branches was statistically significant. Rather, only the attitudinal variable and each of the legal variables (precedent, on-point precedent, and issue evolution) were statistically significant predictors of the Court's constitutional decisions (see Table 4.2). This, we argued, was consistent with the view that separation-of-powers concerns are at their nadir in constitutional cases.

Similarly, when we assessed the model's applicability across issue domains, we highlighted a number of results. The Court's policy preferences and all three legal variables exhibited statistical significance in the hypothesized directions, though precedent's impact was somewhat more pronounced in the economic cases (see Table 4.3). The presidential variable was a statistically significant predictor of civil rights and liberties decisions, but not for the economic cases. Conversely, neither of the congressional variables was relevant to decision making in civil rights and liberties cases, but the House of Representatives appeared as a statistically significant factor in decision making on economic issues.

Unfortunately, the results obtained in those analyses tell us very little about the subset of economic cases that were decided on constitutional grounds. This is so because, of the 1,866 economic cases the Court decided between 1953 and 2000, only 235 (about 12.5 percent) were decided on constitutional grounds. Similarly, the conclusions that emerged from the analysis of constitutional cases in Chapter 4 were disproportionately driven by civil rights and liberties issues – 1,512 of the 1,747 constitutional cases are from the domain of civil rights and liberties.

What does our integrated model suggest for this subset of cases? The constitutional economic cases bring to the forefront opposing theoretical pressures on the Court. On one hand, the constitutional context of this subset of cases should free the Court from worrying about other institutional actors and allow judicial preferences to weigh more heavily. On the other hand, the less-salient nature of the economic issues may lessen the Court's motivation to act on its preferences. In other words, though the constitutional nature of these cases may afford the Court greater freedom to pursue its collective policy preferences, the justices may not possess a strong motivation to do so. If the Court has to strategically

TABLE 7.1. *Integrated Model of Supreme Court Decision Making: Constitutional Economic Cases, 1953–2000 Terms*

	Model	Change in Probability
Supreme Court	2.37	.06
	(1.48)	
President	−.85*	−.10
	(.36)	
House	−.79	−.03
	(1.15)	
Senate	−1.33	−.02
	(2.47)	
Precedent	.52**	.12
	(.15)	
On Point	2.33**	.80
	(1.07)	
Issue Evolution	−.20	−.05
	(.22)	
Constant	1.01	
	(.71)	
Chi²	.00	
Log Likelihood	−144.6	
N	235	

** $p < .01$, * $p < .05$

Probabilities represent the growth (or decline) in the probability of a liberal decision for every one standard deviation change in the independent variable or from 0 to 1 for dummy variables, holding all the other independent variables at their respective means.

choose its separation-of-powers battles, why would it risk retaliation by Congress or the president on an issue area that is less crucial to judicial policy preferences and less critical to its institutional clout? Thus, we consider our model's applicability to these constitutional economic decisions with some uncertainty, not knowing the extent to which the less salient nature of these cases may have consequences for the relative influence of judicial preferences.

Table 7.1 contains the results obtained when our integrated model of Supreme Court decision making is applied to the 235 constitutional economic cases decided between 1953 and 2000. Here, in contrast to the models examined thus far, the only meaningful statistically significant variables are the two representing precedent. Indeed, both the precedent variable and the on-point precedent variable are statistically significant and in the expected direction. This suggests that legal considerations have played an important role in the modern Supreme Court's handling of constitutional economic cases, particularly when precedents exist that are directly on point.

The statistical significance of these legal variables is consistent with the idea that, in general, the modern Supreme Court has endeavored to standardize its treatment of these constitutional economic cases in order to make them a less prominent part of the institution's agenda. The substantive importance of these legal variables is best illustrated by considering the post-*Brown* (more precisely, the post-*Berman*) Court's handing of economic substantive due process cases. In the late nineteenth and early twentieth centuries, the Court styled itself as the ultimate arbiter of the "reasonableness" of economic regulations. Symbolized by the infamous decision in *Lochner v. New York* (1905), the Court brought a scattershot approach to this area of law for some time to come.

By the *Brown* era, however, the Court was adopting a far different attitude toward this issue. As noted, in its first major substantive due process case, *Williamson v. Lee Optical Company* (1955), the Warren Court served notice that it would not be governed by *Lochner*-style jurisprudence. Justice Douglas's opinion laid down the gauntlet, and *Williamson* would remain the authoritative word on economic due process issues for decades to come. The Court also held that states could require railroads to employ a minimum number of workers in the interests of public safety. In doing so, the Court underscored the necessity of deference, noting, "Whether full-crew laws are necessary to further railroad safety is a matter for legislative determination" (*Locomotive Firemen v. Chicago R. I. and Pac. R. Co.*, 393 U.S. at 129 [1968]).

Despite changes, the Court continued to embrace this doctrinal approach to economic due process cases. The Burger Court repeatedly turned back economic due process challenges to state regulations, with liberal Justices Brennan and Marshall joining conservatives including Burger and Rehnquist to uphold governmental regulations in the mining (*Usery v. Turner Elkhorn Mining Co.* [1976]), petroleum (*Exxon Corp. v. Governor of Maryland* [1978]), automotive (*New Motor Vehicle Board v. Orrin W. Fox Co.* [1978]), and agricultural (*Hodel v. Indiana* [1981]) sectors. In *Duke Power Co. v. Carolina Environmental Study Group* (1978), the justices even said the following in dismissing yet another substantive due process challenge to economic regulation: "That the [legislative] accommodation struck may have profound and far-reaching consequences . . . provides all the more reason for this Court to defer to the congressional judgment unless it is demonstrably arbitrary or irrational" (438 U.S. at 83–84).

Notably, the two precedent variables are statistically significant and in the correct direction. Although it is in the expected direction, not even the attitudinal variable has a significant impact on the Court's decisions in these cases. The variables representing the policy positions of the House, and Senate fall short of statistical significance and are in the wrong direction. The presidential variable is significant, but in the wrong direction. Finally, although the issue evolution variable's sign is in the expected direction, it falls well short of significance.

Some of these results may appear surprising at first blush, but they are remarkably consistent with a number of underlying realities. Consider the attitudinal variable's failure to attain statistical significance. In one sense, the variable's lack of statistical significance is surprising. On the one hand, we would expect that, because these economic cases are constitutional issues, the relative absence of institutional constraints would create a favorable climate within which the justices' policy preferences would be of paramount importance. On the other hand, there are several factors that make the variable's overall lack of statistical significance more comprehensible.

On a theoretical level, individual voting patterns in the Court's economic cases tend to scale poorly, as the voting dimensions are more fluid than those in civil rights and liberties cases (Ducat and Dudley 1987; Hagle and Spaeth 1992, 1993; Rohde and Spaeth 1976; Segal and Spaeth 1993, 2002). In addition, a relatively high proportion of the modern Supreme Court's constitutional economic decisions have been unanimously decided (46 percent). By contrast, just 11 percent of the constitutional economic cases were decided by a single vote. That so many of these cases were decided unanimously or near unanimously may help to explain the attitudinal variable's lack of significance.

Although the attitudinal variable did not register as statistically significant, this might be expected to change as general doctrinal patterns begin to support the notion that ideological changes in the Court have influenced recent decision making. In particular, changes in Contract Clause, economic due process, Commerce Clause, and eminent domain doctrine have reflected the Court's ideological changes (Fischel 1995; Keck 2004; Maltz 2000; Olivetti and Worsham 2003; Yarbrough 2000, 104–120). It must also be recalled that the Court's renewed interest in the constitutional economic cases has been comparatively recent and that the bulk of the period we analyze saw the Court attempting to marginalize these cases.

Similarly, the issue evolution variable has no impact in this subset of cases. This indicates that, with respect to constitutional economic cases, the extent to which cases became increasingly difficult did not lead the Court toward more conservative judicial outcomes. The variable's lack of statistical significance in this particular model is likely explained by a combination of empirical and practical factors. As an empirical matter, the dispersion of the issue evolution variable is considerably smaller with respect to this subset of cases than in any of the other three. In other words, the modern Court's constitutional economic case law has exhibited comparatively little fluidity, as the issues relevant to these cases have not evolved to the extent that the issues in the other subsets we analyze have. The fact that this subset of cases has the Court behaving more "liberally" – deferring to governmental regulations on economic activity in three of every five cases – than any other subset of cases buttresses this conclusion.

As a practical matter, it must be reiterated that the post–*Berman* Court's main objective was to marginalize these cases and remove them from their agenda. Arguably, at least until the mid-1980s, the Court accomplished this by attending to precedent. In emphasizing the value of precedent in these economic cases, the Court exhibited great deference to regulation of economic affairs by all levels of government. Regardless of the "difficulty" of the case at hand, then, the Court's desire to extricate itself from economic cases decided on constitutional grounds overrode any impact that might have been generated by increases in case difficulty.

None of the strategic variables (except the president) is statistically significant in this subset of cases, and each of those variables is in the wrong direction. Upon reflection, the presidential variable's unexpected sign are readily explicable. Wanting to free up docket space for civil liberties and rights cases, the post-1953 Supreme Court has been rather consistent in its economic decisions. According to the Supreme Court Data Base, approximately 60 percent of the constitutional economic decisions during this period were decided in a liberal direction. However, during that same period, Republicans occupied the White House much of the time. Similarly, when the Court did begin to rewrite its interpretations of economic areas during the 1990s, it pushed the law in a conservative direction during Democrat Bill Clinton's administration.

Moreover, with respect to constitutional economic cases, there is often a disconnect between the president's ideological stance and the position adopted by the Office of the Solicitor General. In areas such as federal regulation, federalism, and the Commerce Clause, the SG takes a consistent position, regardless of the current president (Pacelle 2003; 2006). In short, because the SG's positions are not dependent on the party in the White House, the president's influence over the Supreme Court's constitutional economic decisions is arguably diluted.

There are at least two potential explanations for why the policy positions of Congress manifest no statistically significant impact in this particular model. First, as we previously noted, modern economic cases tend to be of somewhat lower salience to members of Congress than issues relating to civil rights or civil liberties. In addition to being issues about which legislators tend to care less, they are also visible to comparatively few legislative constituents. Second, as the Court increasingly deferred to legislative judgment in its economic jurisprudence as a general matter, perhaps the justices came to view overall notions of deference – letting Congress do what it pleased with respect to economic matters – rather than more rigid notions of ideological compatibility as the most effective way to placate the legislative branch.

The impact of the strategic variables may also be attenuated by the fact that a number of constitutional economic cases involve state policies and not federal laws. Many of the Takings and Contract Clause cases involve state policy, so the Court's decisions would not engender presidential or Congressional reactions. Therefore, the Court would have further insulation.

All that being said, recent changes in Contract Clause, Takings Clause, and economic due process jurisprudence suggest that precedent is not inviolate. In fact, it may well be that the Court's renewed attention to these legal areas will lead to a magnification of attitudinal considerations and cause the significance of the precedent variables to attenuate. Throughout the bulk of the period we examine, the Court exhibited strikingly high levels of deference to legal precedent in order to focus its attention on other legal areas. During the Rehnquist Court, fissures developed in that consensus as more conservative justices opted to revisit a number of those long-held economic precedents (Schultz and Smith 1996).

To what degree, then, might the results of the preceding analysis be dependent on particular historical periods? We have seen that, in the aggregate, considerations related to legal precedent are the only significant predictors of Supreme Court decision making in this cluster of cases.

However, as we have suggested, the Court's emphasis on economic issues arguably has shifted in recent times. In the 1950s and 1960s, the Court's overriding concern with civil liberties and rights issues led it to marginalize economic cases decided on constitutional grounds. When those disfavored cases did manage to reach the Court's doorstep, the justices disposed of them in the most expeditious fashion possible – they looked to precedent. But by the late 1970s and certainly into the 1980s, more conservative justices began to rethink the wisdom of numerous economic precedents. Is it possible, then, that the influence of precedent is particularly strong in the early years of our analysis but declines or even disappears later? Conversely, might the attitudinal considerations that do not attain statistical significance in the aggregate analysis do so in more contemporary times? In other words, is it possible that modeling 1953 to 2000 as a single period masks a more complicated story of decision making?

To test this possibility empirically, we subdivided the constitutional economic data into two subsets for purposes of an auxiliary data analysis. Specifically, we divided our data using the median year of our analysis – 1977 – as the cut point. Thus, we examined the Court's constitutional economic decisions from 1953 to 1976 in one model and the Court's constitutional economic decisions from 1977 to 2000 in a second model. The results show a transition of the cases. In the early period, only issue evolution is statistically significant, but the ideology of the Court ($p = .053$) and precedent ($p = .067$) are so close that they can be considered to have an influence on decision making. In the more recent time period (1977–2000), only precedent and the Senate have a statistically significant impact on decision making in this subset of cases.

It is difficult to make too many authoritative statements about these data because they encompass a loose conglomeration of different issues. But that has not stopped us to this point. To gain some leverage on these issues, we divide the analysis by Court. If we focus on the Court as a control variable, we have some relatively small numbers of cases, but the results are suggestive. For the Warren Court, we only have fifty-four cases, but the results show that only the attitudinal variable is statistically significant, which makes sense. This is an increasingly liberal Court making liberal decisions (as coded by the Supreme Court Data Base). Indeed, more than two-thirds of the decisions are decided in the liberal direction. The Court continued to press these decisions, deferring to the elected branches and trying to impose some consistency to extricate itself from these areas regardless of the difficulty of the issue. This would explain why issue evolution is not statistically significant (it is in the correct direction but misses significance, even at the .10 level). Similarly, the Warren Court's refusal to adhere to the precedents that got its predecessors in trouble explains why that variable is not statistically significant.

For the Burger Court ($N = 107$), only precedent and issue evolution are statistically significant and in the correct direction. The decline in the percentage of liberal decisions was not great, remaining higher than 60 percent. Thus, by this time, the Court was largely adhering to the precedents that took them out of the constitutional economic cases. For the Rehnquist Court ($N = 74$), only the Senate and precedent variables are statistically significant. There was a decline in the percentage of cases decided in the liberal direction, but the overall total remained higher than 53 percent. The decline coincided with the move of the Senate to the right. Precedent remained an important factor in deciding these cases.

Because these cases are constitutional, it appears that the Court had the opportunity to impose its will with little threat of outright reversal. Yet history taught the justices that the other branches have weapons short of reversing the decisions. The Court had incurred self-inflicted wounds and appeared to have learned its lesson. This was a judicial restraint born of separation of powers and forged in a battle that exposed the weaknesses of an unelected body that possesses neither the sword nor the purse. The Warren and Burger Courts followed precedent and practiced abstinence. The Rehnquist Court showed signs of revisiting these issues. If this is not apparent in the aggregate analysis, there are nevertheless a few important landmark decisions that suggest that decisions and doctrine may begin to diverge from the trends of the past half century.

CONCLUSION

Given the finite nature of agenda space, the competition between civil liberties and economic cases is a zero-sum game. Given the difference in the salience of the issues, it is relatively easy to see who won. To the extent that the Court made a commitment in Footnote Four and *Brown v. Board of Education*, it needed to carve out agenda space to meet its promises. The justices who were selected to protect the New Deal – Douglas, Black, and Frankfurter – would remain on the Court for more than two decades. They became an institutional memory for their junior colleagues. They were associated with the other two branches when the battle between the Court and the president was at its peak and were dispatched to make certain it did not reignite. Roosevelt was famous for putting people on the Court and then convincing them to leave so he could move them elsewhere, but not Douglas, Black, and Frankfurter. Their litmus test was government regulation of the economy.

The results for the constitutional, less salient cases are markedly different than those for the salient cases, whether constitutional or statutory (and, as we will see in the next chapter, the less salient statutory cases as well). Although many of the variables do not show an apparent impact on judicial decision making, we do not merely worship at the altar of statistical significance. There are some hidden effects that are not revealed by the initial coefficients. We find considerable variation by individual Court, reflecting that this subset of issues is shaped by countervailing pushes and pulls, according to our theory – so the fact that we have mixed results is not so surprising.

Soon after the Court capitulated under the threat posed by Roosevelt, the acceptance of big government and regulation became widespread. None of the Republican presidents prior to Reagan made any concerted effort to turn back the clock on the regulatory state (Reichley 1981). This is one of the reasons why the presidential variable does not exert a positive significant impact on the decisions in these areas. Even the later changes that saw the Court reintroduce itself to constitutional economic cases continued to play out while a Democrat was president. The hidden impact here is the attitudinal variable. Many of the changes began to emerge when Scalia came to the Court. If there were not the sheer numbers of decisions to be reflected in the aggregate analysis, there were important landmark decisions that would have a long half-life and serve as influential constraints and opportunities for future justices.

Congress played a modest role at best according to our models, but once again there was a hidden impact. The Court clearly signaled and continually reinforced its deference to Congress and state legislatures. The double standard of Footnote Four promised that the Court would not interfere with the priorities of Congress. The Court generally made good on this promise. If particular decisions did not reflect the median member of the sitting Congress, it was clearly understood that the House and Senate were the primary actors with regard to the constitutional economic cases.[8]

Issue evolution was not statistically significant across the entire period and was only important for an intermittent period. Again, the results

---

[8] Some percentage of these cases involves state laws, mitigating the impact of Congress. The Senate has an impact for part of the period, which may be a function of the fact that the Senate represents state interests better than the House does.

may be a bit misleading. The Court's consistency undercuts the impact of issue evolution. With the Court committed to deference, it was clear that the particular facts of the case were relatively meaningless in structuring decisions. Precedent, however, increasingly played an important role. The hidden impact of precedent was seen mostly during Earl Warren's tenure. The Court was abandoning the old precedents that permitted it to meddle in economic cases. In doing so, the Court was establishing its own precedents and adhering to them. Some may argue that this was simply a manifestation of the attitudinal variable, but we contend that this was the real impact of precedent. The Court was not reading its own preferences into the law. Rather, it was exercising judicial restraint by confining the issues and making the decisions consistent to guide the lower courts and permitting itself to retreat from policing these areas of law.

The Court's decision to confine its review and show deference would play a significant role in structuring its decision making in the statutory economic cases. This could not occur until the Court resolved the threshold question of legislative power and removed the temptation to use the tools of substantive due process. The results of the Court's switch in time will be seen in the next chapter. As soon as Congress and the agencies could write the law and know that it was constitutional, attention focused on the interpretation of statutory provisions and administrative regulations. By settling the law, the Court deconstitutionalized it. The issues were narrower, and the Court had less of an abiding stake in any individual case. The primary motivation was often to settle the law, not to settle it in a particular direction.

More recently, the Court has expressed greater interest in the economic cases. To some justices, these issues are salient. Whereas the majority of the Court began to move to judicial restraint in dealing with civil rights and individual liberties issues, there were signs of a creeping judicial activism in economic issues. Is this an aberration or merely the result of issue evolution? Does it predict a renewed salience for such issues? Whatever the ultimate result, it is certain that the silence if the Court reverts to deference or the aftershocks if it does not will be evident in civil liberties and civil rights as well as the statutory economic cases for decades.

8

Policing the Boundaries

Statutory Economic Issues

Leave it to New Yorkers. Only in New York would a court of original jurisdiction be called the Supreme Court. Of course, this begs the question of what one should call courts higher than the "Supreme Court."[1] It seems that the United States and most states have it right: The Supreme Court is the final court, and its decisions are superior to all others. However, not every case decided by the Supreme Court is a monumental decision that reshapes the legal landscape. Some state supreme courts, like Montana and Wyoming, have mandatory jurisdiction, meaning that they need to hear every case properly brought to the docket. The U.S. Supreme Court faced similar constraints until Congress altered its jurisdiction in 1925 (Estreicher and Sexton 1986; Pacelle 1991).

In 1988, Congress intervened again to cut the Court's mandatory jurisdiction even further (Pacelle 1991; Perry 1991). Nevertheless, it is still possible for the U.S. Supreme Court to end up with some cases that are, shall we say, "less equal than others." Not every case yields a life-altering decision. For every Supreme Court decision that makes the front page of the *New York Times* or the table of contents of a Constitutional law textbook, there are scores of decisions that hardly cause a ripple. The luxurious quarters of the Supreme Court and its modern authority and impact give it a quasireligious aura. When that power and aura are combined with the normative concepts of law and justice, the Court casts a considerable shadow. The justices are often seen as a bevy of Platonic guardians casting their thunderbolts in the form of decisions that

---

[1] It turns out that it is nothing too exciting; New York opted to call its highest tribunal the Court of Appeals.

interpret and fundamentally alter the Constitution, change the nature of federalism, redraw the boundaries of separation of powers, and rebalance the lines between government authority and individual rights. They are, in a sense, modern political theorists, carving out the evolving national identity.

Of course, this is no surprise to proponents of the attitudinal model, who argue that justices are unencumbered in their decision making. This would also explain why the confirmation of a new justice can become a pitched partisan battle. But if that were all there was to it – if justices were super-legislators who wore black robes and had lifetime tenure – we would not have many unanimous decisions. We also would not have many decisions like *United States v. Goodyear Tire and Rubber Co.* (1989), in which Chief Justice Rehnquist assigned the opinion of the Court to Justice Thurgood Marshall. This is noteworthy. First, the opinion of the Court is its official policy statement and offers the reasoning for the decision. More importantly, perhaps, it is precedent for all similar cases and binding on lower courts. What is curious at first glance is that Marshall and Rehnquist were polar opposites ideologically. Therefore, it is hard to imagine why a conservative chief justice would allow a very liberal justice to write a consequential policy statement that would be binding on the Supreme Court, lower courts, and administrators (Rohde 1972). It is curious unless, of course, this was not a consequential case or there is more to Supreme Court decision making than mere ideology (Slotnick 1979).

Consider *United States v. Whiting Pools* (1983). When Lloyd Relin marched up the steps of the Supreme Court on April 19, 1983, he was probably more than a little nervous. This was his first (and it would turn out to be his only) audience before the High Court. Not only had some of the greatest attorneys and most brilliant orators preceded him, but Mr. Relin was also matched up that day against the OSG, arguably the nation's most elite law firm and undoubtedly the most successful (Pacelle 2003; Ubertaccio 2005). When he gave his Gettysburg Address, a modest Abraham Lincoln remarked, "The world will little note, nor long remember what we say here...." History tells us that he was wrong. If anyone had made a similar comment about the *Whiting Pools* case, it would have been much closer to the truth.

The New York Times had a brief article on page 9 detailing the decision on June 9, 1983. Unlike *Brown v. Board of Education*, it was not readily apparent to everyone that millions of lives would be changed by the decision. Certainly, Mr. Relin and Whiting Pools were interested in the outcome (they won, by the way). The SG and the IRS were certainly interested observers and participants. According to Sheppard's citation index, the *Whiting Pools* precedent has been cited just twice in subsequent Supreme Court majority opinions (and another four times in dissents) in more than twenty-five years. (By contrast, *Grove City v. Bell* and *United States v. Leon*, decided in the next term (1984), have each been cited positively more than twenty times, and the latter was cited more than fifty times). The Court's decision was unanimous. Normal adversaries like Justice Brennan and Justice Rehnquist, who voted together less than a third of the time in civil rights and liberties cases, supported the same side in this case (as well as in more than 80 percent of the internal revenue decisions) (Epstein et al. 2003, 572).

So why did the Supreme Court even bother to grant certiorari in *Whiting Pools* or *United States v. Goodyear Tire and Rubber* or even in *Donaldson FKA Sweet v. United States* (yet another economic decision based on statutory grounds)? By any objective measure, there were dozens of "more important" or more visible petitions on the plenary docket. There was a large number of cases that did not attract the four votes necessary to grant cert which certainly would have had greater immediate and more lasting impact. In its decisions, the Court occasionally gives us a glimpse of why it opted to spend a finite resource (agenda space) on a particular case. In each of the three economic cases noted above, the author of the majority opinion revealed that the Court granted the petitions to resolve conflicts between the circuits.

That the Court was unanimous in these cases and in 84 of the 218 internal revenue cases decided in this period is a potential signal that the Court was often less interested in which party won the case than in settling disagreements between the Courts of Appeals. It might also be evidence that the justices care more about settling the case than about being ideologically rigid. If this is the case, it may well be that legal goals trump political ones under some circumstances. And, dare we say, it might mean that there are some limits to the attitudinal model.

In this chapter, we examine cases that are less salient to the Court (economic issues) and also have a statutory basis. The latter means that Congress can overturn a decision more easily if the issue is salient to its members. For these reasons (the lack of salience and the statutory nature of the cases), we expect the Court to hew more closely to precedent and be cognizant of the elected branches of government in making its decisions. Given the primacy of the attitudinal model, we still expect the Court's ideology to play a role, but it may be less dominant than in the constitutional or more salient cases.

CHANGING THE COURT'S AGENDA: THE DECLINE OF ISSUE SALIENCE

In the wake of the partisan realignment that would define politics for at least a generation, the Court stood as the last major barrier to the New Deal (Miller 1968). A partisan realignment juxtaposes two competing ideologies and can lead to a continuing constitutional stalemate or crisis. By definition, a partisan realignment is forged in crisis (Sundquist 1983). A major calamity, usually of an economic nature, unfolds. The minority, or out party, has a huge electoral incentive to embrace the new issue. If the public is sufficiently angry and has transferred blame to the dominant party, an enduring partisan realignment may result.

We typically identify a realignment after the fact, but one of the major signs is when the former out party captures the White House and Capitol Hill, often after a long hiatus (Burnham 1970; Mayhew 2002). Consider the resulting institutional arrangement: The new president and Congress often feel that they have a clear mandate from the people, so they rush in and attempt to solve the nation's economic ills. But their executive orders and legislative pronouncements may provoke judicial review, and therein lies the rub. The Supreme Court that remains proximate to Congress on the map of the city is miles away ideologically. The majority of the Court is part of the old political coalition (Gates 1992; Lasser 1985). Thus, the Court is likely to view bold new initiatives with a skeptical eye.

The Supreme Court of the early 1930s tried to enforce the old norms and struck down a number of components of the economic relief packages that were part of the New Deal. This prompted a reaction from the president and precipitated a constitutional showdown that ended with the Court retreating (Leuchtenburg 1963, 1995; Whittington 2007). We have discussed the ramifications of this battle and how the Court reinvented itself to become the preeminent actor in civil rights and individual liberties. In this chapter, we examine another dimension of that institutional metamorphosis. How did the Court alter its focus as the salience of those issues changed?

A Court that was following the so-called double standard of Footnote Four had to implement a three-pronged strategy. First, it had to clear out the constitutional underbrush that was blocking the New Deal. We examined part of this in Chapter 7, and we mention it a few more times in this chapter. Second, the Court had to make good on its promise to protect the rights of insular minorities and individuals. We dealt with those issues in Chapter 5. Third, and related to the other two, the Court had to carve out the agenda space to attack restrictions on rights and liberties (Pacelle 1991, 1995).

As Roosevelt ultimately did pack the Court, the new members and the holdovers were legally constrained by the work of their predecessors. The Court had to reverse precedents limiting regulatory activities. In areas like antitrust and commerce, existing congressional legislation had been on the books for almost a half century. The problem was that previous Courts had emasculated statutes like the Sherman Antitrust Act (McCloskey 1960, 126–128). The Court had to reinstitute the power and authority of these dormant statutes. In addition, it had to legitimate the newer regulatory schemes that had developed under the New Deal. The Court's supportive decisions encouraged Congress and the president to continue to pursue new areas and expand on existing ones (Baird 2007).

The civil liberties and individual rights cases were slow to materialize. The Court was inconsistent in its early decisions, and any progress was interrupted by World War II, the Cold War, and the Communist scare (Murphy 1972; Rehnquist 1998; Tedford and Herbeck 2009). As soon as the Court determined that Congress had the authority to create the building blocks of the regulatory state, its attention turned to the myriad of challenges to particular regulations. This would consume a great deal of agenda space. Other economic issues, narrower and more private in nature, would need to be removed to create that space (Pacelle 1991).

The Court began to abandon the ordinary economic cases and used the additional space to expand its attention to regulation. The Court's decisions in those cases signaled its intent to eliminate them from the agenda. The most prevalent types of ordinary economic litigation that were decided on the merits of the fact situation stemmed from statutory provisions in the Jones Act (Farber and Frickey 1991; Hill 1995) and the Longshoremen and Harbor Workers Compensation Act (Force 1999; Warshauer and Dittman 2005). These statutes created the authority for compensating some classes of injured workers. Despite the novelty of these acts and the vagueness inherent in the statutes, these cases did not flood the Court's institutional agenda. Apparently, the Supreme Court chose to defer to lower courts in these types of cases. The decline of attention to areas like tax cases, ordinary economic cases, state regulation, and government-as-litigant cases suggests that the Supreme Court made a conscious effort to reduce the agenda space available to those types of issues (Pacelle 1991).

DECISION MAKING IN NONSALIENT CASES

How would each of the traditional models predict decision making in the economic cases? The legal model would argue that the Court will abide by precedent in making its decisions. Particularly in less salient cases, it is more important that the law be settled than that it be settled correctly. The Court will also pay attention to the clear language of statutes and the intent of the framers of that legislation. The attitudinal model would see the individual justices exercise their policy preferences and locate the outcome at the sincere preferences of the median justice. The strategic model would suggest that the Court will carefully weigh the preferences of the president and Congress and try to find a comfortable place between its sincere preferences and the ideal preferences of the other branches. One might think of this strategic context as the Court choosing a policy closest to its ideal policy preferences but also where the incentive for Congress and/or the president to challenge the Court's action remains small. Strategically, the Court might also pay attention to the position of the agency that writes the rules and implements the directives. The Court may do this because the agencies could have powerful allies on congressional committees or throughout the executive branch.

If we had to offer a general hypothesis to express our expectations in the statutory economic cases, we would offer the legal model and Scenario 2. Although the lack of issue salience might argue for the dominance of the legal model, each of the models may have an impact under different circumstances. There are a number of issues that comprise this summary category. Some may be more salient, suggesting that the attitudinal model may also emerge to structure decision making. In some other areas, Congress may find the issues salient, and the Court would be well advised to act strategically. Perhaps the relationships between the agencies and the elected branches establish the context that helps guide the Court in its decision making.

Students of the bureaucracy normally conceptualize the process by which administrative and regulatory policies emerge, change, and are implemented as a function of one of three models: bureaucratic politics, subsystem theory, and a principal-agent model (Eisner, Worsham, and

Ringquist 2006; Ferejohn and Shipan 1990; Fiorina and Shepsle 1989). It is important to appreciate the dynamics of the regulatory process in order to understand what factors would influence the Court in its decision making in this area. On the macro level, it is critical to remember that the bureaucratic structure is nested in a representative government and that agencies are theoretically responsive to elected officials (Lewis 2005; Selden, Brudney, and Kellough 1998).

The bureaucratic politics approach focuses on the constraints and opportunities imposed by the organizational setting (Wilson 1980). It accepts the fact that the agency does not receive clear directives or signals from Congress. This provides bureaucrats and regulators with a fair amount of discretion in discharging their responsibilities.[2] This perspective argues that policy change is a product of the changes within the organization (Wood and Waterman 1994). Part of the potential for policy change could come from the leadership that a new president puts in place or the political context. For example, under unified government, the bureaucratic system is more susceptible to politicization by the president. However, presidents do seem constrained to balance their goals of policy change with concerns for expertise and competence (Lewis 2005). The more entrenched a bureaucracy or the more acute the pressures from Congress and other actors, the less likely it is that the president's new appointee will be able to change the direction of the agency (Eisner, Worsham, and Ringquist 2006, 70; Nathan 1975). This invites judicial activism and the impact of the attitudinal variable on decision making.

The subsystems perspective is the traditional notion of subgovernments (Freeman 1965), issue networks (Heclo 1978), whirlpools of influence, and iron triangles (Cater 1964). The names and the details may vary, but the overall notion is that a series of private actors work closely with public officials to influence public policy. Interest groups work with executive agencies and relevant committees and subcommittees to produce policy through rules and regulations (McFarland 1987; M. Smith 1993). Such a system may be the logical and inevitable outcome of the pluralist Madisonian design laid out in "Federalist 10." McConnell (1966) and Lowi (1969), among others, feel that this creates a situation in which groups are not forced to compete with each other, and government is rendered impotent and unable to plan. Some argue that certain regulatory agencies

---

[2] Of course, some of the classics in the field, most notably Downs (1967), focus on individual-level behavior and the motivations of particular bureaucrats. We are more interested in the organizational opportunities and constraints and how they shape the environment that the Court faces when making decisions.

have been captured by the very industries they are supposed to regulate (Quirk 1981). Presidents have tried, generally without success, to break into these subsystems. Of course, the Court is a threat to such a closed subsystem. The subsystems perspective can constrain the Court and suggests a strategic response. The Court has to be careful not to provoke congressional retaliation.

The principal-agent theory posits a hierarchical relationship in which a principal employs an agent who is an expert. Because of the costs of monitoring and the information asymmetry, the agent may shirk or pursue his or her own agenda. Principals have to monitor the behavior of the agents to rein in their discretion (Brehm and Gates 1997). The oversight mechanisms are often the proverbial fire alarms that go off when a member of the subsystem perceives an impending problem (McCubbins and Schwartz 1984). Principals, like Congress (and its agents, the committees), can rein in the agents through oversight and by rewriting legislation (Bendor and Moe 1985; Ferejohn and Shipan 1990; Hammond 1986; Maltzman 1997; Sinclair 2007). The president may attempt to use the budget or staffing to the same ends, and of course, the courts can be brought in to enforce rules (Wood 1988). Still, this theory seems to argue for a legal model and deference to the agencies. The principal-agent model suggests the need for expertise from the agents. There is an expectation that generalist judges will show deference to these experts.

No single model explains the work of each executive agency and its relationship with other institutional actors. Rather, different agencies have different dynamics and relationships with the elected branches. Therefore, for some issues, the expertise is dominant, in others the subsystem dominates, and in others the more typical bureaucratic politics define the area. It is also likely that the dominant mode of decision making may change over time from one form to another.

ISSUE EVOLUTION AND PRECEDENT

In this section, as in Chapter 6, we examine some of the major statutes and the policy areas that comprise statutory economic issues. Because these issues are less salient than the civil rights and liberties cases, the Court should not be as interested in them. Because they are statutory, the Court will have to share policy making with the other branches. The tax and regulatory cases involve two sets of policy entrepreneurs – congressional committees and bureaucratic agencies. These issues arguably bring the executive and legislative branches into the Court's calculations.

There are long- and short-term factors that influence agencies (Lewis 2005). In the short term, Congress can shift its oversight or budgeting priorities. The president can attempt to exert authority by changing the leadership of the agency. Although that affects the individual bureau, broad-level policy initiatives can sweep across a variety of agencies. The deregulation movement of the 1970s and 1980s ultimately altered the environment for virtually all agencies. The movement started during the Nixon and Ford administrations and picked up steam in the Carter administration, beginning with the transportation and airline industries (Morrison and Winston 1986; Robyn 1987). The Reagan administration pushed the concept even further, pursuing deregulation, devolution, and defunding (Eisner, Worsham, and Ringquist 2006, 175–178). Additional short-term factors could intrude on the individual agencies and influence their environments and the rules and regulations emanating from them. Wood and Waterman (1993, 501–503) argue that bureaus are influenced by discrete events, event progressions, and what they call "tonal" shifts in the policy environment. The responses, they argue, may be immediate or delayed or may unfold over time (Wood and Waterman 1993, 503–504).

The range of economic activity before the Court over the last half century is rather remarkable. The New Deal led to a proliferation of regulatory agencies and spawned a great deal of litigation. Among the major pieces of legislation that were interpreted in more than fifty full decisions in the 1953–2000 period were the Internal Revenue Code of 1939 and 1954 and their amendments (218 cases), the National Labor Relations Act (166), the Interstate Commerce Act (124), the Natural Gas Act (83), the Sherman Antitrust Act (78), the Bankruptcy Act (63), the Securities and Exchange Act (56), and the Clayton Antitrust Act (53). In all, 906 decisions involved regulation. The Court was also asked to interpret provisions of the Federal Rules of Civil Procedure in more than sixty cases. Many of them involved ordinary economic disputes.

We posited that the individual liberties and civil rights cases were salient, which means that they followed different patterns than the cases we examine in this chapter. In stark contrast to the civil rights and individual liberties cases, fully 46 percent of the statutory economic cases were decided unanimously (compared with fewer than 30 percent in civil rights and civil liberties). In addition, the ratio of cases accepted to settle a lower court conflict versus the importance of the case is almost the exact opposite of that found in the civil rights and civil liberties cases. The Court accepted more than twice as many of these cases to settle a lower court conflict than because of the importance of the case (in about

40 percent of the cases, no reason was given). In the civil liberties and civil rights domain, more than twice as many cases were accepted because of the importance of the issue compared with lower court conflicts.

There was also great variance between the different areas within statutory economic cases. Securities regulation, environmental regulation, and antitrust looked more like civil rights and civil liberties cases. The Court took about half of the cases to settle a circuit conflict and half because of the importance of the issue in the case. Contrast that with government liability cases (36/3), internal revenue (144/13), ERISA (16/1), and bankruptcy (41/4) cases (numbers represent the ratio of circuit conflict/important issue), which do not resemble civil rights and individual liberties in any real fashion.

The number of unanimous cases and the rationale for granting most of the cert petitions suggests the reduced salience of these cases. Taken together, this leads us to posit that the relative impact of our independent variables will be different from the analysis of the more salient cases. Specifically, we hypothesize a diminished impact for the president and the Court and greater influence from Congress. We also expect precedent and issue evolution to exert statistically significant effects on decision making, controlling for the other variables.

Ordinary Economic Cases

This loose category of cases involves economic issues without a regulation component. Many of the individual areas share some common elements and similar dynamics. One of the largest categories of cases, those involving the United States as a tort defendant, demonstrates some trends that are tied to legislative actions and judicial responses. The doctrine of sovereign immunity forbids lawsuits against the government without its consent. Congress has periodically passed legislation that voluntarily surrenders some of the government's immunity. Thus, the ability to sue government is a legislatively created right (Schuck 1983, 40–43). The Court, in turn, has had to determine the extent to which the government is liable. In the government liability cases, important legislation like the Federal Tort Claims Act and the Miller Act created conditions for agenda growth. The surge of government-as-litigant cases coincides with the period surrounding the passage of the Federal Tort Claims Act in 1946. The Court was charged with interpreting this new statutory authorization, but again, few cases made it to the Supreme Court's agenda (Pacelle 1991).

The Court was responsible, in large part, for the lack of agenda allocation. In a major decision, *Feres v. United States* (1950), the Court barred the use of the Federal Tort Claims Act in suits by members of the Armed Services for injuries incurred in the military. This closed judicial access to a large number of potential cases. Congressional silence in the wake of *Feres* has left the decision intact. In *Bivens v. Six Unknown Named Federal Narcotics Agents* (1971), the Court appeared to expand federal tort actions by proposing an alternative to the exclusionary rule. Victims of illegal searches could sue the officer who participated in the search. But in *Chappell v. Wallace* (1983), the Court narrowed *Bivens*. In *United States v. Johnson* (1987), the Court expanded the *Feres* doctrine by holding that the death of a pilot caused by a civilian air controller was still a military activity and therefore denied the claim (Ball 1988). Because military injuries are the most significant portion of government tort cases, these decisions over almost four decades kept cases off the Court's docket. The Court has, on average, accepted only one or two government-as-litigant cases per term during the last twenty-five years.

With many of the ordinary economic cases, the Court was able to farm control of the issues out to the lower courts, intervening only when there was a serious circuit conflict. In some of the regulation areas, the Court found other fora such as Bankruptcy Court and the Court of Patent Appeals, later the Court of Appeals for the Federal Circuit. The latter, in particular, had a level of expertise that generalist courts lacked (Miller and Curry 2009). The Supreme Court has delegated decision making in these and other issue areas to other actors like the agencies and the lower courts.

Internal Revenue

Somewhere between the ordinary economic and regulation cases we find internal revenue cases. This is not surprising, as the internal revenue cases have regulatory aspects to them but at the same time often involve individual taxpayers or companies. The treatment of these cases in terms of the reasons for granting the petitions and the patterns of decisions also fell between those of the economic and regulatory cases. Many cases were accepted strictly to resolve a lower court conflict, and many decisions were unanimous. By far, the largest number of statutory economic cases during the last half century came from the Internal Revenue Codes of 1939 and 1954 (218 cases). The salience of internal revenue cases is front-page news. Or, more precisely, it is not. Epstein and Segal (2000) use front-page coverage in the *New York Times* as a proxy for public attention and salience. By that standard, there is little interest in and virtually no attention given to tax cases. In a study of 184 tax cases, a scant 3.8 percent attracted front-page *New York Times* coverage. By contrast, 37.3 percent of the sixty-seven CRA cases got front-page coverage (Epstein, Staudt, and Wiedenbeck 2003). The latter number is compounded when constitutional civil rights cases are added.

Internal revenue policy construction is dominated not by judicial decisions, but by legislative pronouncements. Internal revenue cases involve interpretations of the tax code and IRS policies.[3] Two important Internal Revenue Codes in 1939 and 1954 would be expected to have a major impact on levels of litigation. Clear tax codes would reduce the need for judicial supervision. Vague provisions would invite more litigation. The creation of specialized tax courts, however, would reduce litigation if the Supreme Court could delegate authority and autonomy to these specialized courts. In fact, the decline in the agenda space allocated to internal revenue cases paralleled the changes that created the Tax Court of the United States from the Board of Tax Appeals. Moreover, later changes in the Tax Court were advocated because the Supreme Court often refused to intervene unless there was direct lower court conflict and failed to deal with the ambiguities of the tax code (Dubroff 1979, 177).

In the area of federal taxation policy, "There has been a significant degree of deference on the part of the Court's majority to legislative product and process" in the 1912–2000 period (Staudt et al. 2005, 1946–1947). The Court has never given the executive branch the level of deference awarded to the legislature or the judiciary. The Court appeared to prioritize its own judge-made rules through the 1950s; however, by the 1960s, it became increasingly willing to claim deference to the legislature, thereby constraining its own discretion. This deference is ascribed to the Court's lack of expertise (in sharp contrast to civil rights cases). Tax decisions are particularly susceptible to congressional scrutiny and overrides, despite the deference and respect the Court shows Congress (Alvarez and Brehm 1998). The Court may be seeking to avoid congressional retaliation or may even be inviting Congress to clarify the law (Hausegger and Baum 1999; Staudt et al. 2005, 1969–1970). Whether the Court responds to Congress or the president in federal taxation cases, it is clear that the IRS is responsive to its political principals. According to Scholz and Wood (1998), this is evidence of political control of the IRS.

---

[3] There were some important decisions in the internal revenue area, but none that might qualify as landmark decisions.

Bankruptcy

Bankruptcy cases comprised a great deal of the agenda before the Court had broad discretion over its docket and in the wake of the Depression. As soon as it had discretion, the Court ultimately began to clear these cases off its agenda. When it did grant cert in a bankruptcy case, it was almost always to settle a lower court conflict, and most of the decisions were unanimous. Like the tax cases, the bankruptcy cases look a little like the ordinary economic issues and a little like regulation. Also, the Court was interested in delegating authority over the policing of the regulations to other actors.

The Bankruptcy Reform Act of 1978 represented the first major change in bankruptcy law in eighty years. It had important substantive and procedural elements. The major provision of the act was to set up a series of new bankruptcy courts and expand the responsibilities of the referees. This would presumably keep these cases off the Supreme Court's docket. The conventional wisdom was that the act would serve the public interest by providing an orderly mechanism for resolving disputes between creditors and debtors. However, Eric Posner (1997) argues that the act reflects the interests of organized lobbyists, such as banks and other large creditors, lawyers, bankruptcy judges, and Article III judges, and the institutional interests of members of Congress. Thus, Posner argued, it works to the detriment of debtors.

The 1978 statute has since been replaced by the Bankruptcy Abuse Prevention and Consumer Protection Act of 2005.[4] One of the major changes under the 2005 statute is the use of a strict "means test" to determine whether a debtor's filing under Chapter 7 was an "abuse" and subject to dismissal. Under the 1978 statute, this decision had been made by bankruptcy court judges, who were instructed to take into consideration the particular circumstances that had led to bankruptcy.

Labor Relations

Areas such as antitrust regulation and labor relations engendered substantial interest from the Court, government, and litigants. The treatment of these cases was somewhere between that of the salient civil liberties and rights cases and the other, less salient economic issues. Labor relations litigation includes a variety of individual issues involving unions, the

---

[4] An earlier version of the statute passed in 1997 but was pocket vetoed by President Clinton.

Wagner Act, also known as the National Labor Relations Act (NLRA), and the Fair Labor Standards Act, among others. In totality, labor relations cases represented the largest single area of regulation litigation.

The National Labor Relations Board was one of the creations of the New Deal Congress. It had to walk a line between unions and management and was frequently a target of political pressure. There were a number of amendments to the NLRA as Congress sought to correct perceived problems. In 1947, the Taft-Hartley Amendments shifted the focus of the NLRA to balance the power between labor and management and protect the rights of employees. Numerous other changes were instituted despite the strong opposition of labor (Silver and McAvoy 1987, 183). The periodic attacks however, were often short-circuited by Supreme Court preemption decisions that created a new "no man's land" through which the states were precluded from asserting jurisdiction (Gould 2000, 756). The act is no longer as significant as it once was. Labor policy is now composed of a variety of federal and state statutes, as well as catalogues of judicial decisions. Still, the act remains extremely important for the private sector (Silver and McAvoy 1987, 183).

Antitrust

Antitrust laws, most notably the Sherman Act, are sometimes referred to as "the Magna Carta of free enterprise" (Kahn 2008, 1495). Like most pieces of legislation, Congress constructed the Sherman Antitrust Act in broad and sweeping language. This conferred responsibility on the agencies and the courts to develop standards through case-by-case adjudication. Even when Congress identified specific patterns of behavior in the Clayton Act, it left the courts with the primary responsibility for determining when antitrust issues would be raised. In the Federal Trade Commission Act, Congress was explicit in delegating authority to the newly created Federal Trade Commission (FTC) to define the meaning of the "unfair methods of competition" and develop case law (Gifford 1995, 1678).

There has been a problem, however, with the best-laid plans. According to Daniel Gifford (1995, 1678), the development of law has been "rendered inefficient and inconsistent" because antitrust laws are enforced by two agencies: the Department of Justice and the FTC. Further complicating the development of law is the fact that antitrust regulations are also enforced by private actions, including those brought by state attorneys general. Therefore, there is a lack of coherence in the development of law. Gifford (1995, 1679) argues that the government, which once dominated antitrust through its litigating activities, has lost control over the evolution of that policy. Indeed, most antitrust suits are private actions and currently the source of recent major developments in antitrust case law. The new force in antitrust policy is the state attorneys general. Yet in taking the initiative, they have the potential to disrupt the orderly development of federal law.

The Court played a major formative and supervisory role in this area. The Court's opinions formed the body of antitrust law, and the lower courts attempted to align their own decisions with that core. The Supreme Court gave special deference to the government's positions, in part because the government possessed the capacity and resources to develop a coherent position on antitrust issues. As Wood and Anderson (1993) note, political actors are willing to flex their muscles in this area, giving the courts some pause. Gifford (1995, 680) maintains that Supreme Court precedents ultimately became obsolete. Just when it appeared to establish doctrinal stability, the Court reversed field and rejected the government's position, undoing the work of the past three decades. Despite the fact that the Court overruled just one of its antitrust precedents, it has introduced widespread confusion into the law (Gifford 1995, 1682–1683).

Commerce

The Motor Carrier Act of 1980 reflected congressional dissatisfaction with the Interstate Commerce Commission (ICC)'s deregulatory initiatives. The act was among the most significant statutes of the past half century of transportation regulation. In drafting the new act, Congress reasserted its constitutional primacy by defining the boundaries of regulatory reform as clearly as possible. The act's other principal purpose was to halt the actions of an agency that had become obsessed with deregulation. The White House has been the dominant political force influencing ICC policy, beginning with the Carter administration. As Paul Dempsey (1984, 49) noted: "The Commission has lost the autonomy that traditionally shielded its decision making from the political winds that blow down Pennsylvania Avenue." With the commission dominated by the deregulatory wave and Congress split on deregulation, the sole remaining check on the ICC was the judiciary. Litigants and groups had success using the courts to challenge the ICC's actions (Dempsey 1984, 49–50).

PRECEDENT AND DOCTRINAL CHANGE

During the Warren and Burger Courts, a different type of transition was occurring. The types of regulatory policies emerging from Congress and the administrative agencies had changed significantly. The New Deal regulations tended to be economic in scope, focusing on markets, rates, and the obligation to serve. At their inception, these economic regulations were controversial. The partisan realignment of the 1930s was based, in part, on these types of issues. Soon such policies became widely accepted, even by the Republican Party (Pacelle 1991; Reichley 1981).

The policies of the Warren Court and the programs of the Great Society were responsible for introducing other elements into regulatory schemes. The Warren Court was willing to go well beyond the simple economic effects of regulations to their social consequences. Congressional and executive policies also sought a variety of means of combating poverty. As a result, a new series of regulatory agencies, like the Occupational Safety and Health Administration (OSHA) and the Environmental Protection Agency (EPA), were created, and some existing agencies, like the NLRB and the Food and Drug Administration (FDA), were given different, broader charges (Wilson 1980). Regulations emanating from these and other agencies were social in scope, involving the conditions under which goods and services were produced. Such regulations cut across industries and traditional boundaries, evoking considerable controversy both on and off the Supreme Court (Crowley 1987).

The decisions of the Warren Court in regulation cases reflected the tone and tenor of its policies in civil liberties. The Warren Court used egalitarian principles to govern its decisions concerning the influence of various regulatory schemes. During this period, the Court increasingly supported the underdogs, whether they were involved in disputes concerning individual rights or economic matters. The Warren Court pursued a liberal, populist ideology in deciding regulation cases. In contrast to the Burger and Rehnquist Courts, the Court under Earl Warren was concerned with the qualitative rather than the quantitative aspects of regulatory policies (Pacelle 1991).

During its tenure, the Warren Court decided 72 percent of the regulation cases in favor of the government. Except for bankruptcy cases, the Warren Court was largely supportive of regulations and deferred to the various administrative agencies in its decisions. However, this level of support masked some ideological traits. The Warren Court was likelier to support agency decisions when the agency was anti-business or pro-labor

(Wasby 1989, 332–333). In its decisions, the Court did not solely weigh the economic evidence. The sincere preferences of the individual members and the collective preferences of the institution tended to reflect a distrust of business.

The Burger Court retreated from the decisions of its predecessor. Whereas aggregate levels showed only a moderate reduction, the important landmark decisions emerging from the Burger Court signaled significant departures from the doctrine and ideology of the Warren Court. In addition, support for the agencies was partially a function of the substance of those decisions. The Burger Court upheld almost 90 percent of the decisions that were pro-business or anti-labor, but just more than half of the decisions that favored labor or were anti-business (Wasby 1989, 333).

The Burger Court changed the basis of evaluation for labor relations and antitrust decisions. Organized labor and other workers felt that they suffered under the thumb of this Court, which overhauled long-settled labor policies. The effect was to undermine workers' rights and union democracy. The values that appeared to dominate the Burger Court in labor relations cases were the sanctity of private property and entrepreneurial freedom (Fox 1987, 229–231; Silberman 1987, 221). In antitrust policy, the hostility of the Warren Court toward horizontal mergers was replaced with less suspicious attitudes. The Burger Court insisted that antitrust laws contain economic tests of legality and rejected the Warren Court's assumptions about functions and the competitive impact of various types of business conduct (Malkovits 1983, 182).

The Rehnquist Court joined the retreat from the Warren Court, finding for the government and the liberal side in just half of the cases. The Court has been accused of "toppling doctrines and precedents that had held for decades" while displaying "a disrespect [for Congress] bordering on contempt" (Zeigler 1996, 1367). The decisional trends were consistent in tax cases and most regulatory areas. In each of these, the Court found for the government in about two-thirds of the decisions. With regard to the antitrust, securities regulation, and labor relations cases, the economic cases that are most salient, the decisions better reflect the attitudes of the Rehnquist Court. This was particularly true of labor relations cases, in which the government prevailed in fewer than 40 percent of the decisions. Yet there were very few landmark decisions. The most important decisions had a labor relations connection but were often First Amendment or federalism cases (Tushnet 2005; Yarbrough 2000).

In the aggregate, the Court split its decisions in antitrust and securities regulation evenly in half. In each of the areas, the aggregate numbers do not reflect the importance of some of the landmark decisions. Eleanor Fox (2002, 215) argued that there were three major decisions in this area, which "illustrate the enterprise to defeat antitrust." The securities regulation changes predated the official knighting of Rehnquist as chief justice. But it has not been a linear move toward deregulation. In fact, there was quite a battle going on for control of policy. Before Brennan and Marshall left, the Court generally supported the protective aspects of securities law. The Rehnquist Court moved to limit those protections where possible (Mitchell 2002). Despite the ferment in the law and changes in the composition of the Court, the primary incentive of the justices was to make the law coherent.

STANDARDS OF REVIEW

The judiciary in general, and the Supreme Court more specifically, are in a difficult position when they are asked to interpret regulations or administrative actions. The dilemma for the courts in reviewing such cases concerns the standards of review that are appropriate. Should courts attempt to exercise their sincere preferences, discern congressional intent, show deference to the position of the agency, or rely on precedent? The agency has expertise and often the support, or at least the ear, of a congressional committee. The Court needs to impose consistency on the law and allow the agencies to perform their functions. The standards for judicial review of agencies have changed over time, and with them the activism and restraint of the Court as well as the discretion of the agency. The first important New Deal–era standard came from *Skidmore v. Swift & Co.* (1944). Under the standard of review derived from *Skidmore*, the agency receives neither the strong presumption of validity that attaches under the deferential review of rule making nor the suspicion of invalidity that applies when agencies act near the boundaries of federal authority. Instead, the rule or regulation stands or falls on its own merits.

Under *Skidmore*, the Court would consider the quality of the process: the coherence and consistency of the legal interpretations, the collection and consideration of relevant information, and the reasonableness of its judgments based on that information. If the Court found the agency interpretation to be persuasive and not inconsistent with the meaning of the statute, it would be free to adopt the agency's interpretation as authoritative. But if the Court decided that the agency's interpretation was not persuasive, it would be free to reject that interpretation. *Skidmore* granted an agency nothing more than the power to persuade, allowing courts to substitute their judgment for that of an administrative agency if the court's reading of a statute was "better" than an agency's (Pietruszkiewicz 2006, 4).

It is not surprising that this standard would be adopted by the Supreme Court of the time. It was an activist standard, birthed in difficult economic times and conceived by a Court that was chosen to protect the New Deal. The Court wanted to reserve for itself the ability to monitor agencies and intercede if necessary. The intermediate persuasiveness standard was political expedience, not a comprehensive assessment of administrative efficiency or a theory of the fundamental role of the administrative state launched in the New Deal. The result was a political compromise that viewed the courts as the interpreters of the law. The Supreme Court articulated a standard that favored judicial independence over administrative discretion (Pietruszkiewicz 2006, 4). The *Skidmore* factors eschew deference in favor of de novo determinations by the judiciary despite the fact that the expertise and experience of the agencies give them a broader perspective of the entirety of a statutory scheme.

In federal taxation cases, the Court established a type of moderate deference in *National Muffler Dealers Association v. United States* (1979). *National Muffler* would permit a court to substitute its judgment for that of the agency only if the agency's reading did not implement a congressional mandate in a reasonable manner or contradict past agency positions (Pietruszkiewicz 2006, 44–45). The Court moved more decisively toward a deferential standard in the landmark *Chevron USA v. Natural Resources Defense Council* (1984) decision. The *Chevron* doctrine stands for the principle that the Supreme Court should defer to a reasonable agency interpretation of a statute when the legislation is ambiguous. The Court provided a number of justifications for this position. First, it is the agencies, not the courts, that are the preferable sites for resolving policy conflicts engendered by vague statutory provisions. Second, agency officials have likely been involved in the drafting of the statute. Third, agencies have greater expertise in regulatory areas. Finally, Congress intended that agencies should "fill in the gaps" left when statutes are drafted (Hickman and Krueger 2007). It was a standard that reflected the judicial restraint of the times and limiting review.

According to Orin Kerr (1998), there is a great deal of controversy over the *Chevron* standard. Some analysts use a contextual model and contend that *Chevron* is a "revolution on paper" that has failed to replace the traditional contextual approach to judicial review of agency action. Others interpret *Chevron* through a political perspective that maintains that the *Chevron* doctrine is so indeterminate that it is simply a cover for judges to decide cases based on their personal political preferences. Some commentators rely on an interpretive model and insist that *Chevron* is unstable in that textualist judges apply the doctrine differently from judges who reject a textualist approach.

The Court was not through tinkering, however. In *Lechmere, Inc. v. NLRB* (1992), the Supreme Court held that when interpreting administrative statutes, it should defer to its own precedents rather than to the agency's interpretations of statutes. Thus, the Court determined that *stare decisis* is dominant over deference to administrative agencies (Goplen 1993, 207). If the Court were faithful to its own precedents, this would represent the application of the legal model. Of course, proponents of the attitudinal model would argue that this change was instrumental. This revised standard could be used as a shroud to mask the sincere preferences of the justices who would simply couch their decisions in legitimate normative terms (Eskridge and Baer 2008). Also, it came at a time when there were hints of a resurgence of activism.

Wood and Waterman (1991) argue that there are a number of mechanisms for political control of the bureaucracy. Congressional control is exercised through the institution or the committees. Presidential control comes through appointments. This would suggest that the Court acts strategically. But in his seminal work, Nelson (1982) argues that the development of the bureaucracy is fraught with irony. One irony is that reformers' efforts to make civil service more responsive to the political branches have actually made it less responsive. Client agencies that were created to enhance political representation in government became almost independent from general political branch control. This would free the Court to act on its own designs. Another irony is that regulatory agencies that were created in response to popular political movements often became client agencies of the regulated. As these dynamics waxed and waned, it is not surprising that the Court's standards would also change. Some of the change was strategic and some attitudinal, but underlying the whole period, it appeared that precedent and legal factors remained paramount.

MODELING STATUTORY ECONOMIC DECISIONS

The different theories that underpinned the jurisprudence of the different Courts suggest the impact of the attitudinal variable. The unique position of the agency as part of the executive branch but tied more closely

TABLE 8.1. *Integrated Model of Supreme Court Decision Making: Nonconstitutional Economic Cases*

	Model	Predicted Probabilities
Supreme Court	2.23**	.06
	(.50)	
President	.10	.01
	(.15)	
House	1.21**	.06
	(.45)	
Senate	− 3.67	− .04
	(1.99)	
Precedent	.92**	.17
	(.06)	
On Point	1.27**	.50
	(.44)	
Issue Evolution	− .32**	− .07
	(.08)	
Constant	1.33	
	(.23)	
Chi²	.00	
Log Likelihood	− 935.1	
N	1,632	

** $p<.01$. * $p<.05$.
Probabilities represent the growth (or decline) in the probability of a liberal decision for every one standard deviation change in the independent variable or from 0 to 1 for dummy variables, holding all the other independent variables at their respective means.

to Congress suggests the impact of strategic factors. The fact that the Court wants to move these issues off the agenda, accepts cases almost exclusively to settle circuit conflicts, and decides many of these cases unanimously suggests the viability of the legal model. The shifting standards that go from judicial dominance to agency deference to reliance on precedent reflect the ebb and flow of the different variables. They suggest the complexity of decision making in this area.

The results of the model are shown in Table 8.1. The impact of legal factors, controlling for the other variables, is statistically significant. First, issue evolution has a strong negative impact. As the cases get more difficult, controlling for the other variables, the probability that the Court issues a liberal decision declines. This effect can be seen in Figure 8.1, which indicates that the Court's probability of issuing a liberal decision is approximately .85 in the first stage of issue evolution but declines to less

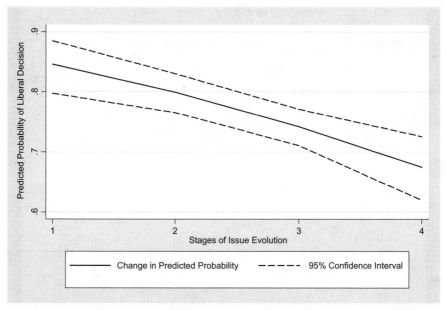

FIGURE 8.1. Effects of Issue Evolution on Statutory Economic Decisions

than .70 under the most difficult factual situation. The Court's probability of deciding the instant case in a liberal direction is higher than 50 percent regardless of the case's difficulty, and we have noted that this result is consistent with the Court's general lack of interest in these issues. Even so, it is evident that as cases become more difficult, the Court becomes less likely to resolve them in a liberal direction. The impact of precedent is particularly strong as well, even controlling for on-point precedents.

The impact of the strategic variables is a combination of some of the results we have seen previously. As with the statutory civil rights and individual liberties cases, the ideology of the House of Representatives (as measured by the median member) has a statistically significant impact on the Court's decisions in this area. Figure 8.2 demonstrates that, although the Court is likelier than not to resolve a statutory economic case in a liberal direction regardless of the House's ideological median, as that median grows more liberal, so, too, does the Court's propensity to issue a liberal decision. The variable for the Senate is not in the predicted direction. The variable for the ideology of the president has no effect on decision making. At first blush, this seems surprising, given the role of the SG in litigating for the government. The attitudinal variable has a

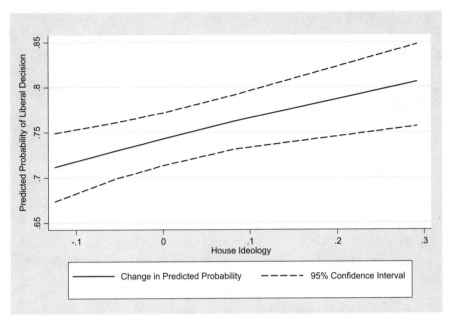

FIGURE 8.2. Effects of House Ideology on Statutory Economic Decisions

statistically significant impact on decisions in these statutory economic cases.

What do we make of these results? On the one hand, the attitudinal variable was expected to exert an impact on decision making, but there were good reasons to think that the impact would be muted in these cases. First, the cases do not scale as well as the more salient civil rights and civil liberties cases (Ducat and Dudley 1987; Hagle and Spaeth 1993; Rohde and Spaeth 1976). Second, a large percentage of these decisions are unanimous. This may be a place where the differences between the levels of analysis come into play. Individual justices may sacrifice their sincere preferences for larger institutional norms like settling lower court conflicts and stabilizing precedent. If we look at the percentages of liberal decisions by time period, we see a relationship between the overall ideology of the Court and the decisions. Over the entire period, 57.1 percent of the Court's statutory economic decisions were decided in a liberal direction. During the Warren Court, that percentage was much more liberal – just slightly less than 70 percent (69.7 percent). Those levels of support declined to 51.5 percent during the Burger Court and just slightly more than 50 percent (50.5 percent) for the Rehnquist Court. The effect of the attitudinal variable is arguably reflected in these percentages, but this impact is a relative one. Each of the Courts issued more liberal than conservative decisions, which is at odds with the notion of the attitudinal model. But if we look at the percentages, we see that the relative effects are significant. As the Court gets more conservative, the decisions get more conservative, even if the percentages are not that conservative in absolute terms.

The impact of the president or, more precisely, the lack thereof, is a bit curious. The regulation and internal revenue cases require the input of the SG. As a presidential appointee who has an unmatched record of success, this lack of impact seems strange. But if we unpeel another layer, we discover the reason for this discrepancy. In the two largest issue areas, tax and regulation cases, the SG supported the government's position in more than 80 percent of the cases across the time period. Nor does this figure markedly change as a function of the party occupying the White House. The issues' lack of salience to presidents means that they do not generally interfere with the OSG in these cases (Pacelle 2006).

Although the regulatory agencies are part of the executive branch, most analysts feel that they are closer to Congress than to the president (Eisner, Worsham, and Ringquist 2006). The proximity of the "executive" agencies to the committees in Congress and the fact that statutory provisions are at issue helps explain why the House has a statistically significant impact on Supreme Court decision making in such cases. Because statutory interpretation is at the heart of many of these cases, the SG is often arguing on behalf of Congress rather than the president (Pacelle 2003). Thus, the OSG can transfer its success and reputation to Congress. In addition, for significant periods, the Court would defer to the wisdom of the agency whose views might well reflect those of Congress. More specifically, in our discussion of issue evolution in these different areas of law, we examined the individual areas and noted that in internal revenue cases and some areas of regulation, the Court seemed very attentive to congressional prerogatives (Staudt et al. 2005).

We consider this a reflection of the impact of the strategic model, but we want to underline the dynamics of the interaction between the Court and, in this case, Congress. There is perhaps an implicit assumption that the Court may tailor its decisions to congressional or presidential prerogatives as a means of avoiding retaliation from its more powerful institutional neighbors. We contend that this defensive posture does not reflect the reality of the statutory economic cases. The Court appears to have a primary interest in settling the law. Thus, it is motivated less by the need to preserve its institutional integrity and more by the desire to get it right and pass the primary policing to Congress, the agencies, and the lower courts. The Court and Congress work together to introduce consistency and fill interstices in the law. Under such conditions, a reversal from Congress or the Court carries little or no stigma (Hausegger and Baum 1999; Murphy 1964; Pickerill 2004; Sager 2004).

These issue areas also show the reemergence of the legal variables. As expected, issue evolution plays a significant role. Other than the on-point precedents, which only occur in a few instances, precedent plays the largest role in influencing the statutory economic decisions. This validates our hypothesis. Because these issues are less salient to the Court, the primary objective is to standardize the law. The Court typically takes these cases in order to resolve lower court conflicts, often narrowing the issues in the case at hand, and often the decision is unanimous (Pacelle 1991; Ulmer 1982). Thus, it relied on *stare decisis* in more than 72 percent of the cases that had an existing precedent.

Our findings provide some support for and a further qualification of the attitudinal model. The fact that the attitudinal variable was statistically significant in the less salient statutory cases speaks to the influence of the Court's collective sincere preferences. The major proponents of the attitudinal model contend that precedent is merely used as a post-hoc justification for decisions that have already been made (Silverstein 2009). We argue that the preponderance of the evidence overwhelmingly rejects this premise. The consistency of the decisions, the consistency of the position adopted by the SG, the rationale for accepting such cases, and the relative lack of interest in the issues suggest that in these areas, law matters, and that the Court is trying to fulfill its role as the arbiter of the federal judicial system.

The percentage of decisions that favored the government (and thus were categorized as liberal) was rather high, considering the ideological composition of the Court. This again speaks to the influence of precedent. The Burger and Rehnquist Courts did reverse field in a few prominent decisions, most notably in labor relations, securities regulation, and environmental issues. For the most part, however, the idea was to stabilize the law and limit attention to such issues.

We examine the underlying relationships more closely, in part because there is a wide variety of issues that comprise the summary category. By examining some of the component parts, we may gain leverage in understanding decision making in economic issues more generally and for some specific issues. We isolate the ordinary economic, judicial power, internal revenue, and regulation cases. Within the regulation area, we examine labor relations, securities regulation, and antitrust cases. For the sake of parsimony, we spare you all of the detailed model results and simply highlight some of the key relationships we find.

The ordinary economic cases do not involve governmental regulation. Among the categories that comprise this area are government liability issues (like contracts and torts), retirement benefits, and Employee Retirement Income Security Act (ERISA) disputes. There were 165 such cases over the 1953–2000 period. None of the strategic variables was statistically significant. The attitudinal variable, precedent, and issue evolution all had an impact on the Court's decision making. The court jurisdiction cases in this category arise out of ordinary economic disputes that are transformed into judicial power or jurisdiction issues. There were 235 cases in this summary category, and the results are very similar, except that the attitudinal variable is not statistically significant. Precedent and issue evolution are the only variables that influence these decisions.

The internal revenue cases make up one of the largest single categories of cases in the statutory economic cases (N = 218). Not a single variable other than precedent has a statistically significant impact on the Court's decision making. This seems at odds with previous studies of attempts to exert political influence on the IRS (Scholz and Wood 1998). Staudt and colleagues (2005) argue that the Court increasingly deferred to Congress. Our results do not show this, but that may be a function of some other dynamics. For example, the Court may be responding to relevant congressional committees. Scholz and Wood (1998) argue that attempts to control the IRS were conditional and dependent on a combination of Congress and the president, and only over certain time periods.

When we aggregate the regulation cases (N = 906), we see patterns that look like the entire group of statutory economic cases. Every variable except the president and Senate is statistically significant. In addition to the attitudinal variable and all of the legal factors, the House variable is statistically significant. We also examine the largest individual areas: labor relations (N = 259 cases) and antitrust (N = 197). The results are almost polar opposites of each other. The results for labor relations look like the broader regulation model – the legal variables are most prominent, and both houses of Congress have statistically significant effects on decision making, controlling for the other variables. By contrast, antitrust decisions are influenced by the Court, president, and precedent (Wood and Anderson 1993). As Wood and Anderson (1993, 34) note, "Decisions by all major U.S. democratic institutions shape both the *level* and *substance* of U.S. anti-trust regulation through time." In this respect, they look more like the salient civil rights and individual liberties cases than the other, less salient economic issues.

A few words of explanation are in order for these two areas of law. There are a number of free speech cases that involve labor relations issues. In our coding, we treat the civil liberties component as dominant over the economic. Because they are salient free speech cases with First Amendment precedents and litigants, the Court and the president would be very likely to exert positive influences on the decisions. The impact of the president is less surprising for the antitrust cases than in any other area. The Department of Justice (DOJ) has the Antitrust Division to enforce the law. The attorney general, the head of the DOJ, is a member of the president's Inner Cabinet and a close advisor. Because the DOJ has jurisdiction over civil rights and antitrust, it would not be a stretch to see presidential influence in these areas. Indeed, many of the attorneys general of the period were aggressive and political in their outlooks (Baker 1992; Clayton 1992; Weaver 1977). In addition, presidents made no effort to hide their ideological stripes in these areas (Wood and Anderson 1993).

Did our little excursion into these subareas elucidate any of the broader trends? We would like to think so. They point out that there is a variety of statutory economic cases and that the impact of the different factors varies by the specific area. But it is important to underline that, almost without exception, the impact of precedent is ubiquitous and stronger than any other variable across these cases.

IMPLICATIONS

Our central thesis has been that different factors influence decision making under different conditions. Our integrated model isolates key factors that explain how legal, attitudinal, and strategic factors condition the Court's decisions. This chapter completes our analysis of these four different conditions, and the results contained herein are different from those we found for the other sets of issues. Precedent and the legal factors are much more pronounced in this area, although strategic and attitudinal factors also play a role.

The agencies and bureaus are typically pulled in two directions. Institutionally, they are part of the executive branch, but since the Legislative Reorganization Act of 1946, they are increasingly responsible to Congress, which has budget and oversight authority over them. Indeed, presidents come and go in four to eight years, whereas the agencies are on the congressional clock. Congress has chosen to delegate extensive power to the agencies and bureaus (Lowi 1969). The vagueness of enabling legislation means that agencies will be called upon to interpret provisions and promulgate rules in furtherance of the existing statutes. Inevitably, this will lead to judicial challenges to the interpretations. This can cause problems for the Court in balancing the designs of the president, Congress, and the agencies. Those potential constraints may give the Court additional leverage under the proper conditions. For instance, for much of the time frame of our study, American politics was defined by divided government (Fiorina 1996; Mayhew 2005). Theoretically and empirically, the president may not be a major factor in the Court's concerns. Presidents tend to find these issues less salient. The fact that the SG, regardless of party, tends to support government regulation also limits the potential harm to the Court (Pacelle 2003). Some studies (Bailey, Kamoie, and Maltzman 2005; Wohlfarth 2009) show that when the SG takes a position seemingly at odds with the administration, the Court is likelier to respect it.

The impact of Congress, particularly the House, is not surprising. Congress is closer to the agencies, and the House starts revenue and tax bills. The relevant committees and subcommittees probably have the most impact over the agencies. Indirectly, they may also have the most strategic impact. As an agent of the institution, the committee will make recommendations that will likely be respected by the larger House or Senate (Maltzman 1997).

There is a heightened sense of legitimacy for the Court in this area as well. Because the Court has defined these cases as being less substantively important, it has exercised judicial restraint in dealing with them. In choosing a standard that focuses on deference to the agencies or relies on precedent, the Court uses legitimate and acceptable grounds for its decisions. The results of our model show the impact of precedent on the Court's decisions in the economic cases.

The Court also gained some autonomy after *Brown v. Board of Education* (and even before that) because these economic issues are not salient to the justices, relatively speaking. They were at one point in time. In nominating the likes of Frankfurter, Black, and Douglas, President Roosevelt was trying to pack the Court with justices who would support his economic policies. The creation of the regulatory state was a significant issue in the partisan realignment of the early 1930s. It was also a litmus test for the president in choosing justices (Abraham 2008). In tracing the background for these issues, we noted that the issues first came to the Court as constitutional questions, often based on federalism or the exercise of national power (McCloskey 1960). As soon as the Court removed that potential obstacle, and it did (see Chapter 7), the narrower statutory questions could populate the Court's agenda. But after the constitutional thicket was cleared, the need for this issue as a litmus test for nominees was reduced and ultimately eliminated.

To accommodate the rising tide of civil rights and individual liberties cases, the Court had to clear agenda space. This would require the Court to take two steps. First, it would have to stabilize the existing law, and everything we saw in this chapter suggests that it tried to do this. Second, the Court would need to trust other actors to monitor these economic cases. It deferred to Congress, the agencies, and the lower courts. It relied on the SG to rein in agencies and help impose stability in doctrine. To monitor, the Court would rely on the proverbial fire alarms rather than police patrols. These economic issues would be salient to someone, whether the agency, the industry, or the congressional subcommittee charged with this issue. The Court would defer to those agencies and respect the province of those committees.

From the Stone Court through the Rehnquist Court, economic issues have largely been treated as part of the institutional rules and norms of the Supreme Court. As a result, the acceptance of these cases is designed almost exclusively to head off problems in the judicial hierarchy. The sincere policy preferences of the justices have little direct real or symbolic impact on economic issues. There are some hints that this may be changing a bit. We saw some evidence of this in Chapter 7. To the extent that it penetrates more deeply, it could have effects on statutory economic cases.

CONCLUSION

This chapter deals with issues that are not particularly salient to the Court but that come with a series of constraints. These are some of the cases that fall through the cracks of the attitudinal model, because so many of the decisions are unanimous. The results of our analysis show a departure from those of the other chapters and speak to the conditional effects of different variables. We argue that in the statutory economic issues, the Court has collective goals that do not focus primarily on its sincere preferences. To be sure, we are painting with a broad brush: Some areas, like antitrust and labor relations, are more salient than tax and bankruptcy cases. Our results seem to support the general doctrinal and substantive analyses of these issues. The Court relies on experts – subcommittees and agencies – to make the fundamental decisions. It relies on precedent to impose some order. It happens to view its role as a supervisor seriously and thus sacrifices its policy preferences to pursue its institutional responsibilities. In this regard, it comes closest to Scenario 2, the primacy of the legal model.

Footnote Four of the *Carolene Products* decision stood for the principles that Congress should be the primary actor in economic issues and that the Court should adopt an interstitial role. Our results suggest that the Court largely made good on this promise. The retreat from the economic issues was coupled with the stated commitment to protect rights and liberties. To fulfill that part of the promise, the Court had to carve out agenda space for rights and liberties cases. This would be accomplished by paring the economic agenda (Pacelle 1991). The process of transforming the agenda would require the Court to be deferential to Congress, respect the prerogatives of the agencies, and permit the lower courts to take the lead in judicial supervision. The Court could do this by carefully regulating access to its agenda, limiting the number of economic cases it would grant cert to review, and trying to impose stability on doctrine by making consistent decisions and following precedent. The results suggest that the Court followed precedent and showed deference to Congress.

We have argued that decision making is a function of substantive preferences and structural considerations. Substantive preferences are at the heart of the attitudinal model. But the Court is also constrained by structural considerations like the need to impose doctrinal stability (Baum 1997). The dominant view is that structural considerations are subordinate to substantive policy preferences. In most of the economic issues, the sincere preferences are subordinate to the structural considerations. This also underlines our overall perspective: Decision making is the result of multiple forces that are intertwined and operate differently under different conditions (Baum 1997, 2006).

The results of our analysis confirm the preponderance of our hypotheses. As with the statutory civil rights cases, Congress and precedent emerge as significant (substantively and statistically) influences on judicial decision making, controlling for all other variables. Because these decisions are based on statutory grounds, the Court has to pay attention to Congress. Interestingly, although we have not tested it directly, our results provide support for the notion that the Court responds to the current Congress (Eskridge 1994). The role of precedent is much greater in these cases and may provide either cover or even some indirect support for the attitudinal variables. By relying on precedent, the Court helps ensure that the law is consistent and predictable. It also relies on a normatively acceptable means of deciding cases. If the Court relies on precedent, it also permits the institution to follow its own counsel rather than relying on the agency. By following precedent in these cases, the Court purchases the opportunity to exercise its prerogatives when issues are more salient to the justices.

The lack of salience also contributes to the influence of these variables. Without an abiding interest in the substantive nature of the decisions, the Court can concentrate on resolving circuit conflicts and imposing stability on the law. These issues may not be particularly salient to the modern president, who has to manage world affairs as well as try to assert some influence in domestic affairs (Marshall and Pacelle 2005; Wildavsky 1969). The president needs to delegate authority to his cabinet and staff to deal with these economic issues. The problem for the president is that the so-called "outer cabinet" departments end up being closer to Congress and the bureau (what is disparagingly referred to as "marrying the natives" [Nathan 1975]). Therefore, the issue ends up being much more salient to the relevant congressional committee or subcommittee than to the president. This reality of American politics is reflected in our results. The Court is attentive to Congress, which is attentive to its relevant subcommittees.

We were a bit agnostic about the influence of the attitudinal variable. The view from the bottom suggests a limited role for the attitudinal variable. The substantial number of unanimous cases means that ideological foes have found common ground more than the attitudinal model would predict. But it is important to remember that we are looking at the institutional level. Here, there is a trend: As the Court gets more conservative and the median moves to the right, the percentage of liberal decisions declines. We want to make two final points about this: First, there is a relative decline in liberal decisions. The Warren Court was deciding more than two thirds of the decisions in a liberal direction. The Burger and Rehnquist Courts issued more conservative decisions but remained at 50 percent or higher in the liberal direction. Second, in the civil rights and individual liberties cases, the attitudinal variable emerged as the most important factor. In the economic issues, it was one of a number of factors competing for primacy. In the statutory economic cases, it finished well behind precedent.

The impact of the legal factors, particularly precedent, played an important macro role in structuring decision making. The Court was making a conscious effort to impose equilibrium on the law. The goal was to let the elected branches of government and agency experts make the important decisions. The Supreme Court also wanted the lower courts to deal with many of these issues. Congress participated by creating new courts or remodeling existing ones to deal with taxes, patents, and bankruptcy. The Supreme Court would be a last sentinel, acting only when necessary – when one of the other actors clearly overstepped the wide boundaries or when the lower courts were confused.

Although the impact of the attitudinal variable was somewhat muted, there was some evidence of it on the macro level. The Court had to formulate an overarching paradigm for dealing with economic issues. Like a pendulum, it has swung in part because of the changing ideological predilections of the Court over time. The Court in 1953 was just beginning to temper a time of judicial dominance. The litmus test for Black, Douglas, Frankfurter and others was government regulation of the economy. They had some expertise in these areas, having served in the Senate (Black), on the Securities and Exchange Commission (Douglas), and as presidential advisors (Frankfurter and Douglas). They were comfortable dealing with these issues and asserting judicial control over the emerging issues. As the Court resolved those issues in favor of the government and turned its attention to other matters like civil liberties and civil rights, it increasingly adopted a deferential stance, first toward Congress and then toward the agencies. More recently, as Chapter 7 details, the Court seems to have a renewed interest in economic matters. This interest has not manifested itself in increased numbers, but it is evident in a few key decisions, which usually represents a harbinger of larger changes. Coincident with this have been the rumblings of a new standard that relies on Court precedent rather than deference. That could portend a move to a new period of Court dominance and a revival of the attitudinal variable's influence in this area.

It helps to view these issues in the context of the constitutional economic cases. Those decisions rejected judicial activism and imposed decades of consistency on the law. Indeed, these cases seemed to disappear, with the occasional reminder that the Court had not changed its mind. Recently, there have been hints of renewed interest, but the steps have been halting – advances coupled with retreats. Still, the future portends some changes, and if they penetrate into the law, the effects will be felt in the statutory cases.

9

Conclusion

Decision Making on the Modern Supreme Court

Is the Supreme Court a bevy of Platonic guardians or the keepers of the covenant, or is it the nation's balance wheel? Does the Court perform a constitutional soliloquy, or is it part of a colloquy in building doctrine? It depends on whom you ask. Attempts to define Supreme Court decision making are vaguely reminiscent of the parable of the blind men and the elephant. The parable, which has many versions (kind of like studies of judicial decision making) in many cultures (like the different approaches), maintains that a number of blind men (from four to nine, depending on the source) are asked to identify an elephant. Each touches the elephant in a different place, so each has a different interpretation. To the one who touches only the leg, it is a tree; to another touching only the trunk, it is a snake; still another grasps the tail and believes the elephant is a rope.

We think many of the existing models resemble this parable. Some analysts have stated a normative view of what decision making should be like but ignore the empirical realities. Others drop unanimous cases and make a judgment despite that limited perspective. Some look at the individual level and try to generalize to the institutional level. We have tried to circumnavigate the elephant and get a broader perspective. As a result, we conclude that no single explanation or model is useful in understanding all decision making. Rather, we see decision making as a function of the opportunities for and the constraints on the Court.

We find merit in each of the different models, but not to the exclusion of the others. When we think holistically about Supreme Court decision making, we find a rather complex process. The Court faces a variety of cases that it likely has not seen. Those cases that are clear applications of past decisions can be handled by the lower courts. To get a case accepted, four justices have to agree. To prevail on the merits, another justice must join them. Perhaps the case will permit the majority to craft an important policy statement that reflects its sincere preferences. The decision not only allocates some authoritative value, but it also establishes a rule for the lower courts to follow and presumably serves as a guidepost for the Supreme Court itself. The Court has to interpret some provisions of the Constitution, written more than 220 years ago in a completely different world, or a statute that was conceived and passed in a pluralist system. Most of those constitutional provisions were vague when they were written and have not acquired additional clarity over the intervening centuries. The statutes were likely forged with separation of powers and checks and balances as a background. Thus, the provisions in these statutes were likely cast in broad, vague terms requiring unelected bureaucrats to interpret them. Many of those interpretations would be challenged and brought to the unelected justices. If all of that were not enough, there are two other branches of government that can respond to any decision.

Other approaches to SC decision making

Too often, scholars have treated the Court as little more than a collection of nine individuals separately pursuing their sincere policy preferences. The results of our analysis suggest that whereas individual justices have a great deal of autonomy and discretion, the Court does not have complete independence. Although its ideological composition is the most important factor, the Supreme Court is not simply a constitutional convention or a super-legislature. We see judicial decision making as a combination of substantive preferences and structural considerations (Baum 1997). Substantive preferences are at the heart of the attitudinal model. However, structural considerations are part of judicial decision making as well. Structural considerations include legal factors as well as concerns about the scope of judicial power. The prevailing view in the literature has been that structural considerations are subordinate to substantive policy preferences.

We posed three questions at the outset. First, does the attitudinal variable crowd out the effect of other factors and lead to what amounts to a judicial soliloquy? The answer, in our view, is decidedly "no." The ideology of the Court is the loudest voice, but it does not work to the exclusion of other factors. Even in those areas that should accentuate the attitudinal variable, its impact was great but not exclusive. Rather, the Court is engaged in an ongoing colloquy with the other branches and with the stability of the law.

Second, are constitutional and statutory cases subject to different factors? Here, the answer clearly is" yes." Whereas some factors, most notably the attitudinal and issue evolution variables, are consistently present, the impact of precedent and the House is positive and statistically significant in the statutory cases. In (the) constitutional cases and in civil rights and civil liberties, the president has a significant impact on decision making. Thus, the generalizations about the greater constraints that are present in statutory cases and the necessity of a colloquy with the other branches are borne out.

Third, we asked whether decision making is a function of issue salience, and we conclude that it is. Issues that are more salient grab closer attention from the Court and the president. In such salient issues, precedent and legal factors take a back seat. In the constitutional civil rights cases, precedent is not even statistically significant. With regard to the less salient issues, precedent moves to the forefront and has an important impact on decision making. In addition, as the issues decline in salience, the impact of Congress rises. Although those issues may be less salient to the Court or a busy president trying to write his pages of history, interest groups, some members of Congress, and committees and subcommittees care deeply about these issues. Decisions in the less salient areas seem responsive to Congress and to precedent.

THE CUBIST'S VIEW OF THE ELEPHANT

In our view, precedent, attitudes, issue evolution, the president, and Congress all influence decision making, but they are conditional parts of the Court's environment. Their relative impacts wax and wane over time and across multiple dimensions. Our study made only passing reference to time. We started with the notion that *Brown* launched the modern Supreme Court, and by implication, this time period is different from others. We did not test this, although we looked at changes within the 1953–2000 period. We found that constitutional cases were treated differently from statutory cases and that salient cases received different treatment than less salient ones. The last four chapters examined the conflation of the grounds of the decision and the relative salience. Now we need to step back and – not to mix our metaphors – look at the forest now that we have studied the trees.

Our results reflect the macro-level institutional changes that were unfolding. *Brown* enhanced the authority of the Court. By providing momentum for civil rights and individual liberties, the Court elevated the issues over which it would exercise dominance. In addition, the Court increasingly became a constitutional tribunal, further exaggerating its influence. Because these issues were the stuff of litmus tests, the impact of the attitudinal variable was expected to be prominent. Similarly, judicial activism and congressional abdication across a number of controversial issues have contributed to the increased power of the Supreme Court (Pacelle 2002). Of course, these issues were not just salient to the justices. It is not surprising to find that in the statutory civil rights and liberties cases, the president and the House had a significant impact on decision making. As the salience declines, so does the influence of the Court's ideology (though it was still significant) and the president. The House, Senate (almost), and precedent played significant roles.

The post-*Brown* period was the second generation of emerging executive power. Crises, foreign affairs, war, technological advances, and Congress's willingness to relinquish some of its powers all have contributed to a stronger American presidency (Barilleaux 2006; Dodd 1986; Fisher 2000). The New Deal and World War II helped to birth the modern presidency. One of the hallmarks of emergent presidential power was the refusal to take no for an answer.

Presidents obviously have an incentive to use their time in the White House to cement their place in history. During the bulk of the past fifty years, a number of presidents have served during periods of divided government, which, of course, complicates their attempts to exert influence and establish their legacies (Fiorina 1996). This has prodded presidents to advance their policy goals in other ways, such as relying on executive orders to circumvent Congress or supplement their legislative initiatives (Deering and Maltzman 1999; Marshall and Pacelle 2005; Mayer 2001) and on executive agreements instead of treaties to bypass the Senate (Howell 2003; Krutz and Peake 2010). Presidents increasingly set the legislative agenda and expanded their constitutional power (Rudalevige 2002, 2005). Presidents have also turned to the Supreme Court in attempting to advance and protect their goals and initiatives. Through appointments and the SG, presidents have sought influence. Indeed, presidents have been accused of politicizing the OSG in an attempt to get the office to do its bidding (Caplan 1987; Wohlfarth 2009).

The institutional relationship between the president and the Court seems almost natural. Scigliano (1971, vii) argues that the framers designed the judicial and executive branches as "an informal and limited alliance against Congress." The rise of presidential and judicial power has largely come at the expense of Congress. The Court has generally been reluctant to challenge the exercise of executive power, particularly in wartime (Fisher 1998, 2000; Howell and Pevehouse 2007; Silverstein 1997). The Court has also facilitated the expansion of presidential power through silent assent (Howell 2003).

Because they spoke with one voice, presidents have been able to wrestle the initiative away from Congress. Congress is hampered by the proverbial collective action problem. We often hear that Congress works for the individual members, but not as a policy-making body. The decentralization of the committee system, the weak leadership, and the primacy of individual electoral goals conspire to reduce the effectiveness of the institution (Marshall and Haney 2010). The expanded power of leadership and the increasing gulf between the parties may enhance the institutional prowess of Congress and make it figure more prominently in the Court's future calculus.

The results also suggest that the legal model deserves more attention. The Court pays attention to precedent and seeks to establish consistency in the law, particularly when the precedent is on point and in the statutory cases. But the application of law is ambiguous. The Court devises tests and tries to build doctrine in a coherent fashion. Richards and Kritzer (2002) identify jurisprudential regimes as influences that structure the Court's decision. The impact of issue evolution supports this conclusion. Indeed, issue evolution and the desire to ensure some consistency in the law represent an additional impact of the legal model.

EXPECTED RESULTS AND SURPRISES

Our results confirm two expected patterns. First, the Court is more vulnerable or open to persuasion in statutory than in constitutional cases, and second, the impact of sincere preferences is greater in salient than in nonsalient cases. But our findings contained a few surprises as well. It was certainly interesting and perhaps unexpected that the attitudinal variable was not statistically significant in the constitutional economic cases. The constitutional nature of the cases freed the Court to act on its preferences. With the recent memory of a bitter confrontation etched in its collective psyche, the Court opted to shift battlegrounds. There are some hints that the Court may reengage these issues, yet there is also a great deal of flux in them. For instance, how does one reconcile decisions like *Nollan* and *Kelo*? This bears future attention.

With very few exceptions, when Congress plays a significant role, it is the House and not the Senate that is involved. Is this a fluke, or are there reasons to think that the more parochial House members would be more vigilant than senators in overseeing the Court? Certainly, members of the House are more closely tied to the people. Members of the House are more tied into the subgovernment phenomenon than senators and likelier to react to the fire alarms. They also have more oversight capacity than their colleagues in the Senate. The role of bicameralism, the committee system, and congressional actions on the Court's decisions certainly merit our future investigation. However, our results suggest that the Senate's influence over the Court may be greatest with the confirmation of new justices but is relatively attenuated, compared with the House, on Court decisions.

The impact of the president, so prominent in civil rights and individual liberties, is absent in economic cases. In the latter, the Court actually seems to work in direct opposition to the president. This is understandable. The Court was largely deferential to the government, even though the Republicans who would rather see regulation rolled back controlled the White House for most of our time period. In addition, the presidents of the last half century were not using economic cases in their calculations when nominating justices. The solicitors general were not bearing the mantel of the presidents; they were more concerned with consistency (fealty to the law) and protecting federal prerogatives.

That brings us back to the legal factors, most notably precedent. Many analysts have argued that precedent matters. We have tried to show how and under what circumstances. Members of the Court admit that precedent does not guide them as much in constitutional cases, and we demonstrate empirical support for this statement. Alternatively, the law does matter in statutory and economic cases. In the latter, the Court seems intent on abiding by precedent with the hope of concentrating on more salient issues.

It is also important to remember than in all of our models, the impact of precedent is measured, controlling for all of the other variables. Thus, when precedent had a statistically significant influence on decision making, it was controlling for the attitudinal variable and issue evolution. Precedent is not etched in tablets so that it can never be modified, but it does offer boundaries and a constraint. It also provides opportunities. The Court can follow precedent to standardize the law. When precedent and policy preferences intersect, the Court can rely on the former and have normative grounds for the decision. Finally, in an instrumental way, the Court can follow precedent when cases fall in a zone of indifference or when congressional or presidential antennae are raised. By doing so, the Court can purchase some goodwill that can be spent on issues it cares about.

In conceptualizing precedent and to avoid the naïve legal model, most analysts focus on *stare decisis* not as a mandate but as a constraint. Precedent eliminates some options and narrows the opportunities for the justices. It establishes some boundaries for the individual justice and for the Court. We have no problem arguing the utility and validity of the institutional perspective on precedent – it is necessary to keep the judicial system functioning and to guide lower courts (vertical precedent). At the individual level, despite the attitudinal model, we are also persuaded of its vitality. From an attitudinal perspective, justices want to read their conception of good public policy into doctrine. Doctrine is composed of a series of precedents that fit together like a jigsaw puzzle. Thus, we find the concept of the "golden rule" of precedent persuasive. Justices need to support precedent so that their decisions will have the respect of their colleagues (horizontal precedent).

Perhaps our biggest point of departure involves the sincere policy preferences of the justices. We accept that they are the most important determinant of individual decision making, but in the end we see them, like precedent, as setting up boundaries. Individual justices would probably like to vote their naked policy preferences, but they understand that they need to attract four more votes, and the language of the opinion is ultimately the most important product (rather than the vote). In addition, each justice is savvy enough to know that there are institutional constraints that have to be part of the collective calculus. Whether it is the migration of a centrist justice or the pendulum swings of the median justice, some members of the Court seem cognizant of the balance between pushing their ideological agenda, weighing their duties as the members of an institution that is at the apex of the judicial system, and the need to respect the turf and the authority of the coordinate branches. The naïve attitudinal model is just too simplistic.

The Court rarely has the unencumbered luxury of simply acting on principle. Instead, it must often anticipate how the other, more powerful institutions could retaliate or threaten its institutional prestige and power (Bickel 1962; Corwin 1984; Strum 1974). Thus, the Court sits in a unique yet precarious position in the context of the separation-of-powers system. Although it is an independent branch of government, it is an institution, and in that sense it is subject to influence through the forces of politics and the heresthetic strategies of other institutional actors competing for power (Riker 1986).

The Court needs to pursue its own institutional responsibilities. Accordingly, it can effectively rely on precedent to make decisions on less salient issues so that it can optimize agenda space for more salient issues and exercise judicial activism. This reflects collective cooperation on the agenda that an institution like Congress is much less likely to achieve. This is another example of the Court as an institution being able to overcome another potential collective action problem (in its use of agenda coordination) to create space so that it can be "judicially active" on the issues it cares about.

In the end, of course, it is hard to disentangle the legal and political factors. Justices often have an abiding philosophy that guides their decision making. Maybe they are activists or restraintists, proponents of originalism, subscribe to legislative intent, or believe the Constitution changes with the times. Somehow knowing that a justice has an abiding philosophy makes the behavior more palatable. But is that philosophy simply a well-dressed political ideology? This is where attention to precedent can combine with sincere policy preferences. The general notion is that the policy preferences beget the philosophy, but what if there is an interactive effect? What if being a member of the Supreme Court really does lead one to modify his or her sincere policy preferences? We think this occurs on the individual level for some of the justices in the middle of the Court. Because those centrists are needed to build a majority, the institution is influenced by this interactive effect by implication.

There are other dimensions to the institutional perspective. The Court has accrued a great deal of legitimacy. Couple that with its accepted preeminence in constitutional matters, and it is clear that the Court has carved out a zone of influence. This means that the Court needs to be cognizant of its limitations as an institution. Therein lies the rub. Through a combination of institutional activism and the abdication of the other branches, particularly Congress, the Court finds itself embroiled in many of the most controversial issues of the time. It is somewhat surprising that the Court remains popular with the public. It deals with the major issues of the day and is certain to be condemned by the president and/or members of Congress when a decision is not to their liking.

The patterns of institutional activity can vary. The Court may remain silent and do nothing, but it does not do this much anymore. It can block the policies of the other branches of government, as it did in the economic cases through the early New Deal. The Court endeavored to learn from its mistake. It can also command or authorize. This is the closest to the constitutional civil rights and civil liberties cases and indeed arose from *Brown*. The Court took the lead and often remained the dominant actor in these issues. In other areas, the Court leaves the work to others. The solutions have been worked out by the other branches of the government, and the Court is willing to defer to them. This describes the economic area, particularly the statutory cases (Silverstein 2009, 29–35).

It is important also to understand the relationship between the Court and the other branches. On the one hand, the Court may react in a constructive fashion if it moves in concert with the other branches toward the same goals. On the other hand, Congress and the Court may work at cross-purposes in what Silverstein (2009) calls a deconstructive mode. Throughout the time period we examined, the relationship between the Court and Congress shifted, particularly in civil rights.

LOOKING ACROSS THE GREAT DIVIDE

It is worth trying to cross or at least look across the Rubicon. We posed a dilemma at the beginning of this study: How do we reconcile studies of decision making that exist at the institutional level with those that examine the behavior of justices at the individual level? We cannot settle this dispute conclusively, but we can speculate a bit about the intersection between the individual and institutional levels. There is one conjunction between the individual and institutional levels – the median justice. Much of the analysis of judicial decision making focuses on the median justice and the need to attract his or her vote. Certainly, those attorneys who populate the OSG admit to this (Pacelle 2003). Attorneys in the OSG invariably talk about the need to earn the vote of the key justice or two in the middle. They comb through their past opinions and pitch their arguments to them with the intent of gaining their precious assent.

Office of the Solicitor General

More to the point, we need to reconcile the fact that, although there are many changes in the composition of the Court, the institution seldom overturns recent precedents. What accounts for this apparent contradiction? The obvious answer is that the action of individual justices is not simply a function of their sincere political preferences. We know this to be true because a significant percentage of cases are decided unanimously. That certainly explains what we have labeled the less salient cases. There are unanimous decisions even in the salient cases, just not quite as many.

What do these dynamics look like? Many analysts examine the process by which the justices vote and bargain (Hammond, Bonneau, and

Sheehan 2005; Maltzman, Spriggs, and Wahlbeck 2000; Murphy 1964).
The implicit notion is that if justices were rigid in their decision making,
bargaining would not be possible. Howard (1968) shows that there is
a significant amount of fluidity in voting (but see Brenner and Spaeth
1995), again suggesting that justices can be loosed from their ideological
moorings under some circumstances. Justices may act strategically among
themselves to move a majority opinion. They may also act strategically
to avoid provoking the ire of the other branches of government (Epstein
and Knight 1998).

Let us posit a scenario to meld the individual and institutional levels
of decision making for the modern Supreme Court. Normally, the Court
has two ideological wings and a center that usually includes the median
justice and is effectively the Court's fulcrum. The Thurgood Marshalls
and the Antonin Scalias are not going to be coaxed to the middle (although
there is occasionally an unusual vote). They will continue to vote their
sincere preferences. The key, then, lies in understanding the justices in the
center.

There is a wealth of evidence at the individual level to support the
broader notions of decision making that animate this study. We argue
that those on the ideological wings of the Court are likelier to attempt
to exert their preferred policy preferences. In our time period, Douglas,
Marshall, Brennan, Scalia, and Rehnquist (before migrating to the center
seat) are the most obvious examples (Brisbin 1997; Tushnet 1994, 1997).
In the civil rights and individual liberties cases, Brennan and Marshall supported the claimants more than 80 percent of the time, whereas Douglas
reached closer to 90 percent support. On the opposite side, Rehnquist's
support hovered at about 20 percent, whereas Scalia was closer to 30 percent. When we shift focus to economic and regulation cases, we see that
Douglas, Brennan, and Marshall supported the liberal side (typically the
government) in fewer than two thirds of the cases. Scalia and Rehnquist
were close to 50 percent for their support of the liberal side in economic
cases (with each at more than 70 percent in federal tax cases) (Epstein
et al. 2007, 486–488).

Whereas these justices were rather consistent in their annual support
(or lack thereof) for individual rights, reflecting the strength of the attitudinal variable, their behavior in economic cases fluctuated dramatically
from term to term. Brennan and Marshall ranged from barely 50 percent
to the low eighties (Clark 1995: Marion 1997). On the other ideological wing, Rehnquist and Scalia ranged from 30 percent to the mid six-
ties. Maybe more to the point are the interagreement scores between the
justices. Rehnquist and Brennan voted together about a third of the time

in civil rights and civil liberties cases. Their agreement on economic cases was more than 70 percent (Epstein et al. 2007, 486–488, 558, 581–582). These same patterns held for the other dyads. Is this a function of issue salience, strategic decision making in bowing to the elected branches, or fealty to the law? We argue that all of these explanations contribute. Because the issues are less salient, the justices care less and are willing to put precedent and coherent doctrine above sincere preferences.

Much was made of the parabolic support of Douglas and Black for civil rights and civil liberties (Ulmer 1973, 1979) and the conservative drift of Frankfurter (Mendelson 1958, 1961; Spaeth 1964) and White (Hutchinson 1998; Nelson 1994). The stories of Black and Douglas neatly parallel the notion of issue evolution. Each was nominated for the express purpose of upholding the New Deal. Their ability to impose doctrinal stability on federalism, regulation, and economic cases and the imperative of the preferred position doctrine pushed civil rights and individual liberties to the center of the Court's concerns. With a World War and then a Cold War being waged and unprecedented issues to consider, both took a while to find their footing (Bartee 1984). Both Black and Douglas came to be known for their support for civil liberties, but as their time on the Court ebbed, they were faced with significantly more difficult questions. Black did not get appreciably less supportive of individual rights because he got older. He was less supportive of free expression because he felt that, although pure speech was entitled to absolute protection, wearing an armband or burning a draft card was not speech. Similarly, Nelson (1994) advances a similar argument to explain White's apparent break from the liberalism of President Kennedy: White did not change; the issues around him changed with the times.

Frankfurter has been the subject of academic jousting for decades. Was he a liberal who suppressed his policy preferences in deference to the law (Grossman 1963; Mendelson 1957) and to avoid provoking the other branches, or was he a conservative hiding behind the cloak of respectability (Spaeth 1964)? Without a detailed examination of his record, we are speculating, but certainly a case can be made that Frankfurter was trying to maintain some stability in the law during a time of significant changes. He, like his colleagues and successors, was influenced by his brethren and in turn had an impact on them. Analysts used to discuss the notion of small-group dynamics as an influence on individual decision making (Snyder 1958; Ulmer 1965). Today, we might consider it to be strategic decision making of a different ilk in that it is endogenous to the Court. Justices bargain with each other about the language of the majority opinion and use the threat of writing separately to exact changes. The fact that justices would bargain suggests that the immutability of judicial attitudes is overstated.

We can conclude that, with regard to the Court as an institution, the median justice really plays a critical role. He (Powell) or she (O'Connor) comes to embody the Court itself. If the median justices are not writing the critical decisions, they are influencing the language of the opinion and may (particularly O'Connor) be writing separately to explain where the Court's median is actually placed. In some ways, their behavior is more consistent than that of those who flank them on the ideological poles. Powell and O'Connor had very similar voting records. Both supported rights and liberties a little less than 40 percent of the time and cast liberal economic votes about 45 percent of the time. Their interagreement scores with their colleagues were almost invariably higher than 50 percent and did not vary widely from civil rights to economic cases (Epstein et al. 2007, 577–581).

It is our contention that the Court is like a cybernetic system. When the balance tips too far to the right or to the left, one of the justices in the center typically shifts to counteract it. Think of the title of Linda Greenhouse's book *Becoming Justice Blackmun.* Analysts will occasionally eschew the typical labeling of the Court (the name of the chief justice) and use the name of the pivotal justice. Thus, it is the Powell Court rather than the Burger Court, the O'Connor Court instead of the Rehnquist Court, and the Kennedy Court as an alternative to the Roberts Court. The biographies and autobiographies of these key justices reflect these metamorphoses. Of course, this belies a central tenet of the attitudinal model – that values and attitudes are long-term and immutable. Stated differently, the justices are said to have fixed preferences in a unidimensional issue space (Pacelle, Marshall, and Curry 2007).

Bailey and Maltzman (2008) find that legal doctrine matters. Some justices are likelier to adhere to *stare decisis* than their colleagues. Not surprisingly, they discover that the Scalia, Thomas, Brennan, and Marshall are not so likely to leave their ideological outposts. The justices who are likelier to follow precedent are Powell, Souter, O'Connor, White, Ginsburg, and Breyer.[1] Not coincidentally, they tend to be the moderates and often the median justice.

---

[1] Bailey and Maltzman (2008) find that Burger is most supportive of precedent and Rehnquist is higher on the list than one might suppose. We attribute this to their position as chief justice. Rehnquist split his time on the Court, serving as an associate before being elevated, which is likely why he is in the middle of the bottom tier. We argue that this is as much a function of strategic decision making as of adhering to precedent. The chief can assign the opinion if he remains with the majority.

Moderate justices, including the median justice, may be more concerned than more ideologically extreme justices with protecting the institutional prestige of the Court in making decisions. Why would the burden of maintaining institutional integrity and thus the power of the Court fall disproportionately on the median? One might think of this as a collective action problem – all justices receive the benefit of a highly respected Court. A highly respected Court decision carries more legitimacy, and so, theoretically, would a unanimous decision. There is no particular evidence to suggest that more extreme conservative or liberal justices seem to care less about the prestige of the Court than do more moderate justices. But there is support for the notion that justices in the center will be more inclined to pay attention to precedent and defer to Congress and the agency in their decisions.

Ideologically polar justices are more interested in policy goals than anything else and likely feel that the Court can survive a few political scraps. As long as they know that one or more of the centrists will protect the Court, they are free to defect from these institutional concerns. And if the centrists do not come through, they might need to temper their behavior and move into the breech and sacrifice their policy goals in favor of institutional legitimacy.

What motivates the justices in the center? Some may desire the power that comes from being the median justice. But more significance is tied to the language of the majority opinion than one's actual vote. The majority opinion is the critical policy statement of the Court. To attract the critical median vote, the author or the assigner of the opinion will need to attend to the views of this justice. The migration of the median justice may be a reflection of that justice's attitudes, but it may also be an individual perspective on the legal or strategic models. Consider the *Board of Regents v. Bakke* (1978) decision. Justice Powell was literally right in the middle of the Court that wrote the opinion that supported Allan Bakke but also permitted affirmative action programs. Similarly, consider the joint opinion in *Planned Parenthood v. Casey* written by O'Connor, Kennedy, and Souter, all of whom had expressed uneasiness with *Roe v. Wade*. These were strategic and legal decisions, and a pure attitudinal decision likely would have been different.

If we generalize (and there is no sense in stopping now), we can argue that the justices in the middle are motivated by the desire to guard the Court as an institution and protect its legitimacy. If membership changes instantly produced major revisions in decisional outputs, the Court would be exposed as a blatantly political institution. Respect for the institution would be jeopardized. Therefore, these justices provide the crucial votes that tip the Court to respect precedent and avoid placing the institution in a precarious position.||

THE LAST WORD . . . FOR NOW

We are pleased that our findings have been consistent with the extant literature. Historically, methodologically, and theoretically, we have confidence in our results. The model and the results are consistent with the notions that have been developed about the process associated with judicial decision making. Our results also reflect the broad doctrinal analyses of the period. We see the ebb and flow of different doctrines and philosophies that have structured judicial decision making since *Brown*. We also feel that our notions of the impact of precedent and attitudes are more realistic and avoid setting up easily toppled straw persons. Our conception of the influence of separation of powers is pragmatic, reasonable, and does not require Herculean efforts from the justices. Theoretically, we adopted a conservative notion of separation of powers. Methodologically, we tested a variety of measures and got consistent and thus robust results.

This study makes a number of important contributions. On epistemological grounds, this integrative model represents a new way to look at institutional decision making. It combines components from the dominant models and tests them. We argue that this integrative model better captures the reality of Supreme Court decision making than does a strict focus on attitudes or legal considerations.||The behavior of the Supreme Court is governed by the substantive preferences of the justices but tempered by structural considerations, the need to attend to precedent, and the institution's sense of duty and obligation to the law and the Constitution.||

These results lend credence to the effects of checks and balances and separation of powers but reflect the impact of different conditions. Finally, the results have implications for the place of the Supreme Court and the normative role of the institution as the protector of rights and liberties. The Court's need to protect its legitimacy serves as a restraint on the institution. The results suggest that institutional contexts, norms, and rules matter. The Court is, as Justice Robert Jackson said, part of "a complex interdependent scheme of government from which it cannot be severed." The Court seems to be the dominant actor in constitutional interpretation and in questions involving rights and liberties. However, although it is the loudest, it is not the sole voice.

Our results also have implications from a broader institutional perspective. For purposes of simplicity and tractability, the congressional literature often assumes that member preferences are exogenous (Krehbiel 1991; Shepsle and Weingast 1995). In other words, individual policy preferences are shaped outside the halls of Congress. Similarly, most advocates of the attitudinal model hold that judicial preferences are preexisting and remain fixed during justices' tenures on the bench. Like many simplified approaches to legislative behavior, the attitudinal model views judicial decision making as the product of purely exogenous forces. In our view, at least with respect to the institutional level, Supreme Court decision making is the product of both exogenous and endogenous considerations. The Court exercises its collective policy preferences, to be sure, but those preferences must be reconciled – at least in some circumstances – with other factors. Those factors, both endogenous and exogenous, appear to include some fidelity to legal precedent, a shared desire to foster the Court's legitimacy, and respect for coordinate branches of government. In that respect, its decision-making calculus is potentially quite different from the way legislative theories treat decision making in Congress.

In sum, our results indicate that untangling the factors relevant to decision making on the modern Supreme Court is arduous. The challenge arises in part from differences in issue salience and levels of constraint on the Court's decision making. That said, we believe that these factors involve more than just judicial policy preferences that have been exogenously predetermined. As C. Herman Pritchett, the founding father of behavioral research in public law, wrote, "Political scientists who have done so much to put the 'political' in 'political jurisprudence' need to emphasize that it is still 'jurisprudence.' It is judging in a political context, but it is still judging; and judging is something different from legislating or administering. Judges make choices, but they are not the 'free' choices of congressmen" (1969, 42).

Measurement Appendix

There is some relative consensus at least regarding the problems faced in measuring political preferences, but a wide-ranging debate remains in the discipline over the best means or approach to do so. Recent work has shown a great breadth of empirical and theoretical innovation in estimating preferences (see for example Poole 2005; Bailey 2007; Epstein, Martin, Segal, and Westerland 2007). Bailey's work develops estimates of preferences by harnessing a variety of behavioral information (e.g. votes, positions, and cases) to bridge institutions and time using a Bayesian Markov Chain Monte Carlo (MCMC) approach. The method provides valid dynamic preference estimates that can be compared across institutions and over time. The NOMINATE Common Space (Poole 2005; Poole and Rosenthal 1997) scaling procedure produces preferences for comparing both chambers and the president. Epstein, Martin, Segal, and Westerland (2005; 2007) have created the Judicial Common Space measure which maps judicial preferences on the same space as the Common Space for the Congress and President.

Scholars have made strong arguments on both sides of the Bailey and Common Space measurement issue. For example, Bailey, Kamoie, and Maltzman (2005) employ Bailey's preference estimates in order to make inter-institutional comparisons between the president and Court. Their model assesses the effect of the solicitor general on the justices' support of *amicus* briefs for all civil liberties cases from the 1953–2002 terms. They make a strong case in support of their choice of the Bailey preference estimates because of the study's need to compare preferences across institutions and over time, but also because of their exclusive focus on civil liberties cases. The Bailey scores are derived from information resulting from civil rights and civil liberties behaviors. In particular, Bailey's estimation procedure utilizes bridge information in the issue areas of crime, civil rights, free speech, religion, abortion, and privacy (see Bailey and Maltzman 2009, p. 56). With their exclusive focus on civil liberties cases, they are in effect holding the agenda relatively constant in this issue area and thus circumventing one of the classic problems in measuring and attributing effects to preferences on decisions (e.g. change in agenda vs. change in preferences). But that strength characteristic in their analysis may represent a weakness in another. For example, Maltzman and Shipan's model explaining variation in legislative enactments requires a design that incorporates a much broader array of issues which is one reason why they argued the Bailey measure was less appropriate for their work (2008).

An important part of our theoretical focus is on how variation in issues may condition the extent that the Court's preferences or other institutional actors' preferences influence the Court's decision making. So, our design seeks to assess a very wide range of possible issues from civil rights and civil liberties all the way to regulation and economic issues.

It is also true that there are potential disadvantages in using the NOMINATE Common Space measures. For example, the Common Space assumes no fundamental change in the voting space which is problematic because of the emergence of a second dimension (race) that became important in the 1950s–1960s and remained present until it converged into the main liberal-conservative dimension in the 1980s (Poole and Rosenthal 1997; Bailey 2007). In addition, the Common Space scaling technique seemingly does not sufficiently resolve the explaining votes with votes problem (Epstein, Martin, Segal, and Westerland 2007; Maltzman and Shipan 2008). But given our theoretical perspective that focuses on how the Court and other institutional actors' preferences will have differential effects across issues, we think the tradeoff remains in favor of using the Common Space measures.

Nevertheless, beyond our theoretical/design focus we have also let the data speak to inform us of differences in the Bailey and Common Space measures. For the general model, there are no substantive differences between the Common Space and Bailey measures. The comparative results are very similar with only a few modest changes where the pattern tends to strengthen the strategic model results. For example, there are no substantive differences in the results between the Bailey and Common Space measures for economic cases, but in the area of civil liberties the Bailey measure strengthens the strategic model effects (e.g. House).

It is less clear in literature on the Bailey vs. Common Space measures how the constitutional vs. statutory decision context should matter to these two different methods of estimating preferences. We have no a priori expectation of how the Bailey preferences should differ from Common Space once the constitutional vs. statutory condition is overlaid across issues. But comparing the preference measures across the constitutional vs. statutory condition also provides relatively modest differences that tend to strengthen the strategic variables. For example, we find no substantive changes for constitutional civil liberties and civil rights cases between Bailey and the Common Space estimates of preferences. However, for statutory civil liberties and civil rights cases, the Bailey measure for preferences makes the president significant—again favoring the strategic model. So, in general, the patterns we find in comparing between the Bailey and Common Space scores tend to support our argument that the Bailey preferences may be more appropriate for civil liberties and civil rights issues. Where there are modest differences, they tend to appear on civil liberties and civil rights cases or when the constitutional vs. statutory condition is overlaid on issue area. Interestingly, this seems relatively consistent with Bailey and Maltzman's findings (2009) and thus gives us even more confidence in our results. The modest differences that do arise make the strategic variable results marginally stronger. However, we think we have marshaled fairly strong evidence showing the effects of the strategic model under certain important theoretical conditions. Using the Bailey measure would allow us to push the strategic line of argument further and make bolder claims, but we prefer to err on the conservative side in line with where our theory has led us. Thus, based on our theoretical focus and the relative robustness we have found empirically across our theoretical conditions, we think the strongest case is to use the Common Space measures.

Cases Cited

Adkins v. Children's Hospital, 261 U.S. 525 (1923).
Agostini v. Felton, 521 U.S. 203 (1997).
A.L.A. Schechter Poultry Corp. v. United States, 295 U.S. 495 (1935).
Alexander v. Holmes County Board of Education, 396 U.S. 19 (1969).
Allied Structural Steel Co. v. Spannaus, 438 U.S. 234 (1978).
Armstrong v. United States, 364 U.S. 40 (1960).
Ashcroft v. American Civil Liberties Union, 535 U.S. 564 (2002).
Ashcroft v. American Civil Liberties Union, 542 U.S. 656 (2004).
Ashwander v. Tennessee Valley Authority, 297 U.S. 288 (1936).
Bailey v. Drexel Furniture Co., 259 U.S. 20 (1922).
Baker v. Carr, 369 U.S. 186 (1962).
Barron v. Baltimore, 32 U.S. 243 (1833).
Bates v. State Bar of Arizona, 433 U.S. 350 (1977).
Batson v. Kentucky, 476 U.S. 79 (1986).
Berman v. Parker, 348 U.S. 26 (1954).
Betts v. Brady, 316 U.S. 455 (1942).
Bivens v. Six Unknown Named Federal Narcotics Agents, 403 U.S. 388 (1971).
BMW Corporation of North America v. Gore, 517 U.S. 559 (1996).
Board of Education v. Dowell, 498 U.S. 237 (1991).
Board of Education v. Mergens, 496 U.S. 226 (1990).
Bowers v. Hardwick, 478 U.S. 186 (1986).
Brandenburg v. Ohio, 395 U.S. 444 (1969).
Brown v. Allen, 344 U.S. 443 (1953).
Brown v. Board of Education, 347 U.S. 483 (1954).
Brown v. Board of Education (Brown II), 349 U.S. 294 (1955).
Buckley v. Valeo, 424 U.S. 1 (1976).
Bush v. Gore, 531 U.S. 98 (2000).
California v. Ciraolo, 476 U.S. 207 (1986).
Camara v. Municipal Court, 387 U.S. 523 (1967).
Carter v. Carter Coal Company, 298 U.S. 238 (1936).

Castaneda v. Partida, 430 U.S. 482 (1977).
Central Hudson Gas and Electric Corporation v. Public Services Commission of New York, 447 U.S. 557 (1980).
Chaplinsky v. New Hampshire, 315 U.S. 568 (1942).
Chappell v. Wallace, 462 U.S. 296 (1983).
Chevron USA v. Natural Resources Defense Council, 467 U.S. 837 (1984).
City of Boerne v. Flores, 521 U.S. 507 (1997).
Cohen v. California, 403 U.S. 15 (1971).
Complete Auto Transit v. Brady, 430 U.S. 274 (1977).
Cooper v. Aaron, 358 U.S. 1 (1958).
Cooper Industries v. Leatherman Tool Group, 532 U.S. 424 (2001).
Daniel v. Paul, 395 U.S. 298 (1969).
Dennis v. United States, 341 U.S. 494 (1951).
Dickerson v. United States, 530 U.S. 428 (2000).
Dolan v. City of Tigard, 512 U.S. 374 (1994).
Donaldson FKA Sweet v. United States, 400 U.S. 517 (1971).
Donovan v. Dewey, 452 U.S. 594 (1981).
Duke Power Co. v. Carolina Environmental Study Group, 438 U.S. 59 (1978).
El Paso v. Simmons, 379 U.S. 497 (1965).
Employment Division v. Smith, 494 U.S. 872 (1990).
Energy Reserves Group, Inc. v. Kansas Power and Light Co., 459 U.S. 400 (1983).
Environmental Protection Agency v. Mink, 410 U.S. 73 (1973).
Escobedo v. Illinois, 378 U.S. 478 (1964).
Ewing v. California, 538 U.S. 11 (2003).
Ex parte McCardle, 74 U.S. 506 (1869).
Exxon Corp. v. Governor of Maryland, 437 U.S. 117 (1978).
Exxon Shipping Co. v. Baker, 554 U.S. 471 (2008).
Fay v. Noia, 372 U.S. 391 (1963).
FCC v. Pacifica Foundation, 438 U.S. 726 (1978).
Federal Aviation Administration v. Robertson, 422 U.S. 255 (1975).
Federal Bureau of Investigation v. Abramson, 456 U.S. 615 (1982).
Felker v. Turpin, 518 U.S. 651 (1996).
Feres v. United States, 340 U.S. 135 (1950).
Ferguson v. Skrupa, 372 U.S. 726 (1963).
First English Evangelical Lutheran Church v. County of Los Angeles, 482 U.S. 304 (1987).
Forsham v. Harris, 445 U.S. 169 (1980).
Flood v. Kuhn, 407 U.S. 258 (1972).
Frontiero v. Richardson, 411 U.S. 677 (1973).
Furman v. Georgia, 408 U.S. 238 (1972).
Gibbons v. Ogden, 22 U.S. 1 (1824).
Gideon v. Wainwright, 372 U.S. 335 (1963).
Ginzburg v. United States, 383 U.S. 463 (1966).
Goldberg v. Sweet, 488 U.S. 252 (1989).
Goldblatt v. Hempstead, 369 U.S. 590 (1962).
Gonzalez v. Raich, 545 U.S. 1 (2005).

Griggs v. Allegheny County, 369 U.S. 84 (1962).
Griggs v. Duke Power Co., 401 U.S. 424 (1971).
Griggs v. Duke Power Co., 420 F. 2d 1225 (1970).
Griswold v. Connecticut, 381 U.S. 479 (1965).
Grove City College v. Bell, 465 U.S. 555 (1984).
Hammer v. Dagenhart, 247 U.S. 251 (1918).
Harris v. McRae, 448 U.S. 297 (1980).
Hawaii Housing Authority v. Midkiff, 467 U.S. 229 (1984).
Heart of Atlanta Motel v. United States, 379 U.S. 241 (1964).
Hill v. Colorado, 530 U.S. 703 (2000).
Hodel v. Indiana, 452 U.S. 314 (1981).
Home Building & Loan Association v. Blaisdell, 290 U.S. 398 (1934).
Huggins v. Raines, 374 U.S. 105 (1963).
Hustler Magazine v. Falwell, 485 US 46 (1988).
Illinois v. Perkins, 496 U.S. 292 (1990).
Jenkins v. Georgia, 418 U.S. 153 (1974).
Jones v. Alfred Mayer, 392 U.S. 409 (1968).
Katz v. United States, 389 U.S. 347 (1967).
Katzenbach v. McClung, 379 U.S. 294 (1964).
Kelo v. City of New London, 545 U.S. 469 (2005).
Keystone Bituminous Coal Association v. DeBenedictis, 480 U.S. 470 (1987).
Kissinger v. Reporters Committee for Freedom of the Press, 445 U.S. 136 (1980).
Kyllo v. United States, 533 U.S. 27 (2001).
Lamb's Chapel v. Center Moriches Union Free School District, 508 U.S. 384 (1993).
Lechmere, Inc. v. N.L.R.B., 502 U.S. 527 (1992).
Lemon v. Kurtzman, 403 U.S. 602 (1971).
Lochner v. New York, 198 U.S. 45 (1905).
Locomotive Firemen v. Chicago R. I. and Pac. R. Co., 393 U.S. 129 (1968).
Lucas v. South Carolina Coastal Council, 505 U.S. 1003 (1992).
Mallory v. United States, 354 U.S. 449 (1957).
Mapp v. Ohio, 367 U.S. 643 (1961).
Marbury v. Madison, 5 U.S. 137 (1803).
Martin v. Hunter's Lessee, 14 U.S. 304 (1816).
Maryland v. Wirtz, 392 U.S. 183 (1968).
McCleskey v. Kemp, 481 U.S. 279 (1987).
McCulloch v. Maryland, 17 U.S. 316 (1819).
Memoirs v. Massachusetts, 383 U.S. 413 (1966).
Meritor Savings Bank FSB v. Vinson, 477 U.S. 57 (1986).
Michelin Tire Corp. v. Wages, 423 U.S. 276 (1976).
Miller v. California, 413 U.S. 15 (1973).
Miranda v. Arizona, 384 U.S. 436 (1966).
Murray v. Carrier, 477 U.S. 478 (1986).
National Bellas Hess, Inc. v. Department of Revenue of Illinois, 386 U.S. 753 (1967).
National Labor Relations Board v. Joues & Laughlin Steel Corp. 301 U.S. 1 (1937).

References

Abraham, Henry J. 2008. *Justices, Presidents, and Senators: A History of the U.S. Supreme Court Appointments from Washington to Bush II* (5th ed.). Lanham, Md.: Rowman & Littlefield.

Aldisert, Ruggero. 1990. "Precedent: What It Is and What It Isn't; When Do We Kiss It and When Do We Kill It?" *Pepperdine Law Review* 17: 605–636.

Aleinikoff, T. Alexander. 2002. *Semblances of Sovereignty – The Constitution, the State, and American Citizenship.* Cambridge: Harvard University Press.

Allen, Charlotte. 2005. "A Wreck of a Plan." *Washington Post*, July 17, B01.

Alvarez, R. Michael, and John Brehm. 1998. "Speaking in Two Voices: American Equivocation About the Internal Revenue Service." *American Journal of Political Science* 42: 418–452.

Anastaplo, George. 2007. *Reflections on Freedom of Speech and the First Amendment.* Lexington: University Press of Kentucky.

Axelrod-Contrada, Joan. 2006. *Internet Censorship: Reno v. ACLU.* New York: Benchmark Press.

Bailey, Michael. 2007. "Comparable Preference Estimates Across Time and Institutions for the Court, Congress and Presidency." *American Journal of Political Science* 51: 433–448.

Bailey, Michael and Forrest Maltzman. forthcoming. *The Constrained Court: Law, Politics and the Decisions Justices Make.* Princeton: Princeton University Press.

Bailey, Michael, Brian Kamoie, and Forrest Maltzman. 2005. "Signals from the Tenth Justice: The Political Role of the Solicitor General in Supreme Court Decision Making." *American Journal of Political Science* 49: 72–85.

Bailey, Michael, and Forrest Maltzman. 2008. "Does Legal Doctrine Matter? Unpacking Law and Policy Preferences on the U.S. Supreme Court." *American Political Science Review* 102: 369–384.

Baird, Vanessa. 2007. *Answering the Call of the Court: How Justices and Litigants Set the Supreme Court Agenda.* Charlottesville: University of Virginia Press.

Baird, Vanessa. 2004. "The Effect of Politically Salient Decisions on the U.S. Supreme Court's Agenda." *Journal of Politics* 66: 755–772.

Baker, Leonard. 1967. *Back to Back: The Duel Between FDR and the Supreme Court.* New York: Macmillan.

Baker, Liva. 1983. *Miranda: Crime, Law, and Politics.* New York: Atheneum.

Baker, Nancy. 1992. *Conflicting Loyalties: Law and Politics in the Attorney General's Office, 1789–1990.* Lawrence: University Press of Kansas.

Ball, Howard. 2000. *The Bakke Case: Race, Education, & Affirmative Action.* Lawrence: University Press of Kansas.

Ball, Howard. 1988. "The United States Supreme Court's Glossing of the Federal Torts Claims Act: Statutory Construction and Veterans' Tort Actions." *Western Political Quarterly* 41: 529–552.

Ball, Howard. 1978. *Judicial Craftsmanship or Fiat? Direct Overturn by the United States Supreme Court.* Westport, Conn.: Praeger.

Ball, Howard, and Philip Cooper. 1992. *Of Power and Right: Hugo Black, William O. Douglas, and America's Constitutional Revolution.* New York: Oxford University Press.

Bamberger, Michael 2000. *Reckless Legislation: How Lawmakers Ignore the Constitution.* New Brunswick: Rutgers University Press.

Barilleaux, Ryan J. 2006. "Venture Constitutionalism and the Enlargement of the Presidency." In Christopher S. Kelley (Ed.), *Executing the Constitution: Putting the President Back into the Constitution,* pp. 37–52. Albany: State University of New York Press.

Barnes, Jeb. 2004. *Overruled: Legislative Overrides, Pluralism, and Contemporary Court-Congress Relations.* Stanford: Stanford University Press.

Bartee, Alice Fleetwood. 1984. *Cases Lost, Causes Won.* New York: St. Martin's.

Bartels, Brandon. 2001. "Supreme Court Outputs and the Political Environment: A Neo-Institutional Macro-Analytic Perspective." Paper presented at the Midwest Political Science Association Meetings, Chicago.

Baum, Lawrence. 2010. *The Supreme Court* (10th ed.). Washington, D.C.: CQ Press.

Baum, Lawrence. 2006. *Judges and their Audiences.* Princeton: Princeton University Press.

Baum, Lawrence. 1997. *The Puzzle of Judicial Behavior.* Ann Arbor: University of Michigan Press.

Baum, Lawrence. 1992. "Membership Change and Collective Voting Change in the United States Supreme Court." *Journal of Politics* 54: 3–24.

Baum, Lawrence. 1988. "Measuring Policy Change in the U.S. Supreme Court." *American Political Science Review* 82: 905–912.

Baumgartner, Frank, and Bryan Jones. 1993. *Agendas and Instability in American Politics.* Chicago: University of Chicago Press.

Beck, James. 1993. *Raphael: The Stanza Della Segnatura.* New York: George Braziller.

Beesley, Susan L., and Theresa A. Newman Glover. 1987. "Developments Under the Freedom of Information Act: 1986." *Duke Law Journal* 1987: 521–567.

Belknap, Michal. 2005. *The Supreme Court Under Earl Warren, 1953–1969.* Columbia: University of South Carolina Press.

Bell, Derrick A., Jr. 1980. *Race, Racism, and American Law* (2d ed.). Boston: Little, Brown.

Bendor, Jonathan, and Terry Moe. 1985. "An Adaptive Model of Bureaucratic Politics." *American Political Science Review* 79: 755–774.

Benecki, Maria H. 1988. "Developments Under the Freedom of Information Act: 1987." *Duke Law Journal* 1988: 566–607.

Benesh, Sara C., and Malia Reddick. 2002. "Overruled: An Event History Analysis of Lower Court Reaction to Supreme Court Alteration of Precedent." *Journal of Politics* 64: 534–550.

Benesh, Sara C., and Harold J. Spaeth. 2001. "Salient to Whom? A Potential Measure of Salience to the Justices." Paper presented at the annual meeting of the American Political Science Association, San Francisco.

Benson, Paul R., Jr. 1970. *The Supreme Court and the Commerce Clause, 1937–1970.* New York: Dunellen.

Berelson, Bernard, Paul Lazarsfeld, and William McPhee. 1954. *Voting: A Study of Opinion Formation in a Presidential Campaign.* Chicago: University of Chicago Press.

Bergara, Mario, Barak Richman, and Pablo T. Spiller. 2003. "Modeling Supreme Court Strategic Decision Making: The Congressional Constraint." *Legislative Studies Quarterly* 28: 247–280.

Berner, Richard Olin. 1976. "The Effect of the 1976 Amendment to Exemption Three of the Freedom of Information Act." *Columbia Law Review* 76: 1029–1047.

Bickel, Alexander M. 1962. *The Least Dangerous Branch: The Supreme Court at the Bar of Politics.* Indianapolis: Bobbs-Merrill.

Bland, Randall W. 1993. *Private Pressure on Public Law: The Legal Career of Justice Thurgood Marshall, 1934–1991* (rev. ed.). Lanham, Md.: University Press of America.

Blasecki, Janet. 1990. "Justice Lewis Powell: Swing Voter or Staunch Conservative?" *Journal of Politics* 52: 530–547.

Blasi, Vincent (Ed.). 1983. *The Burger Court: The Counter-Revolution That Wasn't.* New Haven: Yale University Press.

Blumrosen, Alfred W. 1993. *Modern Law: The Law Transmission System and Equal Employment Opportunity.* Madison: University of Wisconsin Press.

Bork, Robert H. 1996. *Slouching Towards Gomorrah: Modern Liberalism and American Decline.* New York: Harper Collins.

Bork, Robert H. 1971. "Neutral Principles and Some First Amendment Problems." *Indiana Law Journal* 47: 1–35.

Boucher, Richard, Jr., and Jeffrey Segal. 1995. "Supreme Court Justices as Strategic Decision Makers: Aggressive Grants and Defensive Denials on the Vinson Court." *Journal of Politics* 57: 824–837.

Brady, David, and Craig Volden. 2005. *Revolving Gridlock: Politics and Policy from Carter to Clinton* (2d ed.). Boulder: Westview Press.

Branch, Taylor. 1988. *Parting the Waters: America in the King Years 1954–1963.* New York: Simon and Schuster.

Brehm, John, and Scott Gates. 1997. *Working, Shirking, and Sabotage: Bureaucratic Response to a Democratic Public.* Ann Arbor: University of Michigan Press.

Brenner, Saul. 1980. "Fluidity on the United States Supreme Court: A Reexamination." *American Journal of Political Science* 24: 526–535.

Brenner, Saul, and Theodore Arrington. 1987. "Unanimous Decision Making on the U.S. Supreme Court: Case Stimuli and Judicial Attitudes." *Political Behavior* 9: 75–86.

Brenner, Saul, and Harold Spaeth. 1995. *Stare Indecisis: The Alteration of Precedent on the Supreme Court, 1946–1992.* Cambridge: Cambridge University Press.

Brisbin, Richard A., Jr. 1997. *Justice Antonin Scalia and the Conservative Revival.* Baltimore: Johns Hopkins University Press.

Brisbin, Richard A., Jr. 1996. "Slaying the Dragon: Segal, Spaeth and the Function of Law in Supreme Court Decision Making." *American Journal of Political Science* 40: 1004–1017.

Burnham, Walter Dean. 1970. *Critical Elections and the Mainsprings of American Politics.* New York: W.W. Norton.

Caldeira, Gregory, John Wright, and Christopher Zorn. 1999. "Sophisticated Voting and Gate-Keeping in the Supreme Court." *Journal of Law, Economics, and Organization* 15: 549–572.

Campbell, Angus, Philip Converse, Warren Miller, and Donald Stokes. 1960. *The American Voter.* New York: John Wiley and Sons.

Canon, Bradley, and Charles Johnson. 1999. *Judicial Policies: Implementation and Impact.* Washington, D.C.: CQ Press.

Caplan, Lincoln. 1987. *The Tenth Justice: The Solicitor General and the Rule of Law.* New York: Vintage Books.

Carmines, Edward, and James Stimson. 1989. *Issue Evolution: Race and the Transformation of American Politics.* Princeton: Princeton University Press.

Carp, Robert, Ronald Stidham, and Kenneth Manning. 2004. *Judicial Process in America* (6th ed.). Washington, D.C.: CQ Press.

Casper, Jonathan D. 1976. "The Supreme Court and National Policy Making." *American Political Science Review* 70: 50–63.

Cater, Douglass. 1964. *Power in Washington: A Critical Look at Today's Struggle to Govern the Nation's Capital.* New York: Random House.

Chen, Jim. 2003. "Filburn's Legacy." *Emory Law Journal* 52: 1719–1769.

Cheney, Timothy 1998. *Who Makes the Law: The Supreme Court, Congress, the States, and Society.* Upper Saddle River: Prentice-Hall.

Clark, Elias. 1975. "Holding Government Accountable: The Amended Freedom of Information Act – An Article in Honor of Fred Rodell." *Yale Law Journal* 84: 741–769.

Clark, Hunter. 1995. *Justice Brennan: The Great Conciliator.* Secaucus: Carol Publishing Group.

Claude, Richard. 1970. *The Supreme Court and the Electoral Process.* Baltimore: Johns Hopkins University Press.

Clausen, Aage. 1973. *How Congressmen Decide: A Policy Focus.* New York: Palgrave MacMillan.

Clayton, Cornell. 1999. "The Supreme Court and Political Jurisprudence: New and Old Institutionalisms." In Cornell Clayton and Howard Gillman (Eds.), *Supreme Court Decision Making: New Institutionalist Approaches,* pp. 15–41. Chicago: University of Chicago Press.

Clayton, Cornell. 1992. *The Politics of Justice: The Attorney General and the Making of Legal Policy.* Armonk: M.E. Sharpe.

Clayton, Cornell, and Howard Gillman (Eds). 1999. *Supreme Court Decision Making: New Institutionalist Approaches.* Chicago: University of Chicago Press.

Cleary, Edward. 1994. *Beyond the Burning Cross: A Landmark Case of Race, Censorship, and the First Amendment.* New York: Vintage.

Cohen, Linda, and Matthew Spitzer. 1994. "Solving the *Chevron* Puzzle." *Law and Contemporary Problems* 57: 65–110.

Collins, Paul M., Jr. 2008. *Friends of the Supreme Court.* New York: Oxford University Press.

Cortner, Richard. 2001. *Civil Rights and Public Accommodations: The Heart of Atlanta Motel and McClung Cases.* Lawrence: University Press of Kansas.

Cortner, Richard. 1981. *The Supreme Court and the Second Bill of Rights: The Fourteenth Amendment and the Nationalization of Civil Rights.* Madison: University of Wisconsin Press.

Cortner, Richard. 1970. *The Apportionment Cases.* Knoxville: University of Tennessee Press.

Corwin, Edward. 1984. *The President: Office and Powers* (5th ed.). New York: NYU Press.

Cottrol, Robert, Raymond Diamond, and Leland Ware. 2003. *Brown v. Board of Education: Caste, Culture, and the Constitution.* Lawrence: University Press of Kansas.

Coyne, Thomas. 1985. "*Hawaii Housing Authority v. Midkiff:* A Final Requiem for the Public Use Limitation on Eminent Domain." *Notre Dame Law Review* 60: 388–404.

Cox, Gary, and Mathew McCubbins. 1993. *Legislative Leviathan: Party Government in the House.* Berkeley: University of California Press.

Cross, Frank B., and Blake J. Nelson. 2001. "Strategic Institutional Effects on Supreme Court Decisionmaking." *Northwestern University Law Review* 95: 1437–1493.

Crowley, Donald. 1987. "Judicial Review of Administrative Agencies: Does the Type of Agency Matter?" *Political Research Quarterly* 40: 265–283.

Curry, Brett W. 2005. "The Courts, Congress, and the Politics of Federal Jurisdiction." Ph.D. diss., The Ohio State University, Columbus.

Curry, Brett W., Richard L. Pacelle Jr., and Bryan W. Marshall. 2008. "An 'Informal and Limited Alliance': The President and the Supreme Court." *Presidential Studies Quarterly* 38: 223–247.

Cushman, Barry. 1998. *Rethinking the New Deal Court: The Structure of a Constitutional Revolution.* New York: Oxford University Press.

Dahl, Robert. 1957. "Decision Making in a Democracy: The Supreme Court as a National Policy-Maker." *Journal of Public Law* 6: 279–295.

Danelski, David. 1978. "The Influence of the Chief Justice in the Decisional Process of the Supreme Court." In Sheldon Goldman and Austin Sarat (Eds.), *American Court Systems*, pp. 506–518. San Francisco: Freeman.

Davis, Dena. 2000. "Religious Clubs in the Public Schools: What Happened After *Mergens*?" *Albany Law Review* 64: 225–239.

Davis, Michael, and Hunter Clark. 1992. *Thurgood Marshall: Warrior at the Bar, Rebel on the Bench.* New York: Birch Lane Press.

Days, Drew. 1994–1995. "In Search of the Solicitor General's Client: A Drama with Many Characters." *Kentucky Law Review* 83: 485–503.

Deering, Christopher J., and Forrest Maltzman 1999. "The Politics of Executive Orders: Legislative Constraints on Presidential Power." *Political Research Quarterly* 52: 767–83.

Dempsey, Paul Stephen. 1984. "The Interstate Commerce Commission – Disintegration of an American Legal Institution." *American University Law Review* 34: 1–51.

De Sario, Jack P., and William D. Mason. 2003. *Dr. Sam Sheppard on Trial: The Prosecutors and the Marilyn Sheppard Murder.* Kent: Kent State University Press.

Dierenfield, Bruce J. 2007. *The Battle Over School Prayer: How Engel v. Vitale Changed America.* Lawrence: University Press of Kansas.

Dodd, Lawrence. 1986. "A Theory of Congressional Cycles: Solving the Puzzle of Change." In Lawrence Dodd, Gerald Wright, and Leroy Rieselbach (Eds.), *Congress and Policy Change*, pp. 3–44. New York: Agathon Press.

Downs, Anthony. 1967. *Inside Bureaucracy.* Boston: Little, Brown.

Dripps, Donald. 2001. "Constitutional Theory for Criminal Procedure: *Dickerson, Miranda*, and the Continuing Quest for Broad-but-Shallow." *William and Mary Law Review* 43: 1–77.

Dubroff, Harold. 1979. *The United States Tax Court: An Historical Analysis.* Chicago: Commerce Clearing House.

Ducat, Craig, and Robert Dudley. 1987. "Dimensions Underlying Economic Policymaking in the Early and Later Burger Court." *Journal of Politics* 49: 521–539.

Dudley, Robert, and Craig Ducat. 1986. "The Burger Court and Economic Liberalism." *Political Research Quarterly* 39: 236–249.

Dunne, Gerald. 1977. *Hugo Black and the Judicial Revolution.* New York: Simon & Schuster.

Eisler, Kim Isaac. 1993. *A Justice For All: William J. Brennan, Jr. and the Decisions That Transformed America.* New York: Simon and Schuster.

Eisner, Marc Allen, Jeff Worsham, and Evan Ringquist. 2006. *Contemporary Regulatory Policy* (2d ed.). Boulder: Lynne Rienner Publishers.

Ely, James W. 1992. "Property Rights and Judicial Activism." *Georgetown Journal of Law and Public Policy.* Inaugural Issue: 125–127.

Epp, Charles. 1998. *The Rights Revolution: Lawyers, Activists, and Supreme Courts in Comparative Perspective.* Chicago: University of Chicago Press.

Epstein, Lee. 1985. *Conservatives in Court.* Knoxville: University of Tennessee Press.

Epstein, Lee, Valerie Hoekstra, Jeffrey Segal, and Harold Spaeth. 1998. "Do Political Preferences Change? A Longitudinal Study of U.S. Supreme Court Justices." *Journal of Politics* 60: 801–818.

Epstein, Lee, and Jack Knight. 1999. "Mapping Out the Strategic Terrain: The Informational Role of *Amici Curiae*." In Cornell Clayton and Howard Gillman

(Eds.), *Institutional Approaches to Supreme Court Decision Making*, pp. 215–236. Chicago: University of Chicago Press.

Epstein, Lee, and Jack Knight. 1998. *The Choices Justices Make*. Washington, D.C.: CQ Press.

Epstein, Lee, and Jack Knight. 1997. "The New Institutionalism, Part II." *Law and Courts* 7: 4–9.

Epstein, Lee, Jack Knight, and Andrew D. Martin. 2001. "The Supreme Court as a Strategic National Policymaker." *Emory Law Journal* 50: 583–611.

Epstein, Lee, and Joseph Kobylka. 1992. *The Supreme Court and Legal Change: Abortion and the Death Penalty*. Chapel Hill: University of North Carolina Press.

Epstein, Lee, Andrew Martin, Jeffrey Segal, and Chad Westerland. 2007. "The Judicial Common Space." *Journal of Law, Economics, & Organization* 23: 303–325.

Epstein, Lee, and Carol Mershon. 1996. "Measuring Political Preferences." *American Journal of Political Science* 40: 261–294.

Epstein, Lee, and Jeffrey Segal. 2005. *Advice and Consent: The Politics of Judicial Appointments*. New York: Oxford University Press

Epstein, Lee, and Jeffrey Segal. 2000. "Measuring Issue Salience." *American Journal of Political Science* 44: 66–83.

Epstein, Lee, Jeffrey Segal, Harold Spaeth, and Thomas G. Walker. 2007. *The Supreme Court Compendium: Data, Decisions, and Developments* (4th ed.). Washington D.C.: CQ Press.

Epstein, Lee, Jeffrey Segal, Harold Spaeth, and Thomas G. Walker. 2003. *The Supreme Court Compendium: Data, Decisions, and Developments* (3rd ed.). Washington D.C.: CQ Press.

Epstein, Lee, Nancy Staudt, and Peter Wiedenbeck. 2003. "Judging Statutes: Thoughts on Statutory Interpretation and Notes for a Project on the Internal Revenue Code." *Washington University Journal of Law & Policy* 13: 305–333.

Epstein, Lee, and Thomas G. Walker. 2007a. *Constitutional Law for a Changing America: Institutional Powers and Constraints* (6th ed.). Washington, D.C.: CQ Press.

Epstein, Lee, and Thomas G. Walker. 2007b. *Constitutional Law for a Changing America: Rights, Liberties, and Justice* (6th ed.). Washington, D.C.: CQ Press.

Epstein, Lee, and Thomas G. Walker. 1998a. *Constitutional Law for a Changing America: Institutional Powers and Constraints* (3rd ed.). Washington, D.C.: CQ Press.

Epstein, Lee, and Thomas G. Walker. 1998b. *Constitutional Law for a Changing America: Rights, Liberties, and Justice* (3rd ed.). Washington, D.C.: CQ Press.

Epstein, Lee, and Thomas G. Walker. 1995. "The Role of the Supreme Court in American Society: Playing the Reconstruction Game." In Lee Epstein (Ed.), *Contemplating Courts*, pp. 315–346. Washington D.C.: CQ Press.

Epstein, Richard. 2008. "How to Complicate Habeas Corpus." *New York Times*, June 21, B21.

Epstein, Richard. 1993. "*Lucas v. South Carolina Coastal Council*: A Tangled Web of Expectations." *Stanford Law Review* 45: 1369–1392.

Epstein, Richard. 1985. *Takings: Private Property and the Power of Eminent Domain*. Cambridge: Harvard University Press.

Erikson, Robert, Michael MacKuen, and James Stimson. 2002. *The Macro Polity*. New York: Cambridge University Press.

Eskridge, William N., Jr. 1994. *Dynamic Statutory Interpretation*. Cambridge: Harvard University Press.

Eskridge, William N., Jr. 1991a. "Overriding Supreme Court Statutory Interpretation Decisions." *Yale Law Journal* 101: 331–417.

Eskridge, William N., Jr. 1991b. "Reneging on History? Playing the Court/Congress/President Civil Rights Game." *California Law Review* 79: 613–684.

Eskridge, William N., Jr. 1990. "The Case of the Amorous Defendant: Criticizing Absolute *Stare Decisis* for Statutory Cases – April 2001." *Michigan Law Review* 88: 2450–2466.

Eskridge, William N., Jr., and Lauren E. Baer. 2008. "The Continuum of Deference: Supreme Court Treatment of Agency Statutory Interpretation from *Chevron* to *Hamdan*." *Georgetown Law Review* 96: 1083–1226.

Eskridge, William N., Jr., and Philip P. Frickey. 1994. "The Making of the Legal Process." *Harvard Law Review* 107: 2031–2055.

Estreicher, Samuel, and John Sexton. 1986. *Redefining the Supreme Court's Role: A Theory of Managing the Federal Judicial Process*. New Haven: Yale University Press.

Fallon, Richard H., Jr., Daniel J. Meltzer, and David L. Shapiro. 1996. *Hart and Wechsler's The Federal Courts and the Federal System*. Westbury: Foundation Press.

Farber, Daniel A., and Philip P. Frickey. 1991. "In the Shadow of the Legislature: The Common Law In the Age of the New Public Law." *Michigan Law Review* 89: 875–905.

Fenno, Richard F., Jr. 1973. *Congressmen in Committees*. Boston: Little Brown.

Ferejohn, John, and Charles Shipan. 1990. "Congressional Influence on Bureaucracy." *Journal of Law, Economics, and Organization* 6: 1–20.

Fiorina, Morris P. 1996. *Divided Government* (2d ed.). New York: Macmillan.

Fiorina, Morris P., and Kenneth A. Shepsle. 1989. "Formal Theories of Leadership: Agents, Agenda Setting, and Entrepreneurs." In Bryan D. Jones (Ed.), *Leadership and Politics: New Perspectives in Political Science*, pp. 17–40. Lawrence: University Press of Kansas.

Fischel, William A. 1995. *Regulatory Takings: Law, Economics, and Politics*. Cambridge: Harvard University Press.

Fisher, Louis. 2000. *Congressional Abdication on War and Spending*. College Station: Texas A&M University Press.

Fisher, Louis 1998. *The Politics of Shared Power*. College Station: Texas A&M University Press.

Fisher, Louis, and Neal Devins. 1992. *Political Dynamics of Constitutional Law*. St. Paul: West.

Foerstel, Herbert N. 1999. *Freedom of Information and the Right to Know: The Origins and Applications of the Freedom of Information Act*. Westport, Conn.: Greenwood Press.

Force, Robert. 1999. "An Essay on Federal Common Law and Admiralty." *Saint Louis Law Journal* 43: 1367–1387.

Fox, Arthur. 1987. "Showing Workers Who's Boss." In Herman Schwartz (Ed.), *The Burger Court: Rights and Wrongs in the Supreme Court 1969–1986*, pp. 228–239. New York: Penguin Books.

Fox, Eleanor. 2002. "Antitrust and Business Power." In Herman Schwartz (Ed.), *The Rehnquist Court: Judicial Activism on the Right*, pp. 213–225. New York: Hill and Wang.

Franklin, Charles, and Liane Kosaki. 1989. "Republican Schoolmaster: The U.S. Supreme Court, Public Opinion, and Abortion." *American Political Science Review* 83: 751–771.

Freeman, J. Leiper. 1965. *The Political Process: Executive Bureau-Legislative Committee Relations*. New York: Random House.

Friedman, Barry, and Anna Harvey. 2003. "Electing the Supreme Court." *Indiana Law Journal* 78: 123–152.

Galanter, Marc. 1974. "Why the 'Haves' Come Out Ahead: Speculations on the Limits of Legal Change." *Law & Society Review* 9: 95–160.

Gates, John. 1992. *The Supreme Court and Partisan Realignment: A Macro- and Microlevel Perspective*. Boulder: Westview Press.

Gely, Rafael, and Pablo Spiller. 1990. "A Rational Choice Theory of Supreme Court Statutory Decisions with Applications to the *State Farm* and *Grove City* Cases." *Journal of Law, Economics, and Organization* 6: 263–300.

George, Tracey, and Lee Epstein. 1992. "On the Nature of Supreme Court Decision Making." *American Political Science Review* 86: 323–337.

Gerhardt, Michael. 2008. *The Power of Precedent*. New York: Oxford University Press.

Gibson, James L. 1991. "Decision Making in Appellate Courts." In John Gates and Charles Johnson (Eds.), *The American Courts: A Critical Assessment*, pp. 255–278. Washington, D.C.: CQ Press.

Gibson, James L. 1983. "From Simplicity to Complexity: The Development of Theory in the Study of Judicial Behavior." *Political Behavior* 5: 7–49.

Gifford, Daniel J. 1995. "The Jurisprudence of Antitrust." *Southern Methodist University Law Review* 48: 1677–1712.

Gillman, Howard. 1993. *The Constitution Besieged: The Rise and Demise of Lochner Era Police Powers Jurisprudence*. Durham: Duke University Press.

Gillman, Howard, and Cornell Clayton. 1999. *The Supreme Court in American Politics: New Institutional Interpretations*. Lawrence: University Press of Kansas.

Goldman, Robert. 2008. *One Man Out: Curt Flood Versus Baseball*. Lawrence: University Press of Kansas.

Goldman, Sheldon, and Thomas Jahnige. 1985. *The Federal Courts as a Political System* (3rd ed.). New York: Harper and Row.

Goldman, Sheldon, and Austin Sarat. 1989. *American Court Systems* (2d ed.). New York: Longman.

Goldstein, Leslie. 1995. "By Consent of the Governed: Directions in Constitutional Theory." In Lee Epstein (Ed.), *Contemplating Courts*, pp. 275–295. Washington D.C.: CQ Press.

Goldstein, Robert Justin. 2000. *Flag Burning and Free Speech: The Case of Texas v. Johnson*. Lawrence: University Press of Kansas.

Goplen, Susan K. 1993. "Judicial Deference to Administrative Agencies' Legal Interpretations After *Lechmere, Inc. v. NLRB.*" *Washington Law Review* 68: 207–226.

Gormley, William. 1989. *Taming the Bureaucracy: Muscles, Prayer, and Other Strategies*. Princeton: Princeton University Press.

Gould, William B., IV. 2000. "American Regulatory Policy: Have We Found the "Third Way? Labor Policy Beyond the New Deal." *Kansas Law Review* 48: 751–764.

Graber, Mark. 1991. *Transforming Free Speech: The Ambiguous Legacy of Civil Libertarianism*. Berkeley: University of California Press.

Graham, Fred. 1970. *The Due Process Revolution: The Warren Court's Impact on Criminal Law*. New York: Hayden.

Graham, Hugh Davis. 1990. *The Civil Rights Era: Origins and Development of National Policy, 1960–1972*. New York: Oxford University Press.

Greenberg, Jack. 1994. *Crusaders in the Courts: How a Dedicated Band of Lawyers Fought for the Civil Rights Revolution*. New York: Basic Books.

Greenhouse, Linda. 2005. *Becoming Justice Blackmun*. New York: Times Books.

Grey, Thomas. 1975. "Do We Have an Unwritten Constitution?" *Stanford Law Review* 27: 703–718.

Grossman, Joel B. 1963. "Role-Playing and the Analysis of Judicial Behavior: The Case of Justice Frankfurter." *Journal of Public Law* 11: 285–309.

Hagle, Timothy, and Harold Spaeth. 1993. "Ideological Patterns in the Justices' Voting in the Burger Court's Business Cases." *Journal of Politics* 55: 492–505.

Hagle, Timothy, and Harold Spaeth. 1992. "The Emergence of a New Ideology: The Business Decisions of the Burger Court." *Journal of Politics* 54: 120–134.

Haiman, Franklyn. 1981. *Speech and Law in a Free Society*. Chicago: University of Chicago Press.

Hamilton, Alexander. 1982. "Federalist 79." In Garry Wills (Ed.), *The Federalist Papers by Alexander Hamilton, James Madison and John Jay*. New York: Bantam Books.

Hammond, Thomas. 1986. "Agenda Control, Organizational Structure, and Bureaucratic Politics." *American Journal of Political Science* 30: 379–420.

Hammond, Thomas, Chris Bonneau, and Reginald Sheehan. 2005. *Strategic Behavior on the U.S. Supreme Court*. Stanford: Stanford University Press.

Hansford, Thomas G., and David F. Damore. 2000. "Congressional Preferences, Perceptions of Threat, and Supreme Court Decision Making." *American Politics Quarterly* 28: 512–532.

Hansford, Thomas G., and James F. Spriggs II. 2007. "Supreme Court Responses to Congressional Overrides." Paper presented at the Midwest Political Science Association Meetings, Chicago.

Hansford, Thomas G., and James F. Spriggs II. 2006. *The Politics of Precedent on the U.S. Supreme Court*. Princeton: Princeton University Press.

Harriger, Katy. 1997. "The Federalism Debate in the Transformation of Federal Habeas Corpus Law." *Publius: The Journal of Federalism* 27: 1–22.

Harvey, Anna, and Barry Friedman. 2006. "Pulling Punches: Congressional Constraints on the Supreme Court's Constitutional Rulings, 1987–2000." *Legislative Studies Quarterly* 31: 533–562.

Hausegger, Lori, and Lawrence Baum. 1999. "Inviting Congressional Action: A Study of Supreme Court Motivations in Statutory Interpretation." *American Journal of Political Science* 43: 162–183.

Haynie, Stacia. 2004. "The Court's Protection Against Self-Incrimination: *Miranda v. Arizona* (1966)." In Gregg Ivers and Kevin McGuire (Eds.), *Creating Constitutional Change*, pp. 265–280. Charlottesville: University of Virginia Press.

Heclo, Hugh. 1978. "Issue Networks and the Executive Establishment." In Anthony King (Ed.), *The New American Political System*, pp. 87–124. Washington, D.C.: American Enterprise Institute.

Hensley, Thomas, Kathleen Hale, and Carl Snook. 2006. *The Rehnquist Court: Justices, Rulings, and Legacy.* Denver: ABC-CLIO.

Hettinger, Virginia, Stefanie Lindquist, and Wendy Martinek. 2006. *Judging on a Collegial Court: Influences on Federal Appellate Decision-Making.* Charlottesville: University of Virginia Press.

Hickman, Kristin, and Matthew Krueger. 2007. "In Search of the 'Modern' *Skidmore* Standard." *Columbia Law Review* 108: 1235–1320.

Hill, Alfred. 1995. "The Judicial Function in Choice of Law." *Columbia Law Review* 85: 1585–1647.

Hoekstra, Valerie. 2003. *Public Reaction to Supreme Court Decisions.* New York: Cambridge University Press.

Hoff, Joan. 1991. *Law, Gender, and Injustice: A Legal History of U.S. Women.* New York: New York University Press.

Horowitz, Donald. 1977. *The Courts and Social Policy.* Washington, D.C.: Brookings Institution.

Howard, J. Woodford. 1968. "On the Fluidity of Judicial Choice." *American Political Science Review* 62: 43–56.

Howell, William G. 2003. *Power Without Persuasion: A Theory of Direct Presidential Action.* Princeton: Princeton University Press.

Howell, William G., and Jon C. Pevehouse. 2007. *While Dangers Gather: Congressional Checks on Presidential War Powers.* Princeton: Princeton University Press.

Hutchinson, Dennis. 1998. *The Man Who Once Was Whizzer White: A Portrait of Justice Byron R. White.* New York: Free Press.

Ignagni, Joseph. 1994. "Explaining and Predicting Supreme Court Decision Making: The Burger Court's Establishment Clause Decisions." *Journal of Church and State* 36: 301–327.

Ignagni, Joseph. 1993. "U.S. Supreme Court Decision Making and the Free Exercise Clause." *Review of Politics* 55: 511–529.

Irons, Peter H. 2006. *A People's History of the Supreme Court: The Men and Women Whose Cases and Decisions Shaped Our Constitution* (rev. ed.). New York: Penguin Books.

Irons, Peter H. 1994. *Brennan vs. Rehnquist: The Battle for the Constitution*. New York: Knopf.

Irons, Peter H. 1993. *Justice At War: The Story of the Japanese American Internment Cases*. Berkeley: University of California Press.

Johnson, John W. 1997. *Struggle for Student Rights*: Tinker v. Des Moines *and the 1960s*. Lawrence: University Press of Kansas.

Johnson, Timothy R. 2004. *Oral Arguments and Decision Making on the United States Supreme Court*. Albany: SUNY Press.

Kahn, Jacob L. 2008. "From *Borden* to *Billing*: Identifying a Uniform Approach to Implied Antitrust Immunity from the Supreme Court's Precedents." *Chicago-Kent Law Review* 83: 1439–1496.

Kahn, Ronald. 1994. *The Supreme Court and Constitutional Theory: 1953–1993*. Lawrence: University Press of Kansas.

Karst, Kenneth L. 1989. *Belonging to America: Equal Citizenship and the Constitution*. New Haven: Yale University Press.

Katzmann, Robert A. 1997. *Courts and Congress*. Washington, D.C.: Brookings Institution Press.

Keck, Thomas M. 2004. *The Most Activist Supreme Court in History: The Road to Modern Judicial Conservatism*. Chicago: University of Chicago Press.

Kennedy, Randall. 1997. *Race, Crime and the Law*. New York: Pantheon.

Kennedy, Randall. 1988. "*McCleskey v. Kemp*: Race, Capital Punishment and the Supreme Court." *Harvard Law Review* 101: 1388–1443.

Kernell, Samuel. 2006. *Going Public: New Strategies of Presidential Leadership*. Washington, D.C.: CQ Press.

Kerr, Orin S. 1998. "Shedding Light on *Chevron*: An Empirical Study of the *Chevron* Doctrine in the U.S. Courts of Appeals." *Yale Journal of Regulation* 15: 1–60.

Keynes, Edward, with Randall K. Miller. 1989. *The Court Versus Congress: Prayer, Busing, and Abortion*. Durham: Duke University Press.

King, Chad. 2007. "Strategic Selection of Legal Instruments on the U.S. Supreme Court." *American Politics Research* 35: 621–642.

Kingdon, John. 1995. *Agendas, Alternatives, and Public Policies* (2d ed.). New York: Harper Collins.

Kingdon, John. 1989. *Congressmen's Voting Decisions*. Ann Arbor: University of Michigan Press.

Kmiec, Douglas. 2007. "Up In Smoke: The Supreme Court Loses Its Unanimity." *Slate*, 27 February.

Knight, Jack, and Lee Epstein. 1996. "The Norm of *Stare Decisis*." *American Journal of Political Science* 40: 1018–1035.

Kobylka, Joseph. 1989. "Leadership on the Supreme Court: Chief Justice Burger and Establishment Clause Litigation." *Western Political Quarterly* 42: 545–569.

Kobylka, Joseph. 1987. "A Court-Related Context for Group Litigation: Libertarian Groups and Obscenity." *Journal of Politics* 49: 1061–1079.

Konvitz, Milton. 1966. *Expanding Liberties: Freedom's Gains in Postwar America*. New York: Viking Press.

Kort, Fred. 1963. "Simultaneous Equations and Boolean Algebra in the Analysis of Judicial Decisions." *Law and Contemporary Problems* 28: 143–163.

Kort, Fred. 1957. "Predicting Supreme Court Decisions Mathematically: A Quantitative Analysis of Right to Counsel Cases." *American Political Science Review* 51: 1–12.

Krehbiel, Keith. 2007. "Supreme Court Appointments as a Move-the-Median Game." *American Journal of Political Science* 51: 231–240.

Krehbiel, Keith. 1998. *Pivotal Politics: A Theory of U.S. Lawmaking.* Chicago: University of Chicago Press.

Krehbiel, Keith. 1993. "Where's the Party?" *British Journal of Political Science* 23: 235–266.

Krehbiel, Keith, 1991. *Information and Legislative Organization.* Ann Arbor: University of Michigan Press.

Kritzer, Herbert M., and Mark J. Richards 2005. "The Influence of Law in the Supreme Court's Search-and-Seizure Jurisprudence." *American Politics Research* 33: 33–55.

Kritzer, Herbert M., and Mark J. Richards. 2003. "Jurisprudential Regimes and Supreme Court Decision Making: The *Lemon* Regime and Establishment Clause Cases." *Law & Society Review* 37: 827–840.

Krol, John, and Saul Brenner. 1990. "Strategies in Certiorari Voting on the United States Supreme Court: A Reevaluation." *Western Political Quarterly* 43: 335–342.

Krutz, Glen S., and Jeffrey S. Peake. 2010. *Treaty Politics and the Rise of Executive Agreements.* Ann Arbor: University of Michigan Press.

Landes, William, and Richard Posner. 1976. "Legal Precedent: A Theoretical and Empirical Analysis." *Journal of Law and Economics* 19: 249–307.

Lasser, William. 1985. "The Supreme Court in Periods of Critical Realignment." *Journal of Politics* 47: 1174–1187.

Latzer, Barry. 1998. *Death Penalty Cases: Leading U.S. Supreme Court Cases on Capital Punishment.* Boston: Butterworth-Heinemann.

Law, Anna. 2003. "Cracks in the National Consensus – Institutional Norms, the American Judiciary, and Immigration, 1883–1893 and 1990–2000." Ph.D. diss., University of Texas at Austin.

Legomsky, Stephen. 1995. "Ten More Years of Plenary Power: Immigration, Congress, and the Courts." *Hastings Constitutional Law Quarterly* 22: 925–993.

Legomsky, Stephen. 1985. "Immigration Law and the Principle of Plenary Congressional Power." *The Supreme Court Review* 6: 225–307.

Leuchtenburg, William. 1995. *The Supreme Court Reborn: The Constitutional Revolution in the Age of Roosevelt.* New York: Oxford University Press.

Leuchtenburg, William. 1963. *Franklin D. Roosevelt and the New Deal, 1932–1940.* New York: Harper & Row.

Levinson, Sanford V. 1982. "Law as Literature." *Texas Law Review* 60: 373–403.

Lewis, Anthony. 1991. *Make No Law: The Sullivan Case and the First Amendment.* New York: Vintage.

Lewis, Anthony. 1964. *Gideon's Trumpet.* New York: Vintage.

Lewis, David. 2005. "Staffing Alone: Unilateral Action and the Politicization of the Executive Office of the President, 1988–2004." *Presidential Studies Quarterly* 35: 496–514.

Light, Paul. 1982. *The President's Agenda: Domestic Policy Choice from Kennedy to Carter.* Baltimore: Johns Hopkins University Press.

Long, Carolyn. 2006. *Mapp v. Ohio: Guarding Against Unreasonable Searches and Seizures.* Lawrence: University Press of Kansas.

Long, Carolyn. 2000. *Religious Freedom and Indian Rights: The Case of Oregon v. Smith.* Lawrence: University Press of Kansas.

Long, J. Scott. 1997. *Regression Models for Categorical and Limited Dependent Variables.* London: Sage.

Loue, Sana. 1985. "Alien Rights and Government Authority: An Examination of the Conflicting Views of the Ninth Circuit Court of Appeals and the United States Supreme Court." *San Diego Law Review* 22: 1021–1073.

Lovell, George. 2003. *Legislative Deferrals: Statutory Ambiguity, Judicial Power, and American Democracy.* New York: Cambridge University Press.

Lowe, Michael. 1994. "The Freedom of Information Act in 1993–1994." *Duke Law Journal* 43: 1282–1316.

Lowi, Theodore J. 1969. *The End of Liberalism: Ideology, Policy, and the Crisis of Public Authority.* New York: W.W. Norton & Company.

Malkovitz, R. S. 1983. "The Burger Court, Antitrust, and Economic Analysis." In Vincent Blasi (Ed.), *The Burger Court: The Counter-Revolution That Wasn't,* pp. 180–197. New Haven: Yale University Press.

Maltz, Earl M. 2000. *The Chief Justiceship of Warren Burger, 1969–1986.* Columbia: University of South Carolina Press.

Maltzman, Forrest. 1997. *Competing Principals: Committees, Parties, and the Organization of Congress.* Ann Arbor: University of Michigan Press.

Maltzman, Forrest, and Charles R. Shipan. 2008. "Continuity, Change and the Evolution of the Law." *American Journal of Political Science* 52: 252–267.

Maltzman, Forrest, James F. Spriggs II, and Paul J. Wahlbeck. 2000. *Crafting Law on the Supreme Court: The Collegial Game.* New York: Cambridge University Press.

Mann, Thomas E., and Norman J. Ornstein. 2006. *The Broken Branch: How Congress is Failing America and How to Get it Back on Track.* New York: Oxford University Press.

March, James, and Johan Olsen. 1984. "The New Institutionalism: Organizational Factors in Political Life." *American Political Science Review* 78: 734–749.

Marion, David E. 1997. *The Jurisprudence of Justice William J. Brennan, Jr.* Lanham, Md.: Rowman & Littlefield.

Marshall, Bryan W., and Patrick J. Haney. 2010. "Aiding and Abetting: Congressional Complicity in the Rise of the Unitary Executive." In Ryan J. Barilleaux and Christopher S. Kelley (Eds.), *The Unitary Executive and the Modern Presidency,* pp. 188–216. College Station: Texas A&M University Press.

Marshall, Bryan W., and Richard L. Pacelle, Jr. 2005. "Revisiting the Two Presidencies: The Strategic Use of Executive Orders." *American Politics Research* 33: 81–105.

Martin, Andrew D. 2006. "Statutory Battles and Constitutional Wars: Congress and the Supreme Court." In James Rogers, Roy Flemming, and Jon Bond (Eds.), *Institutional Games and the U.S. Supreme Court,* pp. 3–23. Charlottesville: University of Virginia Press.

Martin, Andrew D., and Kevin M. Quinn. 2002. "Dynamic Ideal Point Estimation via Markov Chain Monte Carlo for the U.S. Supreme Court, 1953–1999." *Political Analysis* 10: 134–153.

Mason, Alpheus T. 1956. *Harlan Fiske Stone: Pillar of the Law*. New York: Viking.

Matthews, Donald R., and James W. Prothro. 1966. *Negroes and the New Southern Politics*. New York: Harcourt, Brace & World.

Mauro, Tony. 2008. "Supreme Court Reduces Damages Awarded in Exxon Case." *Legal Times*, 26 June.

Maveety, Nancy. 1996. *Justice Sandra Day O'Connor: Strategist on the Supreme Court*. Lanham, Md.: Rowman & Littlefield.

Mayer, Kenneth. 2001. *With the Stroke of a Pen: Executive Orders and Presidential Power*. Princeton: Princeton University Press.

Mayhew, David R. 2005. *Divided We Govern: Party Control, Lawmaking and Investigations, 1946–2002*. New Haven: Yale University Press.

Mayhew, David R. 2002. *Electoral Realignments: A Critique of an American Genre*. New Haven: Yale University Press.

Mayhew, David R. 1974. *Congress: The Electoral Connection*. New Haven: Yale University Press.

McCann, Michael. 1999. "How the Supreme Court Matters for American Politics." In Howard Gillman and Cornell Clayton (Eds.), *The Supreme Court in American Politics: New Institutionalist Approaches*, pp. 63–97. Lawrence: University Press of Kansas.

McCloskey, Robert. 1960. *The American Supreme Court*. Chicago: University of Chicago Press.

McConnell, Grant. 1966. *Private Power and American Democracy*. New York: Alfred A. Knopf.

McCubbins, Mathew, and Thomas Schwartz. 1984. "Congressional Oversight Overlooked: Police Patrols versus Fire Alarms." *American Journal of Political Science* 28: 165–179.

McFarland, Andrew. 1987. "Interest Groups and Theories of Power in America." *British Journal of Political Science* 17: 129–147.

McGuire, Kevin. 1998. "Explaining Executive Success in the U.S. Supreme Court." *Political Research Quarterly* 51: 505–526.

McGuire, Kevin. 1995. "Repeat Players in the Supreme Court: The Role of Experienced Lawyers in Litigation Success." *Journal of Politics* 57: 187–196.

McGuire, Kevin, and Barbara Palmer. 1995. "Issue Fluidity on the U.S. Supreme Court." *American Political Science Review* 89: 691–702.

McKeever, Robert. 1993. *Raw Judicial Power? The Supreme Court and American Society*. New York: Manchester University Press.

McKenna, Marian C. 2002. *Franklin Roosevelt and the Great Constitutional War: The Court-Packing Crisis of 1937*. New York: Fordham University Press.

McWhirter, Darien. 1994. *Freedom of Speech, Press, and Assembly*. Westport, Conn.: Greenwood Publishing Group.

Meernik, James, and Joseph Ignagni. 1997. "Judicial Review and Coordinate Construction of the Constitution." *American Journal of Political Science* 41: 447–467.

Mendelson, Wallace. 1961. "Mr. Justice Frankfurter Law and Choice." *Vanderbilt Law Review* 2: 333–350.

Mendelson, Wallace. 1958. "Mr. Justice Frankfurter on the Distribution of Judicial Power in the United States." *Midwest Journal of Political Science* 2: 40–61.

Mendelson, Wallace. 1957. "Mr. Justice Frankfurter on Administrative Law." *Journal of Politics* 19: 441–460.

Miller, Arthur. 1968. *The Supreme Court and American Capitalism*. New York: The Free Press.

Miller, Banks and Brett Curry, 2009. "Expertise, Experience, and Ideology on Specialized Courts: The Case of the Courts if Appeals for the Federal Circuit." *Law & Society Review* 43: 839–864.

Mitchell, Lawrence E. 2002. "No Business Like No Business." In Herman Schwartz (Ed.), *The Rehnquist Court: Judicial Activism on the Right*, pp. 227–243. New York: Hill and Wang.

Moe, Terry, and William Howell. 1999. "Unilateral Action and Presidential Power: A Theory." *Presidential Studies Quarterly* 29: 850–873.

Morrison, Steven, and Clifford Winston. 1986. *The Economic Effects of Airline Deregulation*. Washington, D.C.: Brookings Institution.

Motomura, Hiroshi. 1992. "The Curious Evolution of Immigration Law: Procedural Surrogates for Substantive Constitutional Rights." *Columbia Law Review* 92: 1625–1704.

Motomura, Hiroshi. 1990. "Immigration Law After a Century of Plenary Power: Phantom Constitutional Norms and Statutory Interpretation." *Yale Law Journal* 100: 545–614.

Murphy, Paul. 1972. *The Constitution in Crisis Times, 1918–1969*. New York: Harper & Row.

Murphy, Walter F. 1964. *Elements of Judicial Strategy*. Chicago: University of Chicago Press.

Murphy, Walter F. 1962. *Congress and the Court*. Chicago: University of Chicago Press.

Murphy, Walter F., and Joseph Tanenhaus. 1972. *The Study of Public Law*. New York: Random House.

Nathan, Richard. 1975. *The Plot That Failed: Nixon and the Administrative Presidency*. New York: Wiley.

Nelson, Michael 1982. "A Short, Ironic History of American National Bureaucracy." *Journal of Politics* 44: 747–778.

Nelson, William E. 1994. "Justice Byron R. White: A Modern Federalist and a New Deal Liberal." *Brigham Young University Law Review* 1994: 313–348.

Neuman, Gerald. 2002. "Jurisdiction and the Rule of Law After the 1996 Immigration Act." *Harvard Law Review* 113: 1963–1998.

Neuman, Gerald. 1998. "Habeas Corpus, Executive Detention, and Removal of Aliens." *Columbia Law Review* 98: 961–1066.

Neuman, Gerald. 1996. *Strangers to the Constitution – Immigrants, Borders, and Fundamental Law*. Princeton: Princeton University Press.

Newmyer, R. Kent. 2001. *John Marshall and the Heroic Age of the Supreme Court*. Baton Rouge: Louisiana State University Press.

Newton, Jim. 2006. *Justice for All: Earl Warren and the Nation He Made*. New York: Riverhead Books.

Nichols, David. 2007. *A Matter of Justice: Eisenhower and the Beginning of the Civil Rights Revolution*. New York: Simon and Schuster.

Note. 1976. "National Security and the Amended Freedom of Information Act." *Yale Law Journal* 85: 401–422.

Note. 1958. "Congressional Reversals of Supreme Court Decisions: 1945–1957." *Harvard Law Review* 71: 1324–1337.

O'Brien, David. 2008a. *Constitutional Law and Politics: Struggles for Power and Governmental Accountability* (7th ed.). New York: W.W. Norton.

O'Brien, David. 2008b. *Constitutional Law and Politics: Civil Rights and Civil Liberties* (7th ed.). New York: W.W. Norton.

O'Brien, David. 2005. *Storm Center: The Supreme Court in American Politics* (7th ed.). New York: W.W. Norton.

O'Connor, Karen. 1996. *No Neutral Ground? Abortion Politics in an Age of Absolutes*. Boulder: Westview Press.

O'Connor, Karen. 1980. *Women's Organizations' Use of the Courts*. Lexington, Mass.: Lexington Books.

O'Connor, Sandra Day. 2005. "Justice O'Connor Speaks on the Judiciary." *The Third Branch: Newsletter of the Federal Courts* 37: 8.

Olivetti, Alfred M., Jr., and Jeff Worsham. 2003. *This Land is Your Land, This Land Is My Land: The Property Rights Movement and Regulatory Takings*. New York: LFB Scholarly.

Pacelle, Richard L., Jr. Forthcoming. "Rebuilding Institutions and Redefining Issues: The Reagan Justice Department and the Reconstruction of Civil Rights." In Kenneth Osgood and Derrick White (Eds.), *Civil Rights, the Conservative Movement, and the Presidency*. Gainesville: University of Florida Press.

Pacelle, Richard L., Jr. 2009. "The Emergence and Evolution of Supreme Court Policy." In Mark Miller (Ed.), *Rethinking U.S. Judicial Politics*, pp. 174–191. New York: Oxford University Press.

Pacelle, Richard L., Jr. 2006. "*Amicus Curiae* or *Amicus Praesidentis?* Reexamining the Role of the Office of the Solicitor General in Filing *Amici*." *Judicature* 89: 317–325.

Pacelle, Richard L., Jr. 2004. "A *Mapp* to Legal Change and Policy Retreat: *United States v. Leon*." In Gregg Ivers and Kevin T. McGuire (Eds.), *Creating Constitutional Change*, pp. 249–263. Charlottesville: University of Virginia Press.

Pacelle, Richard L., Jr. 2003. *Between Law and Politics: The Solicitor General and the Structuring of Race, Gender, and Reproductive Rights Litigation*. College Station: Texas A&M University Press.

Pacelle, Richard L., Jr. 2002. *The Role of the Supreme Court in American Politics: The Least Dangerous Branch?* Boulder: Westview Press.

Pacelle, Richard L., Jr. 1995. "The Dynamics and Determinants of Agenda Change in the Rehnquist Court." In Lee Epstein (Ed.), *Contemplating Courts*, pp. 251–274. Washington, D.C.: CQ Press.

Pacelle, Richard L., Jr. 1991. *The Transformation of the Supreme Court's Agenda: From the New Deal to the Reagan Administration*. Boulder: Westview Press.

Pacelle, Richard L., Jr., Bryan W. Marshall, and Brett W. Curry. 2007. "Keepers of the Covenant or Platonic Guardians? Decision Making on the United States Supreme Court." *American Politics Research* 35: 694–724.

Pacelle, Richard L., Jr., and Patricia Pauly. 1996. "The Freshman Effect Revisited: An Individual Based Analysis." *Review of Politics* 17: 1–22.

Pack, Bradley. 2004. "FOIA Frustration: Access to Government Records Under the Bush Administration." *Arizona Law Review* 46: 815–842.

Parmet, Herbert S. 1997. *George Bush: The Life of a Lone Star Yankee.* New York: Scribner.

Patchel, Kathleen. 1991. "The New Habeas." *Hastings Law Journal* 42: 941–1066.

Patterson, James. 2001. *Brown v. Board of Education: A Civil Rights Milestone and Its Troubled Legacy.* New York: Oxford University Press.

Pauley, Garth. 2001. *The Modern Presidency & Civil Rights: Rhetoric on Race from Roosevelt to Nixon.* College Station: Texas A&M University Press.

Peacock, James R. III. 1981. "Developments Under the Freedom of Information Act: 1980." *Duke Law Journal* 1981: 338–376.

Perry, Barbara. 2007. *The Michigan Affirmative Action Cases.* Lawrence: University Press of Kansas.

Perry, H. W., Jr. 1991. *Deciding to Decide: Agenda Setting in the U.S. Supreme Court.* Cambridge: Harvard University Press.

Peters, Shawn Francis. 2000. *Judging Jehovah's Witnesses: Religious Persecution and the Dawn of the Rights Revolution.* Lawrence: University Press of Kansas.

Peterson, Andrea. 1989. "The Takings Clause: In Search of Underlying Principles: Part I. A Critique of Current Takings Clause Doctrine." *California Law Review* 77: 1299–1363.

Peterson, Mark. 1990. *Legislating Together: The White House and Capitol Hill from Eisenhower to Reagan.* Cambridge: Harvard University Press.

Phelps, Glenn, and John Gates. 1991. "The Myth of Jurisprudence: Interpretive Theory in the Constitutional Opinions of Justices Rehnquist and Brennan." *Santa Clara Law Review* 31: 567–596.

Pickerill, J. Mitchell. 2004. *Constitutional Deliberation in Congress: The Impact of Judicial Review in a Separated System.* Durham: Duke University Press.

Pietruszkiewicz, Christopher. 2006. "Discarded Deference: Judicial Independence in Informal Agency Guidance." *Tennessee Law Review* 74: 1–45.

Poole, Keith, and Howard Rosenthal. 1997. *Congress: A Political-Economic History of Roll Call Voting.* New York: Oxford University Press.

Posner, Eric. 1997. "The Political Economy of the Bankruptcy Reform Act of 1978." *Michigan Law Review* 96: 47–126.

Powe, Lucas A., Jr. 2009. *The Supreme Court and the American Elite, 1789–2008.* Cambridge: Harvard University Press.

Powe, Lucas A., Jr. 2000. *The Warren Court and American Politics.* Cambridge, Mass.: Belknap Press.

Pritchett, C. Herman. 1984. *Constitutional Law of the Federal System.* Englewood Cliffs, N.J.: Prentice-Hall.

Pritchett, C. Herman. 1969. "The Development of Judicial Research." In Joel Grossman and Joseph Tanenhaus (Eds.), *Frontiers of Judicial Research.* New York: John Wiley.

Pritchett, C. Herman. 1948. "The Roosevelt Court: Votes and Values." *American Political Science Review* 42: 53–67.

Pye, A. Kenneth. 1968. "The Warren Court and Criminal Procedure." *Michigan Law Review* 67: 249–268.

Quirk, Paul. 1989. "The Cooperative Resolution of Policy Conflict." *American Political Science Review* 83: 905–921.

Quirk, Paul. 1981. *Industry Influence in Federal Regulatory Agencies*. Princeton: Princeton University Press.

Raskin, Jamin, and Clark LeBlanc. 2002. "Disfavored Speech About Favored Rights: *Hill v. Colorado*, The Vanishing Public Forum and the Need for an Objective Speech Discrimination Test." *American University Law Review* 51: 179–228.

Rehnquist, William. 2002. *The Supreme Court* (rev. and updated ed.). New York: Vintage Books.

Rehnquist, William. 1998. *All the Laws But One: Civil Liberties In Wartime*. New York: Random House.

Reichley, A. James. 1981. *Conservatives in an Era of Change*. Washington, D.C.: Brookings Institution.

Richards, Mark J., and Herbert M. Kritzer. 2002. "Jurisprudential Regimes in Supreme Court Decision Making." *American Political Science Review* 96: 305–320.

Riker, William. 1986. *The Art of Political Manipulation*. New Haven: Yale University Press.

Ripley, Randall. 1967. *Party Leaders in the House of Representatives*. Washington, D.C.: Brookings Institution.

Ripley, Randall, and Grace Franklin. 1990. *Congress, the Bureaucracy, and Public Policy* (5th ed.). Homewood: Dorsey Press.

Ripley, Randall, and Grace Franklin. 1982. *Bureaucracy and Policy Implementation*. Homewood: Dorsey Press.

Robertson, David Brian. 2005. *The Constitution and America's Destiny*. New York: Cambridge University Press.

Robyn, Dorothy L. 1987. *Braking the Special Interests: Trucking Deregulation and the Politics of Policy Reform*. Chicago: University of Chicago Press.

Roche, John. 1964. "The Expatriation Decisions: A Study in Constitutional Improvisation and the Uses of History." *American Political Science Review* 58: 72–80.

Rogers, James. 2001. "Information and Judicial Review: A Signaling Game of Legislative-Judicial Interaction." *American Journal of Political Science* 45: 84–99.

Rohde, David. 1972. "Policy Goals, Strategic Choice and Majority Opinion Assignments in the U.S. Supreme Court." *Midwest Journal of Political Science* 16: 652–682.

Rohde, David, and Harold Spaeth. 1976. *Supreme Court Decision Making*. San Francisco: Freeman.

Rosenberg, Gerald 2008. *The Hollow Hope: Can Courts Bring About Social Change?* (2d ed.). Chicago: University of Chicago Press.

Rosenberg, Gerald. 1994. "Review Symposium of 1993 Edition of Segal and Spaeth's *The Supreme Court and the Attitudinal Model*." *Law and Courts* 4: 6–7.

Rosenbloom, David, and Rosemary O'Leary. 1997. *Public Administration and Law* (2d ed.). Boca Raton: CRC Press.

Rudalevige, Andrew. 2005. *The New Imperial Presidency: Renewing Presidential Power after Watergate.* Ann Arbor: University of Michigan Press.

Rudalevige, Andrew. 2002. *Managing the President's Program: Presidential Leadership and Legislative Policy Formation.* Princeton: Princeton University Press.

Sager, Lawrence. 2004. *Justice in Plainclothes: A Theory of American Constitutional Practice.* New Haven: Yale University Press.

Sala, Brian R., and James F. Spriggs II. 2004. "Designing Tests of the Supreme Court and the Separation of Powers." *Political Research Quarterly* 57: 197–208.

Salokar, Rebecca Mae. 1992. *The Solicitor General: The Politics of Law.* Philadelphia: Temple University Press.

Savage, David. 1992. *Turning Right: The Making of the Rehnquist Supreme Court.* New York: Wiley.

Sax, Joseph L. 1993. "Property Rights and the Economy of Nature: Understanding *Lucas v. South Carolina Coastal Council.*" *Stanford Law Review* 45: 1433–1455.

Scalia, Antonin. 1997. *A Matter of Interpretation.* Princeton: Princeton University Press.

Scalia, Antonin. 1982. "The Freedom of Information Act Has No Clothes." *Regulation* 6: 14–19.

Schauer, Frederick. 1985. "Easy Cases." *Southern California Law Review* 58: 399–440.

Schmidhauser, John R., and Larry L. Berg. 1972. *The Supreme Court and Congress: Conflict and Interaction, 1945–1968.* New York: Free Press.

Scholz, John T., and B. Dan Wood. 1998. "Controlling the IRS: Principals, Principles, and Public Administration." *American Journal of Political Science* 42: 141–162.

Schubert, Glendon. 1974. *The Judicial Mind Revisited.* New York: Oxford University Press.

Schubert, Glendon. 1965. *The Judicial Mind.* Evanston, Ill.: Northwestern University Press.

Schubert, Glendon. 1962. "The 1962 Term of the Supreme Court: A Psychological Analysis." *American Political Science Review* 56: 90–107.

Schuck, Peter. 1984. "The Transformation of Immigration Law." *Columbia Law Review* 84: 1–90.

Schuck, Peter. 1983. *Suing Government: Citizen Remedies for Official Wrongs.* New Haven: Yale University Press.

Schuck, Peter, and Theodore Hsien Wang. 1992. "Continuity and Change: Patterns of Immigration Litigation in the Courts, 1979–1990." *Stanford Law Review* 45: 115–183.

Schultz, David Andrew. 1992. *Property, Power, and American Democracy.* New Brunswick: Transaction Press.

Schultz, David A., and Christopher E. Smith. 1996. *The Jurisprudential Vision of Justice Antonin Scalia.* Lanham, Md.: Rowman & Littlefield.

Schwartz, Bernard. 1983. *Super Chief: Earl Warren and His Supreme Court – A Judicial Biography*. New York: New York University Press.

Schwartz, Bernard (Ed.): 1998. *The Burger Court: Counter-Revolution or Confirmation?* New York: Oxford University Press.

Scigliano, Robert. 1971. *The Supreme Court and the Presidency*. New York: Free Press.

Scourfield McLauchlan, Judithanne. 2005. *Congressional Participation as Amicus Curiae Before the U.S. Supreme Court*. New York: LFB Scholarly.

Segal, Jeffrey. 1997. "Separation-of-Powers Games in the Positive Theory of Congress and the Courts." *American Political Science Review* 91: 28–42.

Segal, Jeffrey. 1990. "Supreme Court Support for the Solicitor General: The Effect of Presidential Appointments." *Political Research Quarterly* 43: 137–152.

Segal, Jeffrey. 1988. "*Amicus Curiae* Briefs by the Solicitor General During the Warren and Burger Courts: A Research Note." *Western Political Quarterly* 41: 135–144.

Segal, Jeffrey. 1986. "Supreme Court Justices as Human Decision Makers: An Individual Level Analysis of Search and Seizure Cases." *Journal of Politics* 48: 938–955.

Segal, Jeffrey. 1984. "Predicting Supreme Court Cases Probabilistically: The Search and Seizure Cases, 1962–1981." *American Political Science Review* 78: 891–900.

Segal, Jeffrey, and Albert D. Cover. 1989. "Ideological Values and the Votes of U.S. Supreme Court Justices." *American Political Science Review* 83: 557–565.

Segal, Jeffrey, Lee Epstein, Charles Cameron, and Harold Spaeth. 1995. "Ideological Values and the Votes of U.S. Supreme Court Justices Revisited." *Journal of Politics* 57: 812–823.

Segal, Jeffrey, and Harold Spaeth. 2002. *The Supreme Court and the Attitudinal Model Revisited*. New York: Cambridge University Press.

Segal, Jeffrey, and Harold Spaeth. 1996a. "The Influence of *Stare Decisis* on the Votes of United States Supreme Court Justices." *American Journal of Political Science* 40: 971–1003.

Segal, Jeffrey, and Harold Spaeth. 1996b. "Norms, Dragons, and *Stare Decisis*." *American Journal of Political Science* 40: 1064–1082.

Segal, Jeffrey, and Harold Spaeth. 1993. *The Supreme Court and the Attitudinal Model*. New York: Cambridge University Press.

Segal, Jeffrey, Harold Spaeth, and Sara Benesh. 2005. *The Supreme Court in the American Legal System*. New York: Cambridge University Press.

Segal, Jeffrey, Richard Timpone, and Robert Howard. 2000. "Buyer Beware? Presidential Success Through Supreme Court Appointments." *Political Research Quarterly* 53: 557–573.

Selden, Sally Coleman, Jeffrey Brudney, and J. Edward Kellough. 1998. "Bureaucracy as a Representative Institution: Toward a Reconciliation of Bureaucratic Government and Democratic Theory." *American Journal of Political Science* 42: 717–742.

Senate Judiciary Committee. 2006. *Confirmation Hearing on the Nomination of Samuel Alito to be Associate Justice of the United States: Hearing Before the Senate Committee on the Judiciary*, 109th Congress, 2d session.

Shanks, Cheryl. 2001. *Immigration and the Politics of American Sovereignty, 1890–1990*. Ann Arbor: University of Michigan Press.

Shepsle, Kenneth. 2006. "Old Questions and New Answers About Institutions: The Riker Objection Revisited." In Barry Weingast and Donald Wittman (Eds.), *Oxford Handbook of Political Economy*, pp. 1031–1050. Oxford: Oxford University Press.

Shepsle, Kenneth, and Barry Weingast. 1995. *Positive Theories of Congressional Institutions*. Ann Arbor: University of Michigan Press.

Shur, Luba L. 1995. "Content-Based Distinctions in a University Funding System and the Irrelevance of the Establishment Clause: Putting Wide Awake to Rest." *Virginia Law Review* 81: 1665–1720.

Silberman, David. 1987. "The Burger Court and Labor-Management Relations." In Herman Schwartz (Ed.), *The Burger Court: Rights and Wrongs in the Supreme Court 1969–1986*. New York: Penguin Books.

Silver, Edward, and Joan McAvoy. 1987. "The National Labor Relations Act at the Crossroads." *Fordham Law Review* 56: 181–208.

Silverstein, Gordon. 2009. *Law's Allure: How Law Shapes, Constrains, Saves, and Kills Politics*. New York: Cambridge University Press.

Silverstein, Gordon. 1997. *Imbalance of Powers: Constitutional Interpretation and the Making of American Foreign Policy*. New York: Oxford University Press.

Silverstein, Mark. 1994. *Judicious Choices: The New Politics of Supreme Court Confirmations*. New York: W.W. Norton.

Simon, James F. 1995. *The Center Holds: The Power Struggle Inside the Rehnquist Court*. New York: Simon & Schuster.

Sinclair, Barbara. 2007. *Unorthodox Lawmaking: New Legislative Processes in the U.S. Congress* (3rd ed.). Washington, D.C.: CQ Press.

Sinclair, Barbara. 2006. *Party Wars: Polarization and the Politics of National Policy Making*. Norman: University of Oklahoma Press.

Sinclair, Barbara. 1989. "Leadership Strategies in the Modern Congress." In Christopher J. Deering (Ed.), *Congressional Politics*, pp. 135–154. Chicago: Dorsey Press.

Sinclair, Michael. 2007. "Precedent, Super Precedent." *George Mason University Law Review* 14: 363–411.

Skowronek, Stephen. 1997. *The Politics Presidents Make: Leadership from John Adams to Bill Clinton*. Cambridge, Mass.: Belknap Press.

Skrentny, John. 1996. *The Ironies of Affirmative Action: Politics, Culture and Justice in America*. Chicago: University of Chicago Press.

Slotnick, Elliot E. 1979. "Who Speaks for the Court? Majority Opinion Assignment from Taft to Burger." *American Journal of Political Science* 23: 60–77.

Smith, Christopher. 1993. *Critical Judicial Nominations and Political Change: The Impact of Clarence Thomas*. Westport, Conn.: Praeger.

Smith, Martin J. 1993. *Pressure Power & Policy: State Autonomy and Policy Networks in Britain and the United States*. Pittsburgh: University of Pittsburgh Press.

Smith, Rogers M. 1994. "Review Symposium of 1993 Edition of Segal and Spaeth's *The Supreme Court and the Attitudinal Model*." *Law and Courts* 4: 8–9.

Smith, Rogers M. 1985. *Liberalism and American Constitutional Law*. Cambridge: Harvard University Press.

Smith, Steven S. 1989. *Call to Order: Floor Politics in the House and Senate*. Washington, D.C.: Brookings Institution.

Smith, William French. 1991. *Law & Justice in the Reagan Administration: Memoirs of an Attorney General*. Stanford: Hoover Institution Press.

Smolla, Rodney A. 1990. *Jerry Falwell v. Larry Flynt: The First Amendment on Trial*. Champaign: University of Illinois Press.

Snyder, Eloise. 1958. "The Supreme Court as a Small Group." *Social Forces* 36: 232–238.

Songer, Donald, and Susan Haire. 1992. "Integrating Alternative Approaches to the Study of Judicial Voting: Obscenity Cases in the US Courts of Appeals." *American Journal of Political Science* 36: 963–982.

Songer, Donald, and Stefanie Lindquist. 1996. "Not the Whole Story: The Impact of Justices' Values on Supreme Court Decision Making." *American Journal of Political Science* 40: 1049–1063.

Songer, Donald, Jeffrey Segal, and Charles Cameron. 1994. "The Hierarchy of Justice: Testing a Principal-Agent Model of Supreme Court-Circuit Court Interactions." *American Journal of Political Science* 38: 673–696.

Spaeth, Harold. 1995. "The Attitudinal Model." In Lee Epstein (Ed.), *Contemplating Courts*, pp. 296–314. Washington, D.C.: CQ Press.

Spaeth, Harold. 1964. "The Judicial Restraint of Mr. Justice Frankfurter – Myth or Reality." *Midwest Journal of Political Science* 8: 22–38.

Spill Solberg, Rorie L., and Eric S. Heberlig. 2004. "Communicating to the Courts and Beyond: Why Members of Congress Participate as *Amici Curiae*." *Legislative Studies Quarterly* 29: 591–610.

Spiller, Pablo T., and Rafael Gely. 1992. "Congressional Control or Judicial Independence: The Determinants of U.S. Supreme Court Labor Decisions, 1949–1988." *RAND Journal of Economics* 23: 463–492.

Spiller, Pablo T., and Matthew L. Spitzer. 1992. "Judicial Choice of Legal Doctrines." *Journal of Law, Economics, and Organization* 8: 8–46.

Spriggs, James F., II, and Thomas G. Hansford. 2001. "Explaining the Overruling of U.S. Supreme Court Precedent." *Journal of Politics* 63: 1091–1111.

Staudt, Nancy, Lee Epstein, Peter Wiedenbeck, Rene Lindstadt, and Ryan J. Vander Wielen. 2005. "Theories of Statutory Interpretation: Judging Statutes: Interpretive Regimes." *Loyola of Los Angeles Law Review* 38: 1909–1970.

Strum, Philippa. 1974. *The Supreme Court and Political Questions: A Study in Judicial Evasion*. Tuscaloosa: University of Alabama Press.

Sundquist, James. 1983. *Dynamics of the Party System: Alignment and Realignment of Political Parties in the United States* (rev. ed.). Washington, D.C.: Brookings Institution.

Sunstein, Cass. 1999. *One Case at a Time: Judicial Minimalism on the Supreme Court*. Cambridge: Harvard University Press.

Sunstein, Cass. 1993. *The Partial Constitution*. Cambridge: Harvard University Press.

Tate, C. Neal. 1981. "Personal Attribute Models of the Voting Behavior of U.S. Supreme Court Justices: Liberalism in Civil Liberties and Economics Decisions, 1946–1978." *American Political Science Review* 745: 355–367.

Tate, C. Neal, and Roger Handberg. 1991. "Time Binding and Theory Building in Personal Attribute Models of Supreme Court Voting Behavior, 1916–1988." *American Journal of Political Science* 35: 460–480.

Tedford, Thomas, and Dale Herbeck. 2009. *Freedom of Speech in the United States* (6th ed.). State College: Strata Publishing.

Teles, Steven. 2008. *The Rise of the Conservative Legal Movement: The Battle for Control of the Law*. Princeton: Princeton University Press.

Thernstrom, Abigail. 1987. *Whose Votes Count? Affirmative Action and Minority Rights*. Cambridge: Harvard University Press.

Thompson, Kenneth. 1984. *The Voting Rights Act and Black Electoral Participation*. Washington, D.C.: Joint Center for Political Studies.

Tichenor, Daniel. 2002. *Dividing Lines – The Politics of Immigration Control in America*. Princeton: Princeton University Press.

Toma, Eugenia. 1991. "Congressional Influence and the Supreme Court: The Budget as a Signaling Device." *Journal of Legal Studies* 20: 131–146.

Tulis, Jeffrey. 1987. *The Rhetorical Presidency*. Princeton: Princeton University Press.

Tushnet, Mark. 2005. *A Court Divided: The Rehnquist Court and the Future of Constitutional Law*. New York: W. W. Norton.

Tushnet, Mark. 2004. *The NAACP's Legal Strategy Against Segregated Education, 1925–1950*. Chapel Hill: University of North Carolina Press.

Tushnet, Mark. 2003. *The New Constitutional Order*. Princeton: Princeton University Press.

Tushnet, Mark. 1997. *Making Constitutional Law: Thurgood Marshall and the Supreme Court, 1961–1991*. New York: Oxford University Press.

Tushnet, Mark. 1994. *Making Civil Rights Law: Thurgood Marshall and the Supreme Court, 1936–1961*. New York: Oxford University Press.

Ubertaccio, Peter N., III. 2005. *Learned in the Law and Politics: The Office of the Solicitor General*. New York: LFB Scholarly.

Ulmer, S. Sidney. 1984. "The Supreme Court's Certiorari Decisions: Conflict as a Predictive Variable." *American Political Science Review* 78: 901–911.

Ulmer, S. Sidney. 1982. "Issue Fluidity in the United States Supreme Court." In Stephen Halpern and Charles Lamb (Eds.), *Supreme Court Activism and Restraint*, pp. 319–359. Lexington: Heath.

Ulmer, S. Sidney. 1979. "Parabolic Support of Civil Liberty Claims: The Case of William O. Douglas." *Journal of Politics* 41: 634–639.

Ulmer, S. Sidney. 1973. "The Longitudinal Behavior of Hugo Lafayette Black: Parabolic Support for Civil Liberties, 1937–1971." *Florida State University Law Review* 1: 131–153.

Ulmer, S. Sidney. 1965. "Toward a Theory of Sub-Group Formation in the United States Supreme Court: The Case of William O. Douglas." *Journal of Politics* 27: 133–152.

Urofsky, Melvin I. 1998. *Division and Discord: The Supreme Court Under Stone and Vinson, 1941–1953*. Columbia: University of South Carolina Press.

Urofsky, Melvin I. 1997. *Affirmative Action on Trial: Sex Discrimination in Johnson v. Santa Clara*. Lawrence: University Press of Kansas.

Vanberg, Georg. 2001. "Legislative-Judicial Relations: A Game-Theoretic Approach to Constitutional Review." *American Journal of Political Science* 45: 346–361.

Van Hees, Martin, and Bernard Steunenberg. 2000. "The Choices Judges Make: Court Rulings, Personal Values, and Legal Constraints." *Journal of Theoretical Politics* 12: 305–323.

Vose, Clement. 1959. *Caucasians Only: The Supreme Court, the NAACP, and the Restrictive Covenant Cases.* Berkeley: University of California Press.

Wahlbeck, Paul J. 1997. "The Life of the Law: Judicial Politics and Legal Change." *Journal of Politics* 59: 778–802.

Waldron, Gerard J., and Jeff A. Israel. 1989. "Developments Under the Freedom of Information Act: 1988." *Duke Law Journal* 1989: 686–737.

Walker, Thomas G. 2008. *Eligible for Execution: The Story of the Daryl Atkins Case.* Washington, D.C.: CQ Press.

Walker, Jack. 1977. "Setting the Agenda in the U.S. Senate: A Theory of Problem Selection." *British Journal of Political Science* 7: 423–445.

Walker, Samuel. 1994. *Hate Speech: The History of an American Controversy.* Lincoln: University of Nebraska Press.

Walker, Samuel. 1990. *In Defense of American Liberties: A History of the ACLU.* New York: Oxford University Press.

Walker, Thomas G., Lee Epstein, and William Dixon. 1988. "On the Mysterious Demise of Consensual Norms in the United States Supreme Court." *Journal of Politics* 50: 361–389.

Walton, Hanes, Jr. 1988. *When the Marching Stopped: The Politics of Civil Rights Regulatory Agencies.* Albany: State University of New York Press.

Waples, Gregory L. 1974. "The Freedom of Information Act: A Seven-Year Assessment." *Columbia Law Review* 74: 895–959.

Warshauer, Irving J., and Stevan C. Dittman. 2005. "The Uniqueness of Maritime Personal Injury and Death Law." *Tulane Law Review* 71: 1163–1225.

Wasby, Stephen. 1995. *Race Relations Litigation in an Age of Complexity.* Charlottesville: University of Virginia Press.

Wasby, Stephen. 1993. "A Triangle Transformed: Court, Congress, and Presidency in Civil Rights." *Policy Studies Journal* 21: 565–574.

Wasby, Stephen. 1989. *The Supreme Court and the Federal Judicial System* (3rd ed.). Chicago: Nelson Hall.

Wasby, Stephen, Anthony D'Amato, and Rosemary Metrailer. 1977. *Desegregation from Brown to Alexander: An Exploration of Supreme Court Strategies.* Carbondale: Southern Illinois University Press.

Weaver, Suzanne. 1977. *Decision to Prosecute: Organization and Public Policy in the Antitrust Division.* Cambridge: MIT Press.

Wechsler, Herbert. 1959. "Toward Neutral Principles of Constitutional law." *Harvard Law Review* 73: 1–35.

Weingast, Barry, and Mark Moran. 1983. "Bureaucratic Discretion or Congressional Control? Regulatory Policymaking by the Federal Trade Commission." *Journal of Political Economy* 91: 765–800.

White, G. Edward. 1982. *Earl Warren: A Public Life.* New York: Oxford University.

Whittington, Keith. 2007. *Political Foundations of Judicial Supremacy: The Presidency, the Supreme Court, and Constitutional Leadership in U.S. History.* Princeton: Princeton University Press.

Wildavsky, Aaron B. 1975. *Perspectives on the Presidency.* Boston: Little, Brown.

Wildavsky, Aaron B. 1969. *The Presidency.* Boston: Little, Brown.

Wilson, James Q. 1980. "The Politics of Regulation." In James Q. Wilson (Ed.), *The Politics of Regulation,* pp. 357–394. New York: Basic Books.

Wilson, Woodrow. 1885. *Congressional Government.* Boston: Houghton Mifflin.

Woessner, Matthew, and Barbara Sims. 2003. "Technological Innovation and the Application of the Fourth Amendment: Considering the Implications of *Kyllo v. United States* for Law Enforcement and Counterterrorism." *Journal of Contemporary Criminal Justice* 19: 224–238.

Wohlfarth, Patrick C. 2009. "The Tenth Justice? Consequences of Politicization in the Solicitor General's Office." *Journal of Politics* 71: 224–237.

Wolfe, Christopher. 1997. *Judicial Activism: Bulwark of Freedom or Precarious Security?* Lanham, Md.: Rowman & Littlefield.

Wood, B. Dan. 1988. "Principals, Bureaucrats, and Responsiveness in Clean Air Enforcement." *American Political Science Review* 83: 965–978.

Wood, B. Dan, and James E. Anderson. 1993. "The Politics of U.S. Antitrust Regulation." *American Journal of Political Science* 37: 1–40.

Wood, B. Dan, and Richard W. Waterman. 1994. *Bureaucratic Dynamics: The Role of Bureaucracy in a Democracy.* Boulder: Westview Press.

Wood, B. Dan, and Richard W. Waterman. 1993. "The Dynamics of Political-Bureaucratic Adaptation." *American Journal of Political Science* 37: 497–528.

Wood, B. Dan, and Richard W. Waterman. 1991. "The Dynamics of Political Control of the Bureaucracy." *American Political Science Review* 85: 801–828.

Yarbrough, Tinsley E. 2000. *The Rehnquist Court and the Constitution.* New York: Oxford University Press.

Yates, Jeff. 2002. *Popular Justice: Presidential Prestige and Executive Success in the Supreme Court.* Albany: State University of New York Press.

Zeigler, Donald. 1996. "The New Activist Court." *American University Law Review* 45: 1367–1401.

Index